MISSISSIPPI'S
CIVIL WAR GENERALS

RANDY BISHOP

authorHOUSE®

AuthorHouse™
1663 Liberty Drive
Bloomington, IN 47403
www.authorhouse.com
Phone: 1 (800) 839-8640

Published by AuthorHouse   08/02/2017

ISBN: 978-1-5462-0173-1 (sc)
ISBN: 978-1-5462-0171-7 (hc)
ISBN: 978-1-5462-0172-4 (e)

Library of Congress Control Number: 2017911658

Print information available on the last page.

This book is printed on acid-free paper.

To my sons,
Jay and Ben, who have grown into fine young men

CONTENTS

PREFACE

In compiling the biographies of the Mississippi men in this manuscript, I maintained the purpose of briefly exploring the life of each. The intent is to provide a working knowledge of each officer as he lived before and during the great struggle known as the American Civil War. Many of them gave the ultimate sacrifice during the course of the struggle, and such events are duly noted.

While striving to include the major characters from Mississippi, I also felt compelled to include those who, at some point in their time on Earth, made some worthwhile connection to the Magnolia State. Therefore, the last chapter includes personalities who may be more readily recognized as sons from other states, but who also have viable reasons to be included in a work of such a title as this.

I sincerely hope any reader finds the contents educational, informative, and entertaining. If not, I offer my utmost apologies to that person. If so, then my goal in writing about these brave warriors from a long-ago but oft-discussed war was reached.

Randy Bishop
Middleton, Tennessee

WILLIAM WIRT ADAMS, C. S. A.
1819-1888

Judge George Adams and his wife, Anna Weisinger Adams, residents of Frankfort, Kentucky, welcomed a baby on March 22, 1819. Named William Wirt Adams, the boy eventually benefitted from his future political alliances, as well as those of his parents. The elder Adams was a close friend of Henry Clay, the well-known orator and statesman. Anna Weisinger Adams was the daughter of Daniel Weisinger, a prominent pioneer in Kentucky.[1]

William Wirt Adams became a big brother at the age of two with the arrival of Daniel Weisinger Adams. Like William Wirt Adams, Daniel would later hold the rank of a brigadier general in the service of the Confederate States of America. Within a few years after Daniel's birth, the Adams family moved to Natchez, Mississippi. Among other positions, George Adams served as a Mississippi district court judge during the late 1830s.[2]

William Wirt Adams had left the confines of his family's Mississippi home prior to his father's attainment of the judge's post. Wirt, as he was commonly called, had moved from Mississippi in order to attend college in Kentucky. After graduating from the Bardstown, Kentucky institute of

1

higher learning in 1839, Wirt returned to Mississippi. That same year Wirt entered the military, serving as a private under Colonel Edward Burleson in Texas.[3]

Adams was quickly promoted to regimental adjutant. At that rank, he participated in the expulsion of Native Americans from the northern portion of Texas. Adams eventually completed his Lone Star service and returned to Mississippi in the fall of 1839.[4]

In 1843, Wirt Adams's brother Daniel became a major figure of controversy. Defending the honor of Judge Adams, Daniel confronted Dr. Hagan, the editor of *The Vicksburg Sentinel*. That publication had made what Daniel determined as offensive remarks about the judge. Daniel stated the purpose of his visit, at which time "Hogan...closed on him instantly." In the ensuing argument, the twenty-two year old Daniel shot Dr. Hagan in the head, killing him.[5]

Upon his homecoming to Mississippi, William Wirt Adams aggressively entered a variety of successful careers as a planter, slave owner, and in banking. He eventually became the senior member in the banking establishment of Adams and Horn. In 1850, Wirt Adams married Sallie Huger Magrant. The majority of historical sources note that while the couple's relationship lasted almost 40 years, and ended only through the death of Mr. Adams, it produced no children.[6]

In 1858, Wirt Adams began serving his first of two sessions in the Mississippi State Legislature. By 1861, Adams was spending a great deal of time in his $90,000 Louisiana home, acting as a Confederate agent or Commissioner to Louisiana, in an effort to assist that state in its secession from the United States. Adams, a veteran of the struggle for Texas independence, apparently impressed fellow Mississippian Jefferson Davis, as Davis offered Adams the position of Postmaster General of the Confederate States of America.[7] Despite the prominence of the post, Adams declined the request to serve the newly formed government in such a capacity.

Rather than accepting Davis's offer to become Postmaster General, Adams sent a request to the Confederate government on June 6, 1861. Adams asked for permission to recruit soldiers to serve in an independent regiment of mounted riflemen. President Davis met Adams's offer with a mixed response. While the idea of raising a command was approved, Davis denied the aspect of the soldiers working independently. Adams received Davis's consent to recruit a "regiment of mounted men for active operation and constant movement."[8]

Upon the creation of the regiment he largely funded from his personal wealth, Adams was elected colonel of the newly designated 1st Mississippi Cavalry. The companies that comprised the regiment hailed from the states of Mississippi, Alabama, and Louisiana. With Colonel Wirt Adams as the commander of the 1st Mississippi, the regiment became known as Wirt Adams Regiment of Cavalry by year's end.[9]

In August 1861, Brigadier General William Joseph Hardee stated that he was aware of the existence of Adams's regiment. In mid-September Adams, in Jackson, Mississippi at the time, received orders to report to Columbus, Kentucky where Adams was to join Hardee. The following month, Adams took the 1st Mississippi to Bowling Green and met Gen. Albert Sidney Johnston's command. Adams formed the rear guard of Johnston's retreat from the Bluegrass State in December, utilizing the approximate 780 men under Adams's leadership.[10]

Adams joined Lieutenant Colonel Nathan Bedford Forrest and Colonel John Austin Wharton as Confederate cavalry commanders in Johnston's army when it was reorganized in early 1862.[11]

In April 1862, Adams took part in the bloodbath at Shiloh, Tennessee. During the Confederate approach, Adams had led his regiment as a portion of the Confederate rear guard. Holding a position on the right of the Confederate line, Adams and his cavalrymen accompanied the infantry into battle. Serving in an observational capacity after the battle, one of Adams's captains made an attack that resulted in the capture of some 60 prisoners.[12]

The remainder of April, and portions of May 1862, allowed Adams to lead raids along the Nashville and Chattanooga Railroad. By that time, Adams had twelve companies totaling 1,047 men and officers under his command. Later action during the siege of Corinth, Mississippi resulted in his Confederates capturing of approximately 40 Federals "in a gallant fight."[13]

Throughout the summer of 1862, Adams continued to see action in the Mississippi towns of Baldwyn, Saltillo, and Guntown. In July 1862, Adams and his cavalry encountered Federals under the leadership of Phil

Sheridan. Later that summer, Adams, serving under Brigadier General Frank Crawford Armstrong, conducted raids in West Tennessee. In doing so, Adams engaged Federal detachments near Bolivar in late August. In early September, Adams struggled against Federal troops at Britton Lane near Jackson, Tennessee.[14]

Adams soon returned to service in North Mississippi, with the early fall of 1862 witnessing significant action for his regiment. Iuka, Burnsville, and Corinth, Mississippi served as severe tests for Adams. During action at Iuka, Adams led troops in covering the flanks of Confederate general Dabney Maury's skirmish line. Later activities included Adams leading two cavalry regiments in capturing a train and its crew, after which the cars and locomotive were burned. During the heat of the battle in September 1862, Adams led a feint retreat in which pursuing Federal troops fell into a well-planned ambush. Maury reported a total of four casualties, while that of the enemy was "of necessity much greater."[15]

At the Battle of Davis or Hatchie Bridge in early October, 1862, following the Confederate defeat at Corinth, Adams participated in an attack that protected the lone escape route for his compatriots. Earlier, a few dozen of Adams's soldiers were the first to be struck in the Federal advance at Davis Bridge. Some 5,000 men in blue, members of Major General Stephen Hurlbut's Fourth Division of the Army of the Tennessee pushed Adams's pickets three miles toward the village of Metamora, Tennessee. Providing what was called a "spirited defense," and a fight so tenacious that one of Hurlbut's subordinates believed he had encountered an infantry regiment, Adams's troopers convinced Hurlbut that a strong Confederate force was present at Davis Bridge. It has been noted that Adams "regarded it as the most remarkable feat in the history of his regiment."[16]

In early 1863, Adams was assigned the task to provide Confederates at Vicksburg with information about Federal troop movements against the Mississippi River stronghold. In the ensuing months, Adams led his command against the well-known Federal cavalry officer Benjamin Grierson. The two cavalry officers met at Union Church on April 28, with Adams being driven back and unable to retake lost ground the following day. A subsequent struggle involved Adams combating Phil Sheridan at Raymond, Mississippi or Fourteen Mile Creek. On May 16, Adams commanded the Confederate cavalry at Baker's Creek or Champion Hill.

Although he lacked sufficient numbers to do so by that time, Adams was given the assignment of harassing and skirmishing against U. S. Grant's supply lines in the Vicksburg area.[17]

Wirt Adams's Mississippi Cavalry had been attached to Brigadier General John Bowen's Division at Champion Hill. Adams was soon attached to Brigadier General George Cosby's 1st Brigade of Brigadier General William "Red" Jackson's Cavalry Division at Vicksburg. Jackson's division spent most of June 1863 in the area of Vernon, Mississippi.[18]

After the Confederate surrender at Vicksburg, Adams was noted in an official report from Federal general William Tecumseh Sherman who wrote, "Some of Wirt Adams' Cavalry are about Jackson, and the rascals ate some of our bread."[19] While the outcome of the Vicksburg Campaign notoriously failed from the Confederate perspective, Adams's leadership during the months preceding it apparently impressed military officials whose ranks superseded his.

On September 25, 1863, Adams, who had recently been given the responsibility of commanding an additional regiment, received a promotion to brigadier general. Many of his colleagues felt the ascension in rank was long overdue. With this new rank, Brigadier General Adams led demonstrations against Port Hudson and had "the unenviable task" of striking Federal troops under Sherman near Meridian, Mississippi.[20]

The difficulty of Adams's assignment, wherein he worked in conjunction with General Stephen Dill Lee, allowed "but one opportunity to strike effectively." At Decatur, Alabama, Confederates under Adams struck a Union wagon train, but failed to capture a single wagon. However, in his report of the actions during the Confederate raids, Lee wrote, "Adams' Brigade has done the fighting and acted gallantly." Adams reported that the military actions from Champion Hill, Mississippi to Decatur had cost his command 129 casualties.[21]

Subsequent routes took Adams to Starkville and Canton, Mississippi. At Canton he led his troops against Sherman. Adams praised his immediate subordinates in his reports of the action, noting, "In these affairs...were the most conspicuous and gallant participants."[22]

In late March 1864, General S. D. Lee ordered Adams to assume command of the Mississippi Brigade of Jackson's Division. Less than a week into April of the same year, the order was revoked, with Adams replacing Lee. Adams complied with the change, with the stipulation that his brigade remain with him for the remainder of his tenure. By the end of April, Adams had led his regiment to Yazoo City where it captured the gunboat *Petrel*.[23]

On January 2, 1865, Adams encountered Colonel Embury Osband's 1,500 troops of the Third U.S. Colored Cavalry, near Franklin, Tennessee. Fighting for possession of a bridge, Osband wrote, "The desperate nature of the fighting, the superiority of number displayed by General Adams... induced me to attempt to withdraw my men." Osband added, "It was the hardest fought cavalry fight..." in which his U.S. cavalrymen ever participated.[24]

During March 1865, Adams was given orders to join Forrest in attacking Federals of Brigadier General John Thomas Croxton. The recent reorganization of Forrest's cavalry had placed the brigades of Adams, as well as Brigadier Generals Peter Starke and Frank Armstrong in Forrest's division under the leadership of Brigadier General James Chalmers.[25]

On March 25, 1865, Adams received orders from Chalmers to hold his troops at Macon, Mississippi, but to be prepared to move quickly with five days' rations. By April 3, Adams had gained a much needed artillery battery and moved through Columbus, Mississippi with his command bearing only hard bread, cooking utensils, and ordinance. On April 5, Adams arrived in Pickensville, Alabama with some 1,500 cavalrymen.[26]

The following day Adams attacked the 6th Kentucky Cavalry of Cruxton's command, at the Sispey Mills Bridge near Pleasant Ridge, Alabama. Major William Fidler, in charge of the 6th Kentucky, fell captive to Adams, as did a wagon train of flour, bacon, and corn meal. Fidler died aboard *Sultana* a few weeks later. The Confederates devoured the foodstuff not destroyed during the attempt of the Federals to use it as breastworks. Adams's men made three charges before darkness and heavy rains ended the action. Casualties for each side were reported at thirty-four.[27]

One individual wrote of the effort Adams and his troops offered, "Wirt Adams...formed part of the force with which Forrest tried to stem the tide of disaster. Though the Confederates fought with the old-time spirit, it was all in vain."[28]

A Confederate colonel's take on the attack included a statement to Adams, "Should the war cease now, you would have the honor of having won the last victory on Confederate soil and in the Confederate cause." The proclamation was not far from accurate as two later Alabama engagements at West Point and Talladega involved only reserves and not regular troops.[29]

On May 4, 1865, "near Ramsey Station, Sumter County, Alabama" Adams surrendered his regiment. Eight days later the general's parole was written in Gainesville, Alabama. His list of commands during the war was quite impressive. Those units who had served under Adams at various points of the war included the 11th and 17th Arkansas Mounted Infantry Regiments, the Fourteenth Confederate Cavalry, the 9th Louisiana Infantry Battalion and the 9th Tennessee Battalion. Rounding out the list were the Mississippi battalions of Captain Thomas Stockdale and Colonel C. C. Wilbourn, as well as Robert's Mississippi Battery.[30]

The Kentucky-born brigadier general's leadership and service resulted in the praise and admiration of those who knew him. It was stated, "When the war was declared he was one of the first to volunteer, and his record as a soldier will compare with that of any man who bared his breast to shot and shell. Never was produced a better or braver soldier..."[31]

Adams returned to Mississippi, living primarily in Vicksburg and Jackson, where he "resumed the vocations of civil life." In 1880, Adams began serving a five-year tenure as a state revenue agent. In 1885, President Cleveland made Adams postmaster of Jackson, Mississippi, fulfilling the irony of Adams earlier declining a similar offer from Jefferson Davis.[32]

As the years progressed, Adams apparently made friendships and maintained business dealings with individuals of questionable character. One relationship of a controversial nature involved lessees of a penitentiary, while another was connected with a local election. Also involved in the mix was the Jones S. Hamilton murder of R. D. Gambrell. Hamilton was a friend of Adams. The *New Mississippian*, a Jackson, Mississippi periodical, had been strong in its criticism of Adams and his alleged involvement in the affairs.[35]

An article concerning his testimony in the penitentiary-related trial proved particularly bothersome to Adams. The article appeared in the March 27, 1888 edition of the *New Mississippian* and said, "General Wirt Adams, a witness for the defense...ought to remember that character, like charity, should begin at home."[34]

On April 3, 1888, the same publication proclaimed, "Nellie Dinkins's testimony for the state has been impeached, but she has this advantage of General Wirt Adams, a witness for the defense. She never gave certificates and was forced…to admit they were utterly false."[35]

Adams reportedly stated that he had read the articles and desired no confrontation with the newspaper's editor, John H. Martin, a friend of murder victim R. D. Gambrell. An associate of Adams's recorded that Adams "was…restless under the attacks of this editor." Despite his past experience, Adams said, "I do not want to be forced into difficulty with him. I have no quarrel with him, and I actually avoid the public streets that I may not meet him casually and be betrayed into assaulting him."[36]

A subsequent proclamation in the *New Mississippian* said, "…since we exposed… Adams, the postoffice [sic] is endeavoring to wreak its spite against the paper in every possible way. This paper has to be in the postoffice [sic] about a half or an hour sooner than the republican paper… or it is made to lay over for another mail. It is strange how mad some men get when the plain truth is told about them…and yet this paper is feeling remarkably well."[37]

On May 1, 1888, Adams joined his friend Ned Farish for an afternoon walk in Jackson, Mississippi. As the duo approached the corner of President and Amite Streets, they met John Martin, the *New Mississippian* editor. Calling Martin a rascal, Adams then said, "I have stood enough from you." Martin replied with a statement similar to, "If you don't like it," and drew a pistol. Adams responded in a like manner.[38]

It is unclear which of the men fired first, but the combatants shot at each other, with "a large china tree" between them. Martin stood on the tree's south side, Adams to the north. Individuals who arrived at the scene as the gunfire ceased recalled hearing Martin say, "I am dead", while Adams reportedly fell to the ground without uttering a word.[39]

Newspapers of the time reported the mortal wounds inflicted upon both men. It was explained, "General Adams had but one wound and that was directly through the heart. Martin was shot in the right breast…and in the upper part of the right leg…there was also a shot in his hand." The two men were also said to have used six-shooters, Martin's being a forty-one caliber and Adams having a forty-four caliber in his possession.[40]

Adams's funeral "was the largest seen in Jackson for several years.

Almost every carriage and buggy in the city was in the procession...The [Episcopal] church was packed with the best people of the country...there was no man whom Jackson loved more than General Adams." Jones S. Hamilton, one of the men whose association with Adams led to the deadly confrontation with Martin, served as one of Adams's pallbearers.[41]

William Wirt Adams was buried in Greenwood Cemetery in Jackson, Mississippi. Sixty-nine year old Wirt Adams had outlived his younger brother Daniel. The younger former general had spent a portion of his post-war life in England before passing away sixteen years ahead of his older brother.[42]

WILLIAM EDWIN BALDWIN, C.S.A.
1827-1864

On July 28, 1827 Statesburg, South Carolina served as the birthplace of William Edwin Baldwin. The boy's family moved from the Sumter County area to Columbus, Mississippi when he was a child. There is a lack of information regarding William's early life, but it is regularly documented that he operated a hometown book and stationary store in his early adult years.[1]

Baldwin's indoctrination into military life occurred in the pre-Civil War era. William Edwin Baldwin joined a local militia based in Columbus and served as an officer, primarily in the capacity of a company lieutenant for approximately twelve years.[2] His experience in the militia would have a serious impact on his life with the onset of the American Civil War.

The beginning of the war resulted in Mississippi's governor calling for fifty regiments to serve the Confederate government. In May 1861 Columbus, Mississippi furnished a company, the Columbus Rifles. The group became Company K of the 14th Mississippi Infantry Regiment. Baldwin was commissioned colonel of the regiment and it was sent to Pensacola, Florida.[3]

By early August the regiment had moved to Union City, Tennessee, but within two weeks of its arrival it was transferred to East Tennessee. Colonel Baldwin received subsequent orders on August 28 from General Felix Zollicoffer to move the 14th Mississippi to Kentucky. Baldwin arrived at Fishing Creek, or Mill Springs, after the conclusion of the bloody conflict there.[4]

After marching to Greeneville, Tennessee in late September 1861, Baldwin assumed command of an entire brigade in October. The components of Colonel Baldwin's brigade were the 14th, 20th, and 26th Mississippi Infantry Regiments, as well as the 26th Tennessee. Stationed in the Cumberland Gap, Baldwin's brigade reported it actions to General Simon Buckner.[5]

Major Washington Doss was responsible for the leadership of the 14th Tennessee as it moved toward Fort Donelson. Colonel Baldwin, evidently delayed for some reason, eventually reached Donelson where he led the 20th and 26th Mississippi Regiments as well as the 26th Tennessee. Those regiments were assigned to Brigadier General Bushrod Johnson's Division. Baldwin's other regiments, the 2nd Kentucky, the 14th Mississippi, and the 41st Tennessee, were attached to Colonel John Brown's Brigade in Brig. Gen. Simon Buckner's Division.[6] Baldwin's movements received notable recognition and substantial praise in Pillow's report.

Pillow wrote, "I speak of special commendation of…Colonel Baldwin… Colonel Baldwin's brigade constituted the front of the attacking force, sustained immediately by Colonel Wharton's brigade. These two brigades deserve especial commendation for the manner in which they sustained the first shock of battle, and under circumstances of great embarrassment threw themselves into position and followed up the conflict throughout the day…I can speak from personal knowledge of the gallant conduct and bearing of…Colonels Baldwin and Wharton."[7]

Col. Baldwin had participated in an earlier council of war in which confusion reigned. Discussions related to the likely Confederate withdrawal had been avoided, as had "what supplies were to be taken, marching orders for the retreat, and how and when the retreat should commence." In turn, Baldwin's brigade, positioned on the extreme left of the left wing of the Confederate army, took their equipment and rations with them into the heat of battle on the final stand at Donelson.[8] Aside from exemplifying

Baldwin's foresight, the fact bore little significance as the Confederates surrendered with Baldwin being unable to make an escape.

The 14th Mississippi suffered 17 killed, 85 wounded, and 10 missing during the Federal attacks upon Fort Donelson. This resulted in Baldwin's Southern troops numbering 650 men at the time of the surrender of the Confederate garrison. Baldwin joined thousands of other Confederate soldiers in the surrender, the largest of its type to that time in American history. Before gaining freedom through a prisoner exchange, Baldwin was held captive at Fort Warren, Massachusetts for a period of six months.[9]

In September 1862, Baldwin received a promotion to brigadier general, having served in that capacity for months. The 14th, 20th and 26th Mississippi Regiments, as well as the 26th Tennessee compiled Brig. Gen. William Edwin Baldwin's soldiers at his disposal. The new general officer's regiments joined two other brigades as the units assigned to Brig. Gen. Lloyd Tilghman's Division of Gen. Earl Van Dorn's Army of West Tennessee.[10]

Baldwin's first combat as a brigadier general occurred at Coffeeville, Mississippi on December 5, 1862. Information indicated that Federal general Ulysses Simpson Grant was moving from Memphis toward Vicksburg, Mississippi. In the ensuing combat, the Confederates suffered minor casualties with only seven killed and forty-three wounded. Federal losses were far more substantial with ten killed, sixty-three wounded, and forty-captured.[11]

In his official report of the engagement at Coffeeville, Brig. Gen. Tilghman wrote, "I take special pleasure in mentioning...Brig. Gen. W. E. Baldwin, of my own division...displayed the greatest good judgment and gallantry."[12]

In 1863 Baldwin participated in the Vicksburg Campaign, most notably at Port Gibson, Champion Hill, and Big Black River Bridge. Baldwin's command consisted of the 17th, 29th, and 31st Louisiana Infantry Regiments, as well as the 4th and 46th Mississippi Infantry Regiments. Four guns of Capt. T. F. Tobin's Tennessee Artillery finalized Baldwin's troops.[13]

Baldwin spent time in the trenches during the siege of Vicksburg. After the battle of May 22, 1863, the Confederate troops became subjected to a Federal siege that lasted over forty days. Baldwin recalled, "...with but few exceptions, the daily operations were very similar...constant fire of artillery was kept up with considerable briskness early in the morning and late in the evening, slackening and sometimes altogether ceasing during the seven or eight middle hours of the day, and kept up during the night at regular but longer intervals."[14]

General John Pemberton, in command of the besieged troops, called a meeting of the Confederate generals at Vicksburg. The purpose of the council was to discuss the Confederate surrender of the stronghold on the Mississippi River. Reportedly Baldwin, who had been wounded during earlier action during the siege, joined Brigadier General Stephen Dill Lee as the two holdouts in supporting Pemberton's intention to surrender. Unfortunately, the feelings of the two drew little attention, perhaps because "these two had no reasons to offer."[15]

Briefly serving as a prisoner of war a second time, Baldwin was soon exchanged again. Upon his parole Baldwin was sent to Mobile, Alabama and placed in charge of 1,600 men. Sadly "his further participation in the war was...cut short." Leaving the heavily-manned garrison, he encountered personal tragedy on February 19, 1864. Baldwin fell from his horse while riding near the Dog River and was killed when he hit the ground.[16]

As time elapsed after the tragedy, rumors circulated in regard to Baldwin's death. The basic fact that most historians agree with is that Baldwin fell from his horse when a stirrup broke. However, there are other uncertain elements regarding the speed with which he rode his horse and whether or not he was drunk. At least one statement is a generally agreed-upon aspect. That is, "The Confederacy lost a gallant and efficient soldier and Mississippi an illustrious citizen."[17]

Thirty-six year old William Edwin Baldwin was interred in Magnolia Cemetery in Mobile. His body was eventually moved to a family cemetery in Columbus, Mississippi.[18]

WILLIAM BARKSDALE, C.S.A.

(1821-1863)

William Barksdale was born in the Rutherford County, Tennessee town of Smyrna on August 21, 1821. His parents, William and Nancy Hervey Lester Barksdale, had moved from Virginia to Tennessee 13 years earlier, and his father had served in the War of 1812. Within a few years William became an older sibling when his brother Ethelbert was born. William Barksdale's first 16 years were spent in the Middle Tennessee town of Smyrna, but he eventually joined his three brothers and entered the University of Nashville.[1]

Following his law studies in Nashville, Barksdale ended his Tennessee residency and moved to Columbus, Mississippi. An article in *Harper's Weekly* article said, "William removed to Columbus, Mississippi, where he read law, and was admitted to the bar before he was of age." His Columbus law practice became successful, but an apparent disenchantment eventually developed. As evidence, Barksdale gave up his profitable profession as a lawyer and became the editor of a pro-slavery newspaper known as the *Columbus Democrat*. A biographer noted that Barksdale used the paper as a means of printing his own secessionist views.[2]

During the Mexican War Barksdale served as a quartermaster. Initially enlisting in the 2nd Mississippi Infantry Regiment, Barksdale soon reached the rank of captain and saw action during the training ground for the major conflict that laid a decade and a half in the future. It was noted that Barksdale performed "his arduous duties with recognized ability."[3]

After completing his service in the Mexican War William Barksdale used his military exploits to benefit his political ambitions. He served as a member of the Mississippi State Convention in 1851, where he was largely opposed to the concepts contained within the Compromise of 1850. Barksdale also served as a delegate to the 1852 Democratic National Convention that was held in Baltimore. The next year he was elected as a Congressman, and served as a Democratic Representative from Mississippi for 8 years. In the Senate Barksdale earned a reputation as one of the most outspoken members who promoted states' rights.[4]

Barksdale stood near Preston Brooks as Brooks viciously beat Massachusetts abolitionist Charles Sumner with a cane. Barksdale received no censure for the incident. In 1860 Barksdale was quoted as saying, "Never have I desired a dissolution of this Union; but should the Republican Party obtain the control of the Government, I shall be for disunion...the South, with the strong arms and brave hearts of her gallant sons, will build up her own eternal destiny."[5]

The eventual secession of Mississippi caused the pro-secession Barksdale, and his younger brother Ethelbert, to resign their Congressional seats. In turn, William joined the Mississippi Militia as a brigadier general, while Ethelbert became a member of the Confederate States Congress. With his May 1861 appointment in the Confederate States Army, William Barksdale was given the rank of colonel in the 13th Mississippi Infantry Regiment.[6]

A member of the brigade where Barksdale had become a colonel recalled that at the time of Barksdale's promotion the brigade consisted of the 13th, 17th, and 18th Mississippi Infantry Regiments as well as the 8th Virginia. The respective units were under the command of "Cols. Barksdale, Featherstone, Burte, and Eppa Hunton. The first two became generals, the third was killed at Ball's Bluff, and the fourth went to Congress a number of years after the war."[7]

That summer Barksdale led the 13th Mississippi in combat at Manassas. A record of the battle stated, "The Federals...at a distance of about three hundred yards…began…lively sharpshooting…Col. Barksdale, of the Thirteenth Mississippi, ordered his regiment to charge…The Federals… stampeded, and the Thirteenth arrived at the summit of the hill…surprised to find that they [the Federal soldiers] had fled."[8]

Barksdale's Mississippians saw subsequent action in the Peninsula Campaign as well as the Seven Days Battle. During the action at Savage's Station, Barksdale fought in a division under the command of General John Magruder. Barksdale's soldiers of the 13th Mississippi were aligned with the brigades of Semmes and Kershaw to complete the Southern infantry. Cannon crews from Kemper and Hart added to the Confederate fire power.[9]

At Malvern Hill, Barksdale assumed the brigade command of the 13th, 17th, 18th and 21st Mississippi Infantry Regiments, as well as a Virginia Battery, after Brigadier General Richard Griffin was mortally wounded. As the senior ranking colonel in the brigade, due to Featherstone's earlier promotion and movement to another brigade, Barksdale led the brigade in battle. In doing so, Barksdale joined the likes of William Mahone, Marcus Joseph Wright, Robert Ransom, Thomas Reade Cobb, Paul Semmes, Joseph Kershaw, Lewis Armistead, and George Thomas Anderson as commanders in the engagements known as the Seven Days Battles.[10]

A veteran of the brigade recalled that at Malvern Hill Barksdale "mounted his horse and yelled, 'Attention! This brigade must take that battery.'"[11] The order was fully carried out. Robert Edward Lee noted that Barksdale "displayed the highest qualities of a soldier" during this battle. From that point Barksdale's Mississippi Brigade gained a strong reputation as a fighting unit. A Barksdale biographer stated that aside from Second Manassas, where his brigade was not present, "Barksdale distinguished himself on all the early fields of the Army of Northern Virginia." Having been passed on earlier requests from his immediate superiors to be elevated in rank, Barksdale finally gained his recognition and promotion that many considered long overdue. On August 12, 1862, Barksdale was elevated to the rank of brigadier general.[12]

Brigadier General Barksdale helped secure the Federal surrender of Harper's Ferry. Barksdale's brigade joined two others under Brigadier Generals Cadmus Wilcox and Joseph Kershaw in supporting Cobb at Crampton's Gap near Harper's Ferry. Kershaw and Barksdale led their troops against members of Colonel Thomas Ford's 126th New York

Volunteers. The members of the latter regiment had only been in the army twenty-one days when the seasoned Confederate infantrymen slammed into their ranks. The eventual surrender of Federal soldiers at Harper's Ferry would go down in history as the largest surrender of Federal troops in the war.[13]

Barksdale saw action during the September 17, 1862 bloodbath at Antietam or Sharpsburg, Maryland. Barksdale's command at Antietam consisted of the 13th, 17th, 18th, and 21st Mississippi Infantry Regiments. This brigade joined three other brigades and five groups of artillery to compile the division of Maj. Gen. Lafayette McLaws.[14]

C. C. Cummings, a member of Barksdale's brigade, recalled the action at Antietam. He wrote, "...my brigade...had the honor of successfully storming Maryland Heights at Harper's Ferry on Sunday morning the thirteenth...This delayed our entrance on the battlefield" until what Cummings estimated to have been "about ten o'clock on the morning of the 17th."[15]

Cummings added, "We arrived on the field after an all day's and all night's march to get there from the Ferry...We ran up the slope at a double quick and at the crest of the hill, which we gained a little in advance of the blue boys..."[16]

At Major General John Walker's left during the battle, Barksdale later joined Walker in a post-battle ride on the field. Walker said, "...with General Barksdale...I rode over...the battlefield where our own troops had been engaged, to see that none of the wounded had been overlooked... passing along a worm fence, in the darkness, we heard a feeble voice... 'Don't let your horses tread on me.'...This was but one of the very many instances of human suffering we encountered that night." The wounded soldier, a member of the 20th Massachusetts, had a broken back. Barksdale and Walker ordered an ambulance to carry the soldier to a nearby hospital.[17]

Barksdale also participated in the December 1862 action at Fredericksburg. Lt. General James Longstreet wrote that troops under Barksdale were "on picket duty in front of Fredericksburg the night of the advance." According to Major General Lafayette McLaws, it was Barksdale who notified McLaws "that the movements on the other side [of the Rappahannock River] indicated that the enemy were preparing to lay down pontoon-bridges."[18]

Barksdale's snipers were responsible for providing the defense of the town's waterfront, completing the assignment by accurately firing at Federal infantrymen who were attempting to cross the Rappahannock River. Continuing to lead the 13th, 17th, 18th, and 21st Mississippi, Brig. Gen. Barksdale suffered 242 total casualties, with 29 killed, 151 wounded, and 62 missing.[19]

The efficiency of Barksdale's men was noted in Federal reports. It was noted, "Federal accounts show that this determined defense offered by a small fraction of Barksdale's brigade not only prevented Sumner's crossing, but by this delay caused the whole of Franklin's Left Grand Division, except one brigade, to recross the Rappahannock, and thus gave General Lee twenty-four hours'...to prepare for the assault, with full notice of the points of attack."[20]

The tenacity of Barksdale's soldiers was further exhibited at Chancellorsville in May 1863. Most of the Confederate units in Longstreet's Corps were detached for duty in Suffolk, Virginia at the time, with Barksdale holding the honor of being one of the few brigades from Longstreet's command to participate in the battle at Chancellorsville. As in the earlier battle at Fredericksburg, Barksdale was defending the heights above Fredericksburg against a Federal foe. However, in this instance, the men in blue were ten times the size of Barksdale's force. While Barksdale was forced to fall back, his troops regained the lost ground the following day. Casualties for Barksdale at Chancellorsville were 43 killed, 208 wounded, and 341 missing.[21]

Barksdale led his troops northward, arriving in Gettysburg past midnight on July 2, 1863. At Gettysburg, Barksdale's brigade combined with those of Paul Semmes, Wofford, and Joseph Kershaw to constitute the members of the division of Maj. Gen. Lafayette McLaws. Along with the divisions under Lt. General John Bell Hood and Major General George Pickett, these units compiled Longstreet's First Corps of the Army of Northern Virginia.[22]

On the afternoon of July 2, 1863, Barksdale's brigade "burst from the woods and started an irresistible assault" near the Peach Orchard. One of Barksdale's opponents recalled, "It was the grandest charge that was ever made by mortal man." With his subordinates walking during the charge, Barksdale chose to ride his horse. The Confederate assault initially proved successful, as Barksdale's brigade hit the Peach Orchard and soon captured a Federal brigade commander.[23]

With Wofford's brigade close behind, Barksdale's Mississippians charged the Union position in a gathering of fruit trees, breaking the line north of the Peach Orchard. The Confederate left wing wheeled toward the Emmitsburg Road and the buildings on the Sherfy farm. By the time the exchange of fire had ended, Barksdale's men had wounded twenty-one of the twenty-four officers and almost half of the troops of the 2nd New Hampshire Regiment.[24]

Edging toward Cemetery Ridge, Barksdale joined the brigades of Brig. Gen. Cadmus Wilcox and Col. David Lang in crushing the right side of the Federal Third Corps. Barksdale's hair was seen above the increasing level of battle smoke and reportedly shown "like the white plume of Navarre." Barksdale was also heard to have shouted, "Crowd them!" toward his spirited infantrymen.[25] Tragedy awaited Barksdale in the ensuing minutes.

A bullet smashed into Barksdale's left knee. Moments later a cannonball struck his left foot. Another shot hit Barksdale in the chest, knocking him from his horse. The Confederate troops were compelled to retreat, leaving the mortally wounded Barksdale on the field of battle.[26]

A Confederate soldier and veteran of the battle of Gettysburg spoke of the incident to the Barksdale Sons of Confederate Veterans Camp four decades later. The soldier said, "Barksdale...watching the movements of his heroes as they drove the enemy before them. His bright eyes flashed...his thin lip curled with that haughty smile which meant defiance...the flush of victory on his face, shouting, 'They are whipped.'...but the Federal lines, reinforced...poured volley after volley into his lines...Then, waving his sword in the very thickest of the fray, in the last charge upon the enemy's last line...this soldier, patriot, hero fell...."[27]

Another witness recalled how Barksdale, still leading the four Mississippi regiments he commanded at Antietam, heroically led his soldiers at Gettysburg. The soldier remarked that the "barrel-chested" former Congressman possessed "a thirst for battle glory." Epitomizing the thirst and providing supporting evidence for the soldier's proclamation, Barksdale had motivated his troops in a pre-battle speech in which he stated, "We have never been whipped and we never can be." The brigadier general then reportedly asked McLaws and Longstreet at least three times for permission to charge the Federal lines before he was allowed to do so.[28]

Pvt. T. M. Scanlon, 17th Mississippi Infantry Regiment, reminisced of Barksdale's speech that the general gave immediately prior to the charge. Scanlon recalled Barksdale said, "500 yards in front of you at the red barn...as well as the cone mountain...covered with riflemen...and beside that entrenched line there is another 200 yards beyond which we are also expected to take. This is a heroic undertaking and most of us will bite the dust." Barksdale showed no fear, but he made the offer for anyone who "feels this is too much for him" to simply step "two paces to the front" and Barksdale would excuse him from the bloodshed that awaited.[29]

Pointing toward the Massachusetts Battery positioned near the Trostle House, Barksdale emphasized his desire to capture "that little battery across the way" and proclaimed that the group of cannon "could be taken in five minutes." When allowed to advance, Barksdale began repeating the words, "Forward, men, forward" several times.[30]

A witness to the incident, J. S. McNeily, recalled that Barksdale had also shouted, "Advance, advance! Brave Mississippians, one more charge and the day is ours."[31]

An additional soldier added, "At top speed, without firing a shot, the brigade sped swiftly across the field and literally rushed the goal." Yet another stated that the event was, "...the grandest charge that was ever made by mortal man."[32]

Federal troops of Brigadier General Charles Graham received the assault of Barksdale's Mississippians and began reeling from the sudden attack. The area of the battlefield known as the Peach Orchard served as the primary location of the attack and the Federal soldiers began retreating into the yard of the Sherfy homestead. The Confederate progress continued into the Trostle farm where Captain John Bigelow, acting under orders from Colonel Freeman McGilvery of Maine, attempted to hold the Federal position at all costs.[33]

A Confederate recalled, "Barksdale's right had been held in check...'Right wheel, charge!' rang above the roar of battle...Winslow's Massachusetts Battery fell a prize to the sons of Mississippi."[34]

Colonel George Willard's brigade of men in blue reinforced the Federal position and slammed into the center of Barksdale's line. Willard was decapitated when a shell struck him, yet Barksdale, "almost frantic with rage," struggled to rally his men who had been stunned from the arrival of Willard's troops. A legend of the battle holds that a Union officer ordered all members of his company to fire at Barksdale.[35] Regardless of the accuracy of the tale, the former legislator's body was riddled with projectiles.

A Federal account added to the history of Barksdale's wounding. Hunt wrote, "Barksdale's Brigade, except the 21st Mississippi, was held in check only by McGilvery's artillery...Willard...charged Barksdale's brigade and drove it...nearly to the Emmitsburg Road, when he was himself repulsed by a heavy artillery and infantry fire, and fell back to his former position near the sources of Plum Run. In this affair...Barksdale was mortally wounded."[36]

A veteran of the battle noted, "Barksdale, like the fabled god of battle, towering in the front of the advancing column, was seen leading the charge on the last line of the enemy..."[37]

Barksdale's sword was broken in the volley. Shot from his saddle, Barksdale had led his troops in the afternoon charge, but his wounding resulted in the hasty retreat of his brigade.[38]

An account of the incident said, "Barksdale, carrying his sword at an angle of forty five degrees, led those steel nerved veterans on by boldness and heroic inspiration, till he fell mortally wounded near the enemy's works."[39]

Barksdale was reported to have looked at his courier and stated, "I am killed! Tell my wife and children that I died fighting at my post." Reports also circulated that Barksdale, suffering from the pain of his wounds, told a Federal surgeon, "Tell my wife I am shot..."[40]

Of the 1,400 men under Barksdale at Gettysburg, approximately 730 were killed, wounded, or missing. The casualty rate was extremely high for the brigade's officers. Two colonels in the 13th Mississippi, the regiment in which Barksdale began his tenure as an officer, were killed. A third was mortally wounded. Three officers in the 17th Mississippi were wounded, and a fourth was killed. In the 18th Mississippi an officer was captured and a second wounded.[41]

In a letter to his wife, a Vermont private and a soldier from the 148th Pennsylvania recalled his regiment's experience with the mortally wounded

Barksdale. The author of the letter stated that Barksdale, after being wounded, was only able to drink water from a spoon while he lay on a makeshift bed in the home of Gettysburg shoemaker Jacob Hummelbaugh. The man also noted that blood sprayed from Barksdale's chest wound with every breath.[42]

Despite the immense pain which Barksdale was certainly experiencing, the Confederate general remained defiant toward his captors. Barksdale reportedly proclaimed, "You will have Longstreet thundering in your rear in the morning." However, Barksdale, being treated in a field hospital located in the Hummelbaugh house, succumbed to his wounds during the night.[43]

Barksdale's Mississippi buttons and other items, such as his Masonic emblems, were allegedly cut from his clothing as Federal souvenirs. Buried near Hummelbaugh's Gettysburg home, Barksdale was later moved to the Greenwood Cemetery in Jackson, Mississippi.[44]

Praises for Barksdale abounded, including a *Confederate Veteran* article written three decades after Barksdale's death. A member of his brigade wrote, "He was a man of whom it could be truthfully stated, 'Bold as a lion, yet gentle as a lamb.' He was not a military man, but was a pure type of genuine southern chivalry, a southern gentleman of the old school."[45]

Additional accolades added that Barksdale was, "Quick to resent and as quick to forgive, quick to punish disobedience in a subordinate, and a quick to ask forgiveness…No truer patriot ever fell on the field of battle."[46]

SAMUEL BENTON, C. S. A.

1820-1864

Samuel Benton was born on October 18, 1820. The exact location of his birthplace is the object of speculation, but the strongest indications are that the event occurred in Williamson County, Tennessee. Samuel was also a nephew of Missouri Senator Thomas Hart Benton, a veteran of the War of 1812 and a lieutenant colonel and aide-de-camp to Andrew Jackson. Senator Benton had survived a heated brawl with the future seventh President.[1]

Samuel Benton married a lady whose surname was Knox. The couple eventually had one child. As for his professional life prior to the Civil War, Benton briefly taught school before entering the legal profession. After becoming a successful lawyer in the town of Holly Springs, Mississippi, Benton directed his attention toward media and used the town as the site of the 1853 publication of his newspaper, *The Mississippi Time*.[2] These endeavors were all profitable.

The political arena soon attracted Samuel Benton, and the lawyer and publisher yielded to the summons it issued. Classified as a man whose political views were a combination of Whig and States Right's stances, Samuel Benton became a member of the Mississippi State Legislature in

1852. He also served as a member of the 1855 Union Convention. Benton later represented his fellow Benton County Mississippians as a State Legislator during the Secession Convention of 1861. As a member of the Ways and Means Committee of the Secession Convention,[3] Benton contributed to the meetings that eventually resulted in Mississippi severing its ties as a member of the United States, the second Southern state to do so.

With Mississippi's alignment shifting to the newly-formed Confederate States of America, Samuel Benton offered his services to the fledgling government. In doing so, Benton became a member of the 9th Mississippi Infantry Regiment, a unit initially formed under the premise of existing to serve the Confederacy for a period of twelve months. Benton was appointed captain of the 9th Mississippi, and he held that rank for approximately one year.[4]

Captain Samuel Benton returned to Holly Springs and oversaw the formation of the 37th Mississippi Infantry Regiment in April 1862. Benton's previously-exhibited leadership qualities were evidently appreciated as he was elected colonel of the regiment. Sent to Corinth, Mississippi, the 37th Mississippi was assigned to Brigadier General Patton Anderson's brigade, a unit that also contained the 30th and 41st Mississippi Infantry Regiments.[5] Within weeks the unit would see its first combat.

At Farmington, Tennessee, on May 9, 1862, Benton joined skirmishers under the command of Lieutenant John Morgan. After Morgan was wounded, Benton worked with another officer in leading the Confederates in the fight. General Anderson praised the brigade for its conduct at Farmington as well as for its participation during the evacuation of Corinth.[6]

In July 1862, Colonel Benton and his fellow brigade members joined the forces of General Braxton Bragg and marched to the city of Chattanooga, Tennessee. Within weeks, Benton's regiment, known by then as the 34th Mississippi Infantry Regiment, proceeded through Middle Tennessee and into Kentucky.[7] The ensuing action within the borders of the Bluegrass State would have serious effects upon both Benton and the entire regiment.

On October 8, 1862, a major engagement occurred in Perryville, Kentucky. There, the 34th Mississippi worked in conjunction with the 27th and 30th Mississippi Infantry Regiments in a brigade under the command of Colonel Thomas Jones. Col. Benton was responsible for guiding the 34[8]th in the battle.[8]

Benton's troops were engaged in some of the most intense fighting that took place at Perryville. The 34th Mississippi, with the support of troops from Brigadier General James Jackson's Division, made a series of attacks against the Federal cannons under the command of Lieutenant Charles Parsons. The blue clad artillerymen suffered greatly from the Confederate assaults, losing an estimated forty men in their failed attempts to defend the battery. The cost of success was no less severe for Benton's men, as the ranks of his command were also shattered. Company K of his regiment was left with only seven troops after the conclusion of the assaults.[9]

Benton was among the troops who were wounded in the action at Perryville, Kentucky. Jackson, the general with whom Benton's men had joined in the charges against the Federal battery, fell in the series of events as well. As one of the regiments under the command of Colonel Thomas Marshall Jones, a brigade commander in Anderson's Division, the 34th Mississippi sustained one hundred sixty-eight total casualties at Perryville. Benton and some one hundred twenty-four other members of the regiment were wounded. It was recorded that another forty-two men of the 34th Mississippi were killed while one soldier was missing.[10]

The extent of his injury did not allow Benton to rejoin the 34th Mississippi Infantry Regiment as it navigated the Cumberland Gap in route to East Tennessee. The unit spent the remainder of 1862 in the Middle Tennessee area, where it would be reassigned to the command of Colonel Edward Cary Walthall, who, like Benton, was a pre-war Mississippi lawyer. As a part of the recently-promoted Brigadier General Walthall's command, the 34th Mississippi left Shelbyville, Tennessee in time to arrive at Murfreesboro on December 27. The regiment did not see action at the bloodbath at that location.[11]

Benton was finally able to rejoin his troops in time to participate in the battle of Chattanooga. Walthall's Brigade and its regiments were then members of Major General William Henry Talbot Walker's Corps. The men of these units had been among the first Confederates to enter the battle of Chickamauga. Seeing action all three days at Chickamauga and being the recipient of heavy Federal fire, 34th Mississippi concluded the battle with casualties of nineteen missing, ninety-one wounded, and fifteen killed. This was accomplished and suffered without the services of the convalescing Colonel Benton.[12]

At Chattanooga Col. Benton shared command of the 34th Mississippi with Capt. H. J. Bowen. The report of the latter noted the action of the regiment at Chattanooga in writing, "The Thirty-fourth, Col. Samuel Benton commanding, was ordered out about eight in the morning, to strengthen the picket lines at the foot of the mountain's west side, extending along its base about two miles. At about 10 o'clock the enemy, in four lines closely closed up, drove the left of the picket line, and so rapid was their movements that the center and right of the picket lines were cut off and eight colors had passed by the pickets when nearly all surrendered. A small number of the pickets made their escape up the river through the cliffs and cut timber below the Craven house, and…were in the engagements east of the Craven house from four in the evening until eight…"[13]

Only four members of Benton's command were reported as wounded at Chattanooga, but two hundred thirty-one were noted as missing. Certainly suffering from this heavy loss of captives, and the fact that he was among those who managed to escape, Benton and his remaining troops made their way to Dalton, Georgia where they spent the winter of 1863-1864.[14]

In the spring of 1864, witnessed Colonel Benton assumed command of three regiments, the 29th, 30th, and 34th Mississippi Infantry Regiments during the engagement at Rocky Face Ridge, Georgia on May 7, 1864. A week later, Benton led the 34th Mississippi in the battle of Resaca. On the morning of May 14, Benton ordered his troops to establish a line of breastworks. Utilizing dirt and logs, the men were able to do so. They used the safety of the hastily built breastworks as a base from which they were able to drive back a series of Federal assaults initiated in the evening hours.[15]

One historian wrote, "The brigade position was flanked…few if any instances during the war of greater losses from artillery fire than those…at Resaca." Despite casualties of four killed and eleven wounded, the regiment held its ground. At Cassville, the 34th Mississippi was again subjected to heavy fire and continued to endure such fighting in the Confederate lines at locations such as New Hope Church and Kennesaw Mountain.[16]

General Walthall was promoted to the command of a division and

Colonel Benton took over the leadership of Walthall's brigade for the months of June and July, 1864.[17] The intense fighting at locations in and around the city of Atlanta occupied the majority of Benton's waking hours during the hot summer months. These actions provided evidence of his bravery and strong military prowess, but they also took a heavy toll on Benton in the latter portion of July, 1864.

During the July 22, 1864 Atlanta fighting, Benton received a serious wound to his right leg. The injury necessitated the hasty amputation of his severely shattered limb. In addition to the receipt of his critical leg wound, Benton also endured hit from a shell fragment had struck his chest. The latter injury from the projectile inflicted a great deal of discomfort upon the suffering officer, lying prostrate in the strong Georgia heat. A state historical marker, located at Walthall Street and Boulevard Drive in Atlanta, contains a reference to the wounding of Benton and states, "Col. Samuel Benton, wounded in the battle, was carried to the rear and was later removed to a hospital at Griffin, Ga."[18]

On July 26, 1864, Benton received his promotion to brigadier general while recuperating in Griffin, Georgia. There is no recorded information as to Benton's response to this promotion. However, his perception of the event is questionable, as Benton succumbed to the infection from the wound to his right leg and passed away on July 28, 1864. The forty-three year old Benton was initially buried at Griffin, but was reinterred at Holly Springs after the war.[19]

Recognition for Brigadier General Samuel Benton continued after his death. A history of Mississippi indicates that Benton County, Mississippi, formed in 1870, was named him. The area that composed the new county had been formed from regions originally contained in Marshall and Tippah Counties. The name for Benton County has also been linked to Thomas Hart Benton, the senator who was Samuel Benton's uncle. However, the namesake of the county regularly seems to be strongly linked to Samuel Benton. Interestingly, Benton's grave monument in Holly Springs, Mississippi contains no information related to his Confederate service, but a modern headstone added to the site notes his Confederate rank at the time of his death.[20]

WILLIAM LINDSAY BRANDON, C.S.A.
1801-1890

William Lindsay Brandon was born to the well-to-do Adams County, Mississippi residents Gerard and Dorothy Nugent Brandon. Gerard and Dorothy Brandon reportedly parented a total of nine children; William was the youngest. Five boys and four girls filled the Brandon home that had been established when the couple had moved westward and settled on four hundred fifty acres in the Mississippi Territory in 1786.[1]

A fire that occurred several years later destroyed the family's records and creating an uncertainty for William's birthdate. Therefore, the ability to provide his exact date of birth is basically non-existent. Additionally, the years provided his birth generally range from 1800 to1802. However, the year 1801 is the most widely accepted and general date provided for the event that likely occurred near the settlement of Washington, Mississippi.[2]

William Lindsay Brandon lost his mother in 1816. Young William overcame the grief associated with this loss and eventually received an education at Washington College. Additional indications point to the fact that William studied medicine at Princeton, then known as the College of New Jersey. While educated in the medical field, Brandon sought fortune as a planter as well as being at least a part-time member of and lecturer in the medical profession. Information notes that the young farmer and physician also held strong interests in hunting and raising horses. Records indicate Brandon's slave ownership totaled three hundred individuals.[3]

In 1826, three years after the death of his father, William Brandon entered the political field, serving as a member of the Mississippi State Legislature. That same year he married Georgia Ann C. Davis in the small town of Wilkinson, Mississippi. The twenty-seven year old Georgia Ann Brandon passed away seven years later from undisclosed causes. Brandon mourned briefly for his wife; he married Ann Eliza Ratliff the same year Georgia passed away. This second marriage for William Lindsay Brandon took place in West Feliciana Parish, Louisiana.[4]

William Lindsay Brandon's two marriages combined to produce at least four children. William's sons William Ratliff, Lane William, Eugene, and Robert were born in 1834, 1838, 1839, and 1840. Eugene passed away within two years of his birth, while the other sons lived into the early 1900s. In 1840 Ann Eliza Ratliff Brandon, William's second wife, passed away. The exact circumstances surrounding Ann Eliza's death are left to speculation, but the event occurred the same year that Robert was born and when Eugene passed away. Whether the deaths of Ann and Eugene resulted from some type of epidemic, or if Ann lost her life while giving birth to Robert is open to conjecture.[5]

Little additional information about William Lindsay Brandon's antebellum exploits exists, but by the time the American Civil War began Brandon was approaching the age of sixty. That advanced age apparently provided few concerns for the Confederate military officials, as Brandon was assigned the rank of major in the 1st Mississippi Infantry Battalion. Brandon was later promoted to captain in the 21st Mississippi Infantry Regiment, the name which the 1st Mississippi Infantry Battalion held by that time. Captain William Brandon was assigned to command Company D, the Jeff Davis Guards.[6]

In addition to Captain William Brandon's Company D, other companies in the 21st Mississippi Infantry Regiment included ones raised in the counties of Warren, Lawrence, Wilkinson, and Tallahatchie. Other counties represented in the 21st Mississippi included Madison, Sunflower, and Pontotoc. The names of the companies included in the regiment included Hurricane Rifles, Madison Guards, New Albany Greys, and Vicksburg Confederates.[7]

Upon the 21st Mississippi Infantry Regiment's arrival in Virginia, Brandon received a promotion to major. According to a regimental history, "Brandon's battalion was ordered to Manassas… Captain Green's Vicksburg company…with Captain Dudley's company…to form a regiment under the command of Col. B. G. Humphreys.[8]

Illness struck Brandon in June 1861 and chills associated with the undetermined disease necessitated his absence from the regiment until August. The lack of leadership caused the 21st Mississippi Infantry Regiment and Major William Lindsay Brandon to miss the battle of First Manassas.[9] That fact was likely a blessing in disguise for Brandon and his fellow regiment members, as the battle was the largest to have taken place in the United States to that date.

With the rank of lieutenant colonel, William Lindsay Brandon joined his regiment in moving to Leesburg, Virginia on November 19, 1861. One of Lieutenant Colonel Brandon's fellow officers commented on the 21st Mississippi Infantry Regiment's time in Leesburg by writing that it was spent, "…in the drudgery of building forts, rifle pits, and picketing the Potomac with the Federal army in sight."[10]

The next month the unit was ordered to return to Richmond, but it quickly made a return to Leesburg, Virginia. The 21st Mississippi Infantry Regiment, brigaded with the 13th, 17th, and 18th Mississippi Infantry Regiments, remained in Leesburg for the winter of 1861-62. On March 9, 1862 Brandon and his comrades of the 21st Mississippi moved from Leesburg and advanced toward the Rapidan River. On April 7 they moved to the vicinity of Yorktown.[11]

During the battle of Seven Pines Lieutenant Colonel William Lindsay Brandon and his command served as part of the Confederate rear guard, with his regiment, the 21st Mississippi, suffering a minimal loss. One of the major aspects of the action at Seven Pines was the fact that General Joseph Johnston had been disabled when a shell struck his upper body. The resulting wound caused Johnston to relinquish command to General Robert Edward Lee.[12]

In late June 1862 the 21st Mississippi Infantry Regiment, with Brandon in command, was primarily engaged as the advance picket line during the action at Savage Station. Unfortunately, the brigade commander, Brigadier General Richard Griffith, was killed when a shell fragment struck him. Colonel Benjamin Humphreys suffered from the flux during the battle and relinquished command of the 21ˢᵗ Mississippi to Lieutenant Colonel Brandon. With three of his sons serving in the regiment with him, Brandon, weighing approximately 200 pounds and standing 6 feet 2 inches tall, was certainly an imposing sight in battle.[13]

On July 1, 1862 Lieutenant Colonel William Lindsay Brandon led his troops into action at Malvern Hill. Still brigaded with the 13ᵗʰ, 17ᵗʰ, and 18ᵗʰ Mississippi Regiments, Brandon's 21ˢᵗ Mississippi Infantry Regiment was in Griffith's Brigade, under the command of Colonel William Barksdale. As such, Brandon was a member of Major General John Magruder's Division.[14]

At Malvern Hill, Brandon was felled when a ball slammed his ankle and a dud cannon ball struck his hand. The first injury was initially perceived as superficial, but the diagnosis was modified to one more serious as the wounded officer was unable to stand for more than a few seconds. A tourniquet was implemented and Lieutenant Colonel Brandon's critically wounded leg was amputated. Sources have noted that the lack of chloroform, coupled with Brandon's advanced age, created a difficult surgery and an initial prognosis of little chance for survival. The 21ˢᵗ Mississippi suffered twenty-three killed and eighty-three wounded at Malvern Hill.[15]

It would be almost a year before Lieutenant Colonel William Lindsay Brandon had sufficiently recovered from the wound and was able to rejoin the 21ˢᵗ Mississippi Infantry Regiment. Brandon recovered in time to see limited action at Gettysburg. The 21ˢᵗ Mississippi slammed into the Federal line where Major General Daniel Sickle's blue-clad troops were retreating, but the men of the New Jersey Battery managed to keep possession of their guns.[16]

The brigade's monument on the Gettysburg battlefield states that the 21ˢᵗ Mississippi Infantry Regiment arrived at the Peach Orchard near 3 p.m. and, "...at 5 p.m....took part in the assault on the Peach Orchard and adjacent positions, vigorously pursuing the Union forces as they retired. The 21ˢᵗ Regiment pushed on past the Trostle House and captured, but were unable to bring off 9ᵗʰ Mass. Battery and I Battery 5ᵗʰ U. States...a fierce conflict ensued in which Brig. Gen. Wm. Barksdale fell mortally wounded."[17]

Other information related to the participation of the 21st Mississippi Infantry Regiment at Gettysburg states, "When all that was left of Bigelow's battery was withdrawn, it was closely pressed by…Twenty-first Mississippi, the only regiment which succeeded in crossing Plum Run… men had entered the battery and fought hand-to-hand…"[18]

The death of the highly-respected Brigadier General William Barksdale, a Mississippi politician before the war, led to Colonel Benjamin Humphreys being promoted to brigadier general. That had an impact upon the military career of Lieutenant Colonel William Brandon. On August 14, 1863, William Lindsay Brandon was promoted to colonel. The effect of the action at Gettysburg was great upon the 21st Mississippi Infantry Regiment. Of the four hundred twenty-four regiment members present at the battle, eighteen were killed, and eighty-five wounded.[19]

Colonel William Lindsay Brandon, a member of Longstreet's 1st Corps, fought in the Chickamauga and Knoxville Campaigns in September and November of 1863. In these actions, Brandon was on detached service from the Army of Northern Virginia and under the direct command of Brigadier General Benjamin Humphreys. At Chickamauga the 21st Mississippi Infantry Regiment suffered casualties of seven killed and forty-three wounded. Colonel Brandon eventually returned to Virginia where he served with General James Longstreet.[20]

When the Confederate 1st Corps returned to Virginia, Colonel William Brandon's military promotions took a final step. Effective to rank from June 18, 1864, William Lindsay Brandon became a brigadier general. Brigadier General William Lindsay Brandon returned to Mississippi and, beginning on July 23, 1864, commanded the Reserve Corps of Mississippi.[21]

Brigadier General William Lindsay Brandon was given the responsibility of securing needed military personnel as he had been appointed the director of the Mississippi Bureau of Conscription on October 8, 1864. It was stated, "He labored unceasingly to bring out every man needed for the service of the Confederacy." The lack of able-bodied candidates, coupled with the increase of desertions in the final year of the war limited Brigadier General Brandon's effectiveness. As a result, the bureau was suspended before the war reached its conclusion.[22]

Upon the conclusion of the war, Brigadier General William Lindsay Brandon returned to *Arcole*, his Mississippi plantation, where he resumed his planting endeavors. A summary of his post-war life proclaimed, "He zealously promoted the cause of the South, but when that cause was lost accepted the result in good faith and turned his attention to rebuilding of the ruined fortunes of his State." Brandon eventually retired, but remained at his Wilkerson County, Mississippi plantation until his death on October 8, 1890. The former politician, soldier, physician, and planter was buried in the family plot located at *Arcole*.[23]

WILLIAM FELIX BRANTLEY, C.S.A.

1830-1870

William Felix Brantley was born in Green County, Alabama on March 12, 1830. His parents, William and Marinda Jolly Brantley, were originally from Georgia and Alabama, respectively. The couple young moved to Mississippi while William was still a child, and the Magnolia State served as the location of his formative years.[1]

William Felix Brantley eventually had a total of four brothers and two sisters. His two sisters were named Missouri and Mary, while William's brothers were known as Edmund, Albert Horton, Arnold, and John Ransom. The Brantley children received high levels of education, as John became a physician; William and Albert became attorneys.[2]

William Brantley began his study of law in Carroll County, Mississippi, and lived with his brother John. William eventually moved from Carroll County and established his legal practice in Greensboro, Mississippi in 1852. Brantley's career flourished, and the 1860 census listed William Felix Brantley as a lawyer living in Choctaw County, Mississippi.[3]

In the meantime, Brantley wed Cornelia S. Medley on December 27, 1855. The couple produced three children, but only one of whom would survive to adulthood. The firstborn child of William and Cornelia was Mary Thomas Brantley, a daughter named after one of William's aforementioned sisters. Mary Thomas Brantley, William and Cornelia's daughter, was born September 5, 1858. Upon reaching adulthood, Mary married and had five children, but records indicate that at least three of her offspring passed away prior to their mother's death. William and Cornelia also had a son, Joseph Ransom Brantley, born on September 5, 1859. Joseph died at the age of ten. Another child died as an infant in June 1861.[4]

Tragedy continued to beset the Brantley family when William's brother, Edmund, was killed in a duel in Tennessee. In 1859, John Ransom Brantley, another of William Felix's brothers and a physician in Texas, was killed in Gonzales. John Ransom Brantley was the victim of a man named David Balzell.[5]

During the course of these events, the state of Mississippi held its secession convention in January 1861. William Felix Brantley represented Choctaw County at the meeting held in Jackson. The decision of the convention's attendees was overwhelmingly in favor of breaking the ties that had existed between Mississippi and the United States. The final count of the corresponding votes revealed a strong pro-secession tally of eighty-three to fifteen. With that outcome, Mississippi became the second state, following South Carolina, to leave the Union.[6]

With the secession of Mississippi completed, Brantley offered his services to the Confederate States of America. On April 20, 1861, he enlisted in the Mississippi State Militia and was assigned the rank of captain. That rank remained Brantley's when his company, the Wigfall Rifles, officially joined the Confederacy as the 15th Mississippi Infantry Regiment.[7]

The 15th Mississippi was organized in Corinth, Mississippi in May 1861, and the field officers were elected the next month. Following stops in Union City, Tennessee and Knoxville, the members of the 15th Mississippi began a march into Kentucky. On October 21, 1861, the regiment participated in the battle of Camp Wildcat or Wildcat Mountain, and suffered minor casualties[8] in the Confederate victory.

In January 1862, the 15th Mississippi met a strong Federal force at Fishing Creek, Kentucky. In addition to the military loss, a major tragedy occurred when the Confederates suffered the death of their beloved commander, General Felix Zollicoffer. Reporting on the regiment's role in the engagement, Major General George Crittenden wrote, "For an hour...the Fifteenth Mississippi...had been struggling with the superior force of the enemy. I cannot omit to mention the heroic valor of these two regiments."[9]

Armed primarily with flintlock muskets, the tenacity of Captain William Brantley and his fellow members of the 15th Mississippi received praise from Crittenden. The major general said, "The reputation of the Mississippians for heroism was fully sustained by this regiment. Its loss in killed and wounded, which was far greater than that of any other regiment, tells sufficiently the story of its discipline and courage..." Crittenden's words were substantiated in the tally of the 15th Mississippi's casualties with forty-four killed and one hundred fifty-three wounded.[10]

By April 1862, and the onset of the battle of Shiloh, Captain Brantley was a member of the 29th Mississippi Infantry Regiment. During the fighting at Shiloh, Brantley was wounded, but the severity was minimal. He was rewarded for his gallantry at Shiloh when he received a promotion to lieutenant colonel in May 1862.[11]

On December 13, 1862, Lieutenant Colonel Brantley rose to the rank of colonel. The promotion took place approximately two weeks before the onset of the carnage at Stones River or Murfreesboro, Tennessee. On Wednesday, December 31, Colonel Brantley received his second wound of the war when a projectile struck his shoulder at Stones River.[12]

Regarding the wound received at Stones River, Colonel Brantley and his adjutant, Lieutenant John Campbell, were "knocked down by concussion produced by the explosion of a shell very near them...The casualties of the Twenty-ninth were 34 killed...202 wounded...The total killed and wounded was exceeded by only one regiment in the army..."[13]

The brigade commander's report of the incident said, "It is due in particular to commend Col. W. F. Brantley...for the skill, activity, zeal and courage I have ever observed...under similar circumstances, but which in an especial degree signaled...actions on this occasion."[14]

The performance of the 29th Mississippi was noted in General Leonidas Polk's official report of the action at Murfreesboro. Polk wrote, "The fire of the enemy...was terrific... evidences of destructive firing as were left on the forest, from which this brigade emerged, have rarely if ever, been seen. The timber was torn and crushed...but the onward movement of the Mississippians...was irresistible."[15]

Recovering from his Stones River wound in a rapid manner, Colonel William Brantley was in Shelbyville, Tennessee in mid-January 1863. There, the 29th Mississippi was temporarily combined with the 24th Mississippi Infantry Regiment and placed under Brantley's command.[16]

Leading the 29th Mississippi at Chickamauga in September 1863, Colonel Brantley was in the brigade of Brigadier General Edward Walthall of Brigadier General St John Liddell's division. The units under Liddell were members of Major General William Walker's corps. During the battle of Chickamauga, there was another commendation for Brantley's performance, as Colonel Walthall, the brigade commander at Chickamauga, praised Brantley's efforts.[17]

At Chickamauga, Colonel Brantley, "...advanced to Chickamauga Creek at Alexander's Bridge, and a fight ensued, the brunt of which fell upon the Twenty-ninth Regiment, under Colonel Brantley. It was a fierce engagement...and the regiment had 56 killed and wounded."[18]

In the subsequent action at Chickamauga, Brantley and the men of the 29th Mississippi, positioned near Byram's Ford, "...were in battle... where brigades of both armies were charging in different directions in the woods, flanking each other in turn, and friend often firing on friend... In this engagement the Twenty-ninth suffered severely. Next day they moved further to the north and pushed across the Chattanooga road... Here they came under an artillery fire that could not be endured and fell back hurriedly, losing a few killed and 15 or 20 captured."[19]

Reports of the battle clearly indicate the ferociousness of the combat that took place at Chickamauga. The casualties of the 29th Mississippi at Chickamauga were among the heaviest casualties of either side for that campaign. During the three days of fighting, the three hundred sixty-eight men of the regiment who reported for duty endured a total casualty figure of one hundred ninety-four killed, wounded, and missing.[20]

The 29th Mississippi was also involved in the action on and around Lookout Mountain, the eminence overlooking Chattanooga, Tennessee. Still in Walthall's brigade, Brantley's troops performed well in what came to be known as the "battle above the clouds." The brigade's casualties, for 1,489 active soldiers, were eight killed, forty-eight wounded, and a staggering eight hundred forty-five captured.[21]

As for the conduct of Colonel William Brantley and the 29th Mississippi, perhaps the best description is found in the report of General Walthall. The brigade commander said, "I directed Colonel Brantley to advance his left as far as it could be done without leaving an interval between his line and the cliff, so as to get the benefit of an oblique fire upon the line that was pressing upon us. The order was executed with that officer's characteristic promptness."[22]

More accolades for Brantley and his fellow Mississippians were noted in General Walthall's additional comments that Colonel Brantley exhibited "skill, activity, zeal, and courage" during the fighting at Chattanooga. General Braxton Bragg proclaimed that a particular Federal assault was contested "by one brigade only, Walthall's, which made a desperate resistance, but was finally compelled to yield ground." Another officer noted the Mississippians "gallantly contested" the advance of General Joseph Hooker's Corps at Chattanooga.[23]

In 1863, in the midst of some of the most contested battles of the American Civil War, William Felix Brantley suffered another personal loss when his wife Cornelia passed away.[24] The dedication of the Confederate officer resulted in Brantley foregoing a lengthy period of mourning. In turn, he would not seek another wife until the war's conclusion.

Among military engagements Colonel William Brantley experienced during 1864, the May 13 through 15 action at Resaca, Georgia resulted in high praises, while the regiment endured heavy Federal artillery fire. An official report said Brantley was, "...commended for his gallantry, after leading a charge on the enemy that repulsed Federal assaults three times."[25]

An official report stated, "Brantley's command was the extreme left of Hood's Corps, adjoining Hardee's Corps, in a part of the works exposed to an enfilading fire of artillery, but they held the position with remarkable coolness and repulsed the infantry attacks in front...Some of [Federal] troops obtained lodgment in a depression within 150 yards of the guns but were driven out by Brantley...the brigade was under the enfilading fire of twenty-four cannon, and their breastworks of logs and earth were set on fire by shot...they held fast through a day and a half...of the Twenty-ninth 5 were killed, 23 wounded."[26]

Resaca was one of the numerous locations where Brantley's 29[27] Mississippi experienced battle during the early phases of the Atlanta Campaign. A history of the regiment recorded that while its members were participating in the engagements around Atlanta, "...there was hardly a day when the Twenty-ninth Mississippi was not under fire."[27]

On June 22, 1864, Colonel Brantley and the men in his regiment participated in the fighting at Kolb's Farm. At that location, Federals under Generals Hooker and Schofield struck the Confederate position. In turn, Brantley managed to lead his soldiers as they captured the Federal works, "but could not maintain its position in them for lack of support."[28]

A month later, on July 22, 1864, Brantley's brigade commander, Colonel Samuel Benton, was mortally wounded at Ezra Church. As a result, Colonel William Felix Brantley assumed command of the 29[29] Mississippi. Brantley held that post for the remainder of the war.[29]

Colonel Brantley's performance and leadership skills that were exhibited in battle, combined with his leadership abilities, earned him a final promotion on July 26, 1864. On that day William Felix Brantley became a brigadier general in the Confederate Army.[30]

Two days later Brigadier General William Felix Brantley led his brigade of battle-hardened Mississippians into an engagement on the Atlanta-area Lickskillet Road. According to Brantley, the events of the day included the Federal troops being driven from their works, "but being greatly weakened by the killed and wounded, and the innumerable cases of utter exhaustion among the best men of my command, as well as by the absence of a goodly number who had no legitimate excuse...I was unable to hold the works."[31]

A lack of water, combined with the extreme heat of the late July day, as well as the previously noted situations, canceled any successful renewal on the part of the Confederates. The casualties for the 29[32] Mississippi were combined with those of the 30th Mississippi in the report for the action. The two regiments suffered a total of five killed and twenty-four wounded from the two hundred seventy-seven men who were present on the field. They also managed to capture approximately twenty Federal prisoners.[32]

Following the Confederate exodus from Atlanta, Brigadier General Brantley led his infantrymen in a skirmish at Snake Creek Gap. That action preceded their move to Gadsden, Alabama. In the last days of

October 1864, Brantley crossed the Tennessee River and awaited orders for additional offensives.[33]

In November 1864, Brigadier General Brantley led his brigade toward Franklin, Tennessee. The units under his command were the 24th, 27th, 29th, 30th, and 34th Mississippi Infantry Regiments, as well as a dismounted cavalry company.[34]

The ensuing battle of Franklin followed far-less injurious engagements at Columbia and Spring Hill. General Stephen Dill Lee wrote about Franklin, a battle which took place in hours near and after sunset. Lee said, "The brigades of Sharp and Brantley and of Deas particularly distinguished themselves. Their dead were mostly in the trenches and on the works of the enemy, where they fell in a desperate hand-to-hand conflict. Brantley was exposed to a severe enfilade fire. These noble brigades never faltered in this terrible night struggle. I have never seen greater evidences of gallantry than was displayed by this division [Major General Edward Johnson]."[35]

The struggle at Franklin had riddled the ranks of Brantley's brigade. It was recorded that Brantley's troops suffered more casualties than did any other in their division. While "the strength of the brigade was about that of a full regiment, but less than that in line of battle," Brigadier General Brantley's brigade was the unfortunate recipient of seventy-six killed, one hundred forty wounded, and twenty-one missing at Franklin.[36]

Brigadier General William Felix Brantley followed the Federals in a movement toward Nashville and began to create entrenchments in the area on December 2, 1864. On the night of December 15, Federal soldiers attacked Brantley's command that was positioned near the Franklin Pike. General Stephen Lee recalled, "One feeble effort to use this force…was readily repulsed by Stovall's and Brantley's Brigades, which had been moved to the right."[37]

Following a series of skirmishes and battles in the Nashville area, Confederates under Brantley crossed the Tennessee River on December 26 and made winter quarters in northeast Mississippi. A month earlier, General John Bell Hood had issued a plea for recruits to join Brantley's command. Hood wrote, "The brigade…the State of Mississippi may justly feel proud of, and the present state of its ranks is due to the severe losses it has sustained in the many battles in which it has been engaged, in all of which it has borne a conspicuous part."[38]

On February 12, 1865, the brigade was furloughed, but it was reassembled two days later at Meridian, Mississippi. Moving toward North Carolina on February 18, 1865, Brigadier General Brantley was delayed in Montgomery, Alabama, a result of the Mobile fighting. Eventually reaching Smithfield, North Carolina, Brantley recorded his brigade's strength at only two hundred eighty-three on March 31, 1865.[39]

The spring of 1865 witnessed Brigadier General Brantley participating in the Carolina Campaign. Leading the former brigade of Walthall, Brigadier General Brantley was in the division of General Edward Johnson. On April 26, 1865, Brantley joined General Joseph Johnston in the massive Confederate surrender in North Carolina. Brantley was soon paroled in Greensboro, North Carolina and began making his way toward Mississippi.[40]

With the conclusion of the war, William Felix Brantley returned to Choctaw County, Mississippi and resumed the practice of his once-lucrative legal profession. Less than four years later Brantley married for a second time, making a commitment to a lady named Julia. Late in 1869 the couple had a son, but the tragedy that had made its presence felt in the Brantley family's past once again reared its ugly head. On November 10, 1869, the Brantley infant died.[41]

On August 16, 1870, Arnold Brantley, another of William's brothers, met a tragic and untimely death when he was shot, reportedly in cold blood. Arnold had served as the mayor of Winona, Mississippi, and that position had apparently led to the creation of an enemy bent on murdering the politician. William Brantley made it known that he would use his legal expertise to bring justice to the person or people responsible for Arnold's death.[42]

On November 2, 1870, Brantley was about one half mile east of Winona, Mississippi, the Montgomery County, Mississippi town where his brother Arnold had been murdered less than three months earlier. Although William had reportedly been warned of the dangers associated with being in the area, he had also made a vow to avenge his brother's untimely death.[43]

A period newspaper recorded that William Brantley was known to make sound judgments and would not allow any form of danger to deter him from accomplishing any task. He was also noted as stating that he would conduct business at whatever location he was summoned. Unfortunately, that mindset led to more tragedy for the Brantley family as William rode into an ambush and was killed when a shotgun blast struck his body as he drove his buggy toward his house. No one was ever arrested or tried for Brantley's murder.[44]

William Felix Brantley was buried next to Cornelia in Greensboro, Mississippi, a town in Webster County, Mississippi. Today, the cemetery is the primary visible artifact of the settlement that once served as the county seat for Webster County. The location of Brantley's grave, which has a headstone containing a carved image of him is situated, "…behind the church at Old Greensboro, about three miles north of Tomnolen, Webster County, Mississippi."[45]

Sadly, the unfortunate events that had plagued the Brantley family did not end with William Felix's death. Two years after the former general's murder, William Dunn, the son of William Brantley's sister Missouri, was killed in Greensboro, Mississippi. A man surnamed Story shot Dunn and ended the life of the man named after his uncle, William Felix Brantley.[46]

JAMES RONALD CHALMERS, C.S.A.
1831-1898

On January 11, 1831, the Halifax County, Virginia couple Joseph Williams Chalmers and Fannie Henderson Chalmers, welcomed their first child, James Ronald Chalmers. A few years later, James moved to Jackson, Tennessee with his family. By the end of the decade the Chalmers were residing in Holly Springs, Mississippi.[1]

Judge Joseph Williams Chalmers eventually represented Mississippi in the United States Senate. While working with the James Knox Polk administration, Judge Chalmers and his wife eventually had seven children, four sons and three daughters. In the meantime, James Ronald Chalmers attended St. Thomas Hall in preparation for college.[2]

At the age of twenty, Chalmers graduated from South Carolina College, now known as the University of South Carolina. Having studied law, James finished second in a class of fifteen students. Upon his graduation, Chalmers returned to Holly Springs and entered politics. He also studied law in the well-known firm of Barton and Chalmers. James Chalmers served as an 1852 delegate to the Democratic National Convention and entered the legal profession in the following months. The practice evidently flourished as James Chalmers became the district attorney for Mississippi's Seventh Judicial District in 1858 at the young age of twenty-seven.[3]

In the meantime, James Chalmers and his wife, Rebecca Arthur Chalmers, had their first child, Susan Arthur Chalmers. Sadly, the daughter, born in 1855, passed away in 1856. The following year, the couple had another daughter, Kate Henderson Chalmers Rogers. The younger daughter, the last for the Chalmers, lived until the last full year of the Second World War.[4]

"Soon recognized as one of the ablest prosecuting attorneys" in the Magnolia State, Chalmers proved his worthiness, despite having to battle allegations of having been elected over "several worthy and popular competitors." In addition to his legal practice, Chalmers served as a DeSoto County delegate to the Mississippi State Convention. Chalmers was classified as "an ardent State rights Democrat" and voted in favor of Mississippi seceding. In January 1861, the body, of which Chalmers had served as chairman of the military committee, passed the ordinance of secession.[5] With that decision, Mississippi officially broke its ties with the United States.

In March 1861, thirty year-old James Chalmers joined the Confederate Army and, although he had no previous military experience, was soon elected colonel of the 9th Mississippi Infantry Regiment. That regiment was reportedly the first from the state of Mississippi to enter the Confederate service and was sent to Pensacola, Florida.[6]

The initiation into combat for Colonel Chalmers came during the Confederate attack against Fort Pickens, a Federal fort located on Santa Rosa Island, south of Pensacola. The 1861 raid took place on the night of October 8 and 9 and resulted in an unsuccessful Confederate attempt at victory. With the Federal occupants suffering less than seventy casualties, the outcome of the battle is clearly demonstrated with the related numbers of the Confederates, under Brigadier General Robert Anderson, having lost some one hundred seventy-five men.[7]

Colonel James Ronald Chalmers was promoted to brigadier general on February 13, 1862. Moving his "Pensacola Brigade" northward, Chalmers intended to join the Confederates encamped in North Mississippi. In the month of March he had the 2,500 members of his brigade positioned at Iuka, Mississippi. The troops were moved to Eastport, Mississippi where the units under his command included troops recently relocated from East Tennessee as well as the 9th Texas and soldiers of the 5th, 7th, and 10th Mississippi Infantry Regiments.[8]

Brigadier General Chalmers commanded the Confederate forces that battled and defeated General William Sherman at Eastport, Mississippi. During the March 12, 1862 battle, Chalmers managed to instigate Sherman's gunboats to retreat, saving a bridge across Bear Creek. In addition the Memphis and Charleston Railroad remained in Confederate possession.[9]

On March 31, 1862, Chalmers commanded his brigade, in addition to one hundred members of Colonel James Clanton's 1st Alabama Cavalry. These infantrymen and horsemen reconnoitered the Federals who were positioned along Lick Creek in the vicinity of Pittsburg Landing, near the Shiloh Methodist Church in Tennessee.[10]

Only two months after his promotion, Brigadier General Chalmers led the Second Brigade of General Jones Mitchell Withers Division, Army of Mississippi, at Shiloh, Tennessee. The 8:30 a.m. order from Chalmers requested the men of his "Pensacola Brigade" to charge, but the ranks of the 10th Mississippi were the only ones to initially hear the order. When the additional members of his brigade responded, the result was the quick exodus of the Federal troops of the 18th Wisconsin Infantry from their post. Later activities for Chalmers at Shiloh included suffering additional casualties at the Daniel Davis Wheat Field, the cotton field of Sarah Bell, and the infamous area later known as the Hornet's Nest.[11]

Positioned on the extreme right of the Confederate line, Chalmers joined his troops in the last Confederate charge on the battle's second day, April 7, 1862. Chalmers managed to escape injury, despite having his horse shot from under him and his clothing bearing the marks of projectiles that brushed his body. His bravery resulted in a commendation in the days after the conflict on the banks of the Tennessee River.[12]

Three months later, on July 1, 1862, Brigadier General Chalmers, with a command of approximately five thousand, fought Federal colonel Phil Sheridan near Booneville, Mississippi. Sheridan was able to give the appearance of possessing a far-superior force, as he had his troops conduct a series of boarding and disembarking moves from trains. In fact, Sheridan has less than eight hundred fifty soldiers at his disposal during what was termed as a "stubborn engagement" that lasted from 8:30 that morning until late in the evening.[13] The resulting Confederate loss would prove to be a sore spot for Chalmers for some time.

Brigadier General James Chalmers participated in the 1862 invasion of Kentucky, having been temporarily assigned to a cavalry unit. Reassigned to the leadership role in an infantry brigade at his own request, Chalmers was under the command of General Braxton Bragg. Chalmers was given recognition for his service at Munfordville, Kentucky, where he reportedly performed his "duties with courage and zeal."[14]

Prior to the battle at Munfordville, Chalmers had been ordered to Cave City, Kentucky to protect the area railroad. Brigadier General Chalmers readied his troops for the fifteen-mile march to Fort Craig, located near Munfordville, where he was told to expect an encounter with a small Federal force. When Chalmers reached the fort he determined that an attack upon the force would be advantageous and he began the same without permission from, or taking the time to notify, his superiors. The smoke from cannon fire added to the low visibility the September morning's fog created, and Chalmers men walked into an onslaught of Federal fire.[15]

Being subjected to what came to be labeled as "Chalmers Great Blunder," the Mississippians of Chalmers command encountered an event that one witness recalled as being "a most severe and galling fire." A member of Chalmers's command said, "We were so cut up...no telling what would have become of us if Chalmers had not hoisted the white flag."[16]

Despite the initial situation, Chalmers and his Confederate counterparts managed to overcome the Federal fire and eventually attained the capture of Fort Craig. The hoisting of the white flag had created a cessation in the battle during which Chalmers requested the surrender of the fort. More shots were soon fired and men of both sides became casualties, but the sought after victory was eventually achieved on the part of the Confederates.[17]

An evaluation of Chalmers's performance at Munfordville stated, "He attacked with vigor, but was repulsed." This was rationalized in that the brigadier general had been "misinformed regarding the strength of the garrison and the character of the defensive works." Of the one thousand nine hundred thirteen men who Chalmers reported as fit for duty at

Munfordville, the casualty figures were thirty-five killed and two hundred fifty-three wounded.[18]

In the aftermath of the Kentucky Campaign, Chalmers seemed to have lost control of his troops who had become enraged at area bushwhackers. Members of Chalmers's command captured sixteen of the bushwhackers and hanged them in a tree. The bodies were left to swing in the air as a reminder to those who attempted to inflict harm upon Confederates in Kentucky.[19]

At Murfreesboro, Tennessee, Chalmers was severely wounded in the head. The incident occurred in the area of the battlefield known as Hell's Half Acre on December 31, 1862. Various statements regarding Chalmers included, "Chalmers's Confederate Brigade...arose at the order, and, under terrific fire, dashed forward across the open field...Chalmers's attack was made with great fury...they came forward like a pack of hounds in full cry...in the field between the Round Forest and the wood...[the Federals] repulsed Chalmers..."[20]

Four months elapsed before Brigadier General Chalmers was able to return to his command. Prior to that point of his recovery, Chalmers was assigned the command of the District of Mississippi and East Louisiana, with Bragg as his superior. The request to place Chalmers into that position had come from Governor John Jones Pettus of Mississippi.[21]

During the spring of 1863, Brigadier General Chalmers made an unsuccessful attempt to arrest fellow Confederate officer Robert Vinkler Richardson. The latter had apparently been operating as a partisan ranger, an act that had agitated the Confederate high command.[22]

In January 1864, Chalmers received the leadership position of two cavalry brigades of the First Cavalry Division in General Nathan Bedford Forrest's Cavalry Corps, and he was given the nickname "Little 'Un." As such, Chalmers led the heralded First Division of Forrest's Cavalry from that time until the conclusion of the war.[23]

The battle of Fort Pillow, Tennessee in April 1864, resulted in criticism of Forrest that exists to the present time. The killing of a large number of African American troops in the final stages of the fight created a high level of negative comments directed toward General Forrest, under whom Chalmers served. More insight into the action at Fort Pillow can be gained through the reading of the official report Chalmers compiled.

Chalmers stated, "On the morning of the 11th...I moved...in the direction of Brownsville ...and thence by a continuous route back again to the Fort Pillow road. I moved from Brownsville...at 3:30 p.m...and reached Fort Pillow, a distance of 40 miles, at daylight next morning."[24]

Chalmers continued, "The works at Fort Pillow consisted of a strong line of fortifications ...stretching from Coal Creek bottom...to the Mississippi River...in length about 2 miles and at an average distance of about 600 yards from the river...About 300 yards in rear of this...stood the last fortification...a strong dirt fort in semicircular form, with a ditch in front of it 12 feet wide and 8 feet deep."[25]

In reviewing the onset of the attack, Chalmers noted, "The fight was opened at daylight by McCulloch. He moved cautiously through the ravines and short hills which encompassed the place...he succeeded about 11 o'clock in taking the work...and the flag of the Eighteenth Mississippi Battalion...the first regiment to enter the fort, was quickly flying above it."[26]

According to Chalmers, the Confederates, "...took possession of all the rifle-pits around the fort...The enemy made no attempt to surrender, no white flag was elevated, nor was the U. S. flag lowered until pulled down by our men. Many of them were killed while fighting, and many more in the attempt to escape. The strength of the enemy...was probably about 650 or 700...69 wounded were delivered to the enemy's gun-boats the next day...One hundred and sixty-four white men and 40 negroes were taken prisoners...half a dozen men may have escaped. The remainder of the garrison were killed."[27]

Chalmers compiled an April 20, 1864 letter in which he praise the effectiveness of recent West Tennessee actions. He wrote, "I congratulate you upon your success in the brilliant campaign...under the guidance of Major-General Forrest...whose restless activity, untiring energy, and courage baffled...and paralyzed...our enemies."[28]

Fully discussing the campaign, Brigadier General Chalmers stated, "In a brief space of time we have killed 4,000 of the enemy, captured over 1,200 prisoners, 800 horses, 5 pieces of artillery, thousands of small-arms, and many stand of colors, destroyed millions of dollars' worth of property, and relieved the patriots of West Tennessee from the hourly dread in which they have been accustomed to live."[29]

Chalmers concluded the letter in saying, "While we rejoice over our victories, let us not forget the few gallant spirits who yielded up their lives to their country, and fell as brave men love to fall, 'with their backs to the field and their feet to the foe'."[30]

In June 1864 Brigadier General Chalmers managed to once again march a great distance in an amazingly short duration of time. A history of Forrest's exploits stated, "Chalmers...left Monte Vallo...on the 10th of June, to return by forced marches to Mississippi. Notwithstanding the heavy rains...muddy roads and swollen streams encountered, he was at Columbus, Miss., one hundred and twenty miles from Monte Vallo, by one p.m. on the 13th."[31]

By the end of June 1864, Chalmers's Division consisted of brigades under Colonels Edmund Rucker and Robert McCulloch. The approximate manpower of Chalmers's Division at the time was comprised of one thousand four hundred of McCulloch and a recorded variation of nine hundred to two thousand three hundred from Rucker's brigade. Stationed in Verona, Mississippi, the division joined two others that were in the areas of Tupelo and Corinth to complete the composition of Forrest's Cavalry at the time.[32]

When General Forrest was wounded in action at Okolona, Mississippi, Chalmers took temporary charge of Forrest's Cavalry. The situation the unit faced was noted in an August 1, 1864 Chalmers letter. He wrote, "...fourteen thousand infantry and cavalry...at Lagrange...If the enemy moves in three columns...it will be impossible for us to meet him... our effective strength is 5,357, but we are very much crippled...both of my brigade commanders are wounded...most of the field-officers of the command were either killed or wounded..." [at Okolona].[33]

In August 1864, lawyer-turned-soldier James Ronald Chalmers was present at one of the most lopsided Confederate victories of the war, the battle of Johnsonville, Tennessee. During that engagement, Chalmers was recorded as having ordered the renowned Morton's Battery to position their guns on the opposite side of the Tennessee River from which Johnsonville was located. A witness recalled, "Precisely at two o'clock all the guns were discharged with such harmony that it sounded like one report, one heavy gun."[34]

Brigadier General Chalmers saw action at the November 1864 battle of

Franklin, Tennessee where his command suffered another round of heavy losses. With his forces severely dwindled, Chalmers spent the spring of 1865 fighting a series of skirmishes against the Federal command of Major General James Harrison Wilson. Chalmers surrendered his command at Gainesville, Alabama, and he was paroled on Mary 10, 1865.[35]

In the post-war years, James Chalmers returned to his lucrative legal practice and served a series of terms as a Congressman for the State of Mississippi. In 1872 he was elected to the Senate and was also on the Horace Greeley electoral ticket. In both 1876 and 1878, without an opponent, Chalmers was elected to represent the area of the state known as the "shoe-string district." In 1880, as well as 1882, Chalmers was popularly elected, but a duality of "some sort of manipulation and legerdemain at Jackson by the Governor and Secretary of State" resulted in his elections being overturned. The 1880 election was ruled to have been James R. Lynch's victory, while the 1882 decision was given to V. H. Manning. In the latter campaign's aftermath, Chalmers was asked to occupy a Democratic seat in the State Senate.[36]

Chalmers also maintained his desire to again serve in the Mississippi Congressional body. In 1884, as well as 1886, he ran against J. B. Morgan, a fellow Democrat, for his party's nomination. A period writer noted, "… there is but little doubt in the minds of his friends that he was elected both times, yet the certificate of election was given to his opponent."[37]

An evaluation of Chalmers, written in 1887, noted various aspects of his character. The synopsis said, "General Chalmers is fluent, bold, pointed, and fearless. In his style he draws occasionally upon a cultivated and exuberant fancy, but indulges more frequently in pointed and racy anecdote." The writer added, "As a friend, he is sincere, true, and devoted; as an enemy, fearless and inflexible, but at all times just and generous, as ready to atone for a wrong, when he is convinced that he has committed one, as he is, upon the other hand, steadfast and immovable when satisfied he is right."[38]

Another commentary on Chalmers came from Clark Russell Barteau, a one-time Confederate lieutenant-colonel. Barteau stated, "I love and appreciate the man. His talent is of high order, his character spotless, and his moral courage beyond all question."[39]

In 1888, James Chalmers moved to Memphis and continued to practice law. He joined with Thomas W. Harris, another former Confederate and "lifetime friend." It was said of the legal team, "They are recognized as among the leaders and most efficient of the Southern bar."[40]

Former Congressman, Confederate brigadier general, and attorney James Ronald Chalmers died in Memphis on April 9, 1898. The sixty-year old warrior was buried in the city's Elmwood Cemetery.[41] As a fitting memorial to the man who had strong ties to the state of Tennessee, and called Mississippi home, Chalmers is the namesake of a Sons of Confederate Veterans Camp in Tennessee. The camp is active to this day.

CHARLES CLARK, C.S.A.
1811-1877

Charles Clark was born in the Warren County, Ohio town of Lebanon on May 24, 1811. The Clark lineage could reportedly be traced to the *Mayflower*. Clark eventually undertook what has been termed a southward migration, and he left the Cincinnati-area town to attend school in Kentucky. In 1831 Clark moved to Mississippi where he briefly served as a school teacher and studied law. The education profession gave way to Clark's stint as a planter and to his eventual evolution toward the primary vocation of an attorney.[1]

A pivotal incident in Clark's law career occurred when he successfully represented a man in a Mississippi Delta land dispute with the Choctaw Indians. Clark's client donated a massive land grant as the young lawyer's legal fee. Clark named his newly-acquired plantation *Doe Roe*. Through a combination of literacy and pronunciation issues, the name and spelling were usually listed as *Doro*. The Bolivar County, Mississippi land holding "grew to over 5,000 acres and became the most prosperous in the region... in the social and economic affairs..."[2]

Entering the political arena, Clark served in the Mississippi Legislature from 1838 to 1844 and was regarded as a steadfast member of the Whig Party. The young lawyer also held a stint under the command of Jefferson Davis in the Mexican War, during which he rose to the rank of colonel in the 2nd Mississippi Infantry. Although he had raised a state regiment, there are indications that Clark never saw combat during his service in the war.[3]

After the Compromise of 1850, Clark shifted his allegiance to the Democratic Party. This political realignment was primarily due to Clark's disenchantment with the Whig Party's strong Unionist view. It was in the Democratic Party where Clark served as a delegate to the Charleston Convention of 1860. He supported John Breckinridge in Breckinridge's bid for the President.[4]

Clark made a determined effort to represent his area residents in the Mississippi Secession Convention, but he lost to a moderate opponent. With Mississippi's secession in 1861, Clark was given the rank of brigadier general in the militia group known as the Mississippi 1st Corps. As such, he served as one of four brigadier generals in the state. He quickly climbed to the rank of major general of the troops for Mississippi before the various Mississippi regiments were accepted into Confederate service. When that event took place Clark was appointed brigadier general, a decreased rank he agreed to hold in the new government's military.[5]

Brigadier General Charles Clark's early days of service in the Confederate Army were hectic for a man who had reached the age of fifty. He was mustered into the Confederate service in Pensacola, Florida before being sent to Virginia. Within a short period of his arrival in Virginia, Clark received orders to move to Kentucky.[6]

After he reached Kentucky, Clark was assigned to command a brigade of Mississippi troops, effective November 1, 1861. The brigade was placed into John Floyd's division of the Central Army of Kentucky, under the leadership of General William Hardee. Throughout the winter of 1861-1862 Clark remained in that position, but by March 1862 he had been reassigned to General Leonidas Polk's Corps where Clark was given command of the 1st Division.[7]

In April 1862 Brigadier General Charles Clark participated in the battle of Shiloh. In his official report of the engagement Clark noted that his division contained the Second Brigade, under the leadership of Brigadier General Stewart, as well as the First Brigade, with Colonel R. M.

Russell, of the 12th Tennessee Regiment, in command. On April 6, "the two brigades, the Second in front, marched to the field…in line of battle."[8]

Another account of the battle of Shiloh noted, "The third [Confederate] line…was composed of the First Corps, under Polk…Polk's corps, 9,136 strong in infantry and artillery, was composed of two divisions: Cheatham's on the left…and Clark's on his right, formed of A. P. Stewart's and Russell's brigades."[9]

Clark recorded his movements in writing, "When we arrived within 300 yards of Major-General Bragg's line, General A. Sidney Johnston ordered me to send the Second Brigade, by a flank movement, to the right…and to remain with the First Brigade in position and await orders. He led the Second Brigade in person…"[10]

Brigadier General Clark continued, "I was ordered to move to the edge of the open fields in front, and was…informed…that the battery on the left and front of my line was enfilading [Bragg's] troops, and directed me to charge it with one of my regiments. The Eleventh Louisiana, being most convenient, I led it forward."[11]

The Federal battery Clark spoke of was positioned behind a ridge some 300 yards from Clark's line. He ordered an advance upon the battery. Clark noted, "The battalion moved up the ascent, with fixed bayonets, at a double-quick…on the crest of the ridge we were opened upon by the enemy's battery with shot and canister and by a large infantry support with musketry at easy range." Clark's men were forced to fall behind the ridge, where they reformed.[12]

Eventually the Federal forces facing Clark were driven from the field. Clark wrote, "We pursued them at double-quick for some 500 yards…A brisk interchange of musketry continued for about fifteen minutes…I… was proceeding along the line… when I received a severe wound in the right shoulder." Clark went to the rear where his wound was dressed.[13]

Recovering from his wound, Brigadier General Charles Clark returned to command a division at the battle of Baton Rouge in August 1862. There, Clark was under the corps command of his former political cohort, John C. Breckinridge. A life-altering event lay in store for the recently-recovered Charles Clark. Unfortunately, Clark was seriously wounded again during the action at Baton Rouge when a ball shattered his hip. The severity of the second combat wound in a few months prevented Clark from being taken from the field when his division was suddenly forced from the area. In turn, he fell captive to the advancing Federal forces. Brigadier General Clark was sent to New Orleans to receive better treatment. This act reportedly took place because his Federal captives believed Clark's injury was fatal.[14]

One account of the action at Baton Rouge provided more details of Clark's activities in the battle. The author stated, "Breckinridge organized his force in two divisions, the first commanded by Brigadier-General Charles Clark...Shortly after daylight on the 5th of August, a dense fog prevailing, Breckinridge moved to the attack" with Clark's command to the right of the road that ran from Greenwell Springs to Baton Rouge.[15]

A report said, "Clark took up the attack; and falling on fiercely they at first carried everything before them...the 4th Wisconsin went to the aid of the 14th Maine, which had been stoutly holding its own against the onset of Clark."[16]

Clark's wounding was recalled, "Brigadier-General Charles Clark, commanding the First Division, was severely wounded and made prisoner." Clark was among the Confederate casualties of eighty-four killed, three hundred fifteen wounded, and fifty-seven missing.[17]

Brigadier General Clark's wife made a trip to New Orleans in order to attend her gravely wounded husband. Although he received a high level of medical attention, and was allowed to receive clothing and money from other Confederates, Clark was unable to make a full recovery. Considered an invalid, Brigadier General Clark used crutches for the remainder of his life.[18]

In February 1863 Clark was released from captivity and made his way to Mississippi. Bad health, combined with the aged soldier's inability to move about as well as he desired, caused Brigadier General Charles Clark to come to the decision to resign his commission in October 1863.[19] However, Clark was not finished with his service to the citizens of Mississippi.

Charles Clark was elected governor of Mississippi. An evaluation of his tenure in office proclaimed, "Clark was active in communicating with Confederate military officials regarding the defense of the state. He protested the impressment of slaves into Confederate service."[20]

Charles Clark remained in the governor's office until the spring of 1865. Having continued to provide troops for the Confederate cause, Clark ordered a special session of the state legislature in May 1865. At that time Governor Clark acknowledged his personal sadness related to Lincoln's assassination. Within a short period of time Clark was arrested and sent to Fort Pulaski, Georgia. He remained incarcerated at that location until October 1865.[21]

Clark returned to *Doro* and resumed his law practice. In the next decade he continued to be active in the profession that had made him wealthy before the war. As Reconstruction ended, Charles Clark returned to politics and served as Chancellor of his district until his death on December 18, 1877. The former Confederate brigadier general was buried on the grounds of his plantation in Bolivar County, Mississippi.[22]

DOUGLAS HANCOCK COOPER, C.S.A.

1815-1879

The life of Douglas Hancock Cooper was full of contradictory ideals. He was born into wealth and privilege, but he died poor and was buried in an unmarked grave. Although a Southern-born white, he appeared to be more comfortable living with the Native Americans of Oklahoma. His father was a minister; Douglas Hancock Cooper was not an active member of any church. He did seek to assist others through his affiliation with the Masonic Lodge.

Douglas Hancock Cooper was born to Dr. David Cooper and his wife, Sarah Hancock Davenport Cooper, on November 1, 1815. The future Confederate general was the couple's only child, and he experienced the comforts provided in his father's varied vocations as both a Baptist preacher and a practicing physician. The Wilkinson County, Mississippi couple and their son enjoyed long-standing connections to the elite level of the United States, as Sarah was a relative of John Hancock. Dr. Cooper, according to family records, spent thirty years of his life in the ministry and was regarded as "an educated, polished man."[1]

Douglas Cooper's mother died when he was a child, and his father remarried in 1824. Magdaline Hutchins Claiborne Cooper, the second wife of David Cooper, moved with the family to their new home, *Soldier's Retreat*, near Natchez, Mississippi. Dr. David Cooper passed away at the home in 1830, leaving the fifteen year-old Douglas in the care of his stepmother. Dr. Cooper's will reportedly provided generously for young Douglas, who attended Liberty, Mississippi's Amite Academy before entering the University of Virginia in 1832.[2]

Upon completing his college education in 1834, Douglas Cooper became a lawyer and planter in Wilkinson County, Mississippi. The nineteen year-old graduate married seventeen year-old Frances Martha Collins, an Adams County, Mississippi resident, on March 26, 1834. The newlyweds established their residence in the Woodville, Mississippi area and named their home *Mon Clova*. The marriage of Douglas and Frances produced seven children, a number far above that which Douglas had experienced as an only child. The names of the Cooper children were Sarah, Frances, Douglas Hancock, Jr., David, Elizabeth, Emma, and William.[3]

The plantation life Cooper provided for his family at *Mon Clova* was indicative of the stereotype many individuals continue to hold for the Antebellum South. Individuals such as Jefferson Davis visited. Almost one hundred slaves resided on the grounds. The Cooper girls, educated at a female academy, learned French and "had to read the classics, learn to play the piano, sing, dance correctly, master the technique of the hoop skirt, and how to coquette with the boys without begin forward or immodest. The boys were taught the arts of a gentleman…how to manage a plantation… and always show great consideration for the ladies and the aged."[4]

Douglas Hancock Cooper entered the political arena of Mississippi in 1844 as an elected Wilkinson County representative to the State Legislature. He later formed the Woodville Company for service in the Mexican War and was elected captain of the unit. The company was assigned to the Mississippi Rifle Regiment, under the command of Colonel Jefferson Davis, a relationship that benefitted Cooper throughout the majority of his life.[5]

During his time spent in the Mexican War, Captain Cooper was praised for his performance in the battles of Buena Vista and Monterey. In the latter engagement, Cooper's conduct for gallant action received praise from Colonel Jefferson Davis.[6]

Davis and Cooper maintained a working relationship during the growing crisis of the slavery issue and the increasing sectional tension that existed between the Northern and Southern sections of the nation. Cooper was a committee member during the 1849 Southern Convention in Jackson, Mississippi, while Davis attended as a convention guest. The next year, Cooper attended a related 1850 gathering in Nashville. With the election of Franklin Pierce as President in 1852, Jefferson Davis was appointed Secretary of War.[7]

The influence of Jefferson Davis upon the national political arena affected Cooper in a positive manner, as Cooper was appointed United States Agent to the Choctaw in the Indian Territory in June 1853. Interestingly Cooper's plantation *Mon Clova* was located on land that once belonged to the Choctaw and was ceded in a treaty with the United States. Further exposure of Cooper to the Choctaw lay in the fact that his late father, Dr. David Cooper, was a founder of the Choctaw Academy in Kentucky, an institute that served to educate future Choctaw leaders.[8]

The year of Douglas Cooper's appointment as Indian Agent to the Choctaws, Lieutenant A. W. Whipple, the supervisor of the Pacific Railroad survey that traversed Choctaw land holdings in the area that would become Oklahoma, complimented Cooper's relationship with the people that the new agent was assigned to supervise. Whipple wrote, "Cooper has been here but a few weeks. He seems a high minded and honorable gentleman and bids fair to succeed his lamented predecessor in the deep affection of the people."[9]

In addition to Douglas Cooper's assumption of his father's concern for education, he was highly mindful of the issue of alcohol trafficking. In 1855 Cooper wrote, "The Choctaws are steadily advancing in the arts of civilized life...[and] deserve credit for what they have been doing during a whole generation in the cause of temperance...Their laws have been quite well executed...[and they] deserve credit for not ever having had a distillery...as well as for doing so much in the cause of education..."[10]

That same year Cooper helped negotiate a treaty to disagreements between the Choctaw and Chickasaw. The tension was related to the treaty the two nations had signed years earlier. The situation necessitated Cooper spending several grueling months in Washington, D.C. Upon his return to Oklahoma, Cooper was sent to Louisiana, Mississippi, and Alabama for the purpose of distributing bounty claims to the Choctaw who had remained in those lands rather than making their way to what was then identified as Indian Territory. In his 1856 Annual Report Cooper noted the peoples he visited were "vagrants" and that the Indian Office should see that the individuals "should be forced to come to the Indian Territory… and have a better chance."[11]

Cooper was viewed among his contemporaries as, "Kind and sympathetic by nature, generous to a fault…an honest man of noble impulses, and born and bred a gentleman," Perhaps this reputation, combined with his exposure to the situations of the Native Americans with whom he had lived three years, led to his supervisory position in which the Choctaw and Chickasaw were combined into one agency. The agency office was located at Fort Washita, Oklahoma.[12]

When Agent Cooper was finally able to return to Fort Washita in the fall of 1857, he found the Choctaw embroiled in conflict. Comanche, Kiowa, and other Native American groups were regularly witnessed roaming the "outlying part of the Choctaw Nation," necessitating "some action to protect the recently established" nation the Chickasaw had created. Cooper contacted Washington, D.C. and pleaded for military protection. In his request Cooper stated that, as the agent of the Chickasaw and Choctaw, he should be given "jurisdiction over all their country, and… be furnished…a constabulary force to guard the region against undesirable characters and liquor traffic along the borders of Arkansas and Texas."[13]

Cooper soon made the request for Choctaw and Chickasaw volunteers to join an armed guard that would be under the direction of Secretary Thompson in Washington, D. C. The group traveled for sixteen days along the Washita and Canadian Rivers. He used the opportunity to speak with members of various Native American leaders in an effort to restore peace.[14]

In his 1858 report Cooper recalled the events of the Washita and Canadian River area. Cooper wrote, "Although…unable to discover any Comanches…the effect of the expedition upon the Indians of the plains will be good…[and] disabuse their minds…that the Chickasaw or Choctaws…are afraid to go out on the plains and convinced them that no depredations on the frontier will be allowed to pass unpunished."[15]

In the continued praise Douglas Cooper received from the Choctaw people, none was more candid than that offered in October 1858. The

Choctaw Council called for the district of their residence be renamed Cooper County in honor of Douglas Hancock Cooper.[16] The resolution of the Choctaw Council was in its intent and full of praise for Cooper.

The resolution stated in part, "The General Council of the Choctaw Nation…are hereby cordially tendered to General Douglas H. Cooper… resident among us, for the greater part of the past six years, for the very able, highly efficient, purely disinterested and successful manner in which he has discharged many trying and laborious duties required of him…for the benefit of the Choctaw people, his urbanity of manner, his unequaled readiness to accommodate all, his generous hospitality to our people…"[17]

In the ensuing months a series of fights with the Comanche took place. Additional tension resulted from the Choctaw desire to remove various settlements from the area of Cooper County. Those groups who were unwelcomed in the region included certain bands of Shawnee, Kickapoo, and Delaware. While those struggles continued for years, the emergence of the slavery issue contributed to the additional problems Cooper encountered.[18]

In July 1859 the American Board for Foreign Missions ended its support of schools and missions, including those of the Choctaw. Cooper seemed to approve the action as the Board was reportedly abolition minded. Within a year the influence of the Knights of the Golden Circle, a secret organization that was strongly pro-Southern, was gaining influence among slaveholders in Indian Territory and was also hinted to be operating among the Native American farmers.[19]

By April 1861 Indian Territory Agents were expressing a pro-Southern stance, making their preference of supporting the Confederate government. Many of them were replaced as the U. S. officials saw the changing allegiances as dangerous to the cause of the Union. Douglas Cooper was asked "to continue his position" of the Choctaw Agent because of the fact that he "was highly regarded and had the confidence" of both the United States and the Choctaw.[20]

Events transpired quickly when, on May 13, 1861, Confederate Secretary of War LeRoy Pope Walker wrote a letter to "Major Douglas Cooper, Choctaw Nation." The contents of the correspondence allowed Cooper to raise a Choctaw and Chickasaw mounted regiment which Cooper, working with Brigadier General Benjamin McCulloch, would command. The note provided Cooper with the rank of colonel and assigned the unit "to the command of the district embracing the Indian Territory lying west of Arkansas and south of Kansas."[21]

On May 25, 1861 the Chickasaw Legislature also expressed its confidence in Douglas Cooper. The legislative declaration adopted Cooper as a member of the Chickasaw and, as such, he would be "entitled to all the rights, privileges and immunities of a citizen..." An article published in the *National Register*, printed at Boggy Depot, also declared the independence of the Chickasaw Nation and aligned it with the Confederate States of America.[22]

The Choctaw Nation declared itself a free and independent nation, and noted a preference to align with the Confederate States in June 1861. The General Council and Principal Chief George Hudson signed the proclamation that required all males between 18 and 45 to military service. Some 700 men comprised the immediate goal to be called the Mounted Regiment of Choctaw and Chickasaw Riflemen and serve under "Col. D. H. Cooper... C.S. Army."[23]

The effects of recent developments had a profound effect upon Cooper. As the highly respected and visible Indian Agent, he was setting an example for the other Chickasaw and Choctaw citizens. In July, Cooper signed the treaty that solidified the Chickasaw and Choctaw alliance with the Confederacy. Cooper also took an oath of allegiance to the same, and pledged to "accept the duties of Choctaw and Chickasaw Agent under the new government."[24]

A trend that hampered the Confederates serving in the Indian Territory was clear from the onset. Neither proper horse feed, ammunition, nor weapons were provided to the Choctaw or Cherokee soldiers as Arkansas tended to be the destination of any such materials shipped west of the Mississippi. Cooper took exception to this policy and advocated that the Native Americans be given a more responsible role in the Confederate war effort. In addition, the lack of timeliness regarding pay for the Native Americans was another point of contention for Cooper.[25]

On July 25, 1861, Colonel Cooper wrote Confederate President Jefferson Davis a plea to gain more favorable provisions for his command and to bring the poor relationship with a fellow officer to the forefront. Cooper stated, "There seems to be a disposition to keep the Indians at home. This seems to me a bad policy. They are unfit for garrison duty and would be a terror to the Yankees...Captain Pike has intimated that the holding for the agency...and that of colonel of the regiment are incompatible. It has been the effort...for years to break me down...to get control of the Choctaw and Chickasaw agency. Pike has not entered into this scheme heretofore, but his hint shows that an excuse is only wanted to do so."[26] The tension between Cooper and Pike that was exhibited in the letter to Davis would remain throughout the American Civil War.

Colonel Cooper's initiation to fighting was in the fall of 1861. Opothleyahola, a Creek leader with 5,000 warriors, had not agreed to the treaty the Creek had made regarding service with the Confederate States of America. Cooper tried to negotiate a peaceful solution to the situation, but he determined the Creek leader would have to be forced to recognize the authority of the Creek leaders who represented the majority pro-Confederate group.[27]

According to reports of ensuing battles, three different engagements took place by the end of December. In the first, which took place at Round Mountain, the fighting resulted in a draw. On December 26, 1861, Cooper's troops had to withdraw due to a lack of ammunition. The third battle was more successful for Cooper and his soldiers who forced Opothleyahoa and his followers to move northward during a strong winter storm. The objects of Cooper's attacks eventually made their way to Kansas and remained there as refugees.[28]

In March 1862, Cooper's Regiment saw action at Pea Ridge, Arkansas. The defeat of the Confederates at that location resulted in a confused retreat of the men in gray. Colonel Cooper led the Native Americans as they covered the retreat of General Earl Van Dorn's troops.[29]

In mid-August, 1862, Cooper was notified he had been promoted to brigadier general. At Newtonia, Missouri, Cooper commanded approximately two thousand three hundred Missouri troops and two thousand man force of Choctaw, Chickasaw, and mixed-blood Cherokee soldiers. While taking part in the battle of Newtonia, Cooper received a special order that stated, "Brig. Gen. D. H. Cooper is assigned to duty as Superintendent of Indian Affairs..."[30]

By the fall of 1862, the strained relationship between Brigadier Generals Albert Pike and Douglas Cooper took a new slant. Allegations regarding Pike's poor mental state resulted in General Thomas Hindman sending a stern order to Cooper. The October 31 letter stated that Cooper should disregard orders from Pike and "resist any interference, using the force necessary for the purpose." However, by December the charges against Pike had been dropped and he resumed his military exercises.[31]

Pike's arrest created the possibility of Cooper gaining command of the Texas and Indian troops in the Indian Territory. Sadly, Cooper was passed over in favor of General William Steele. The rationale for the denial of promoting Cooper to the leadership role was due to the regular rumors that Cooper had personal issues with controlling his consumption of alcohol.[32]

Subsequent action at Neosho, Missouri took place on April 26, 1863. In recording the skirmish, Brigadier General Cooper wrote, "Too much praise cannot be awarded Col. Stand Watie and his brave men for their ceaseless vigilance…and their gallantry in attacking and routing a superior force of regular, well-drilled Federal troops."[33]

An event in April 1863 centered upon the push to remove Cooper from his position with the Indian Brigade. To refute the leaders of the movement, Captain James Gamble, a member of the Chickasaw Battalion, wrote General E. Kirby Smith. Gamble said, "Whatever reports may be in circulation intended to lower the standing of General Cooper… to cause his removal from his present position…cannot emanate from the Chickasaw people…I do not remember having heard a Chickasaw express any dissatisfactory language toward General Cooper."[34] This and other notes of support ended the subversive acts regarding the removal of Cooper.

On July 17, 1863, Brigadier General Cooper commanded the Indian Brigade at the battle of Honey Springs. That engagement is usually regarded to be "the major engagement…in the Indian Territory."[35] The details of the confrontation reveal the severity of the action that took place between the forces of Cooper and the Federal cavalrymen of Major General James Blunt.

Two days earlier, Blunt used cavalry and artillery to push Confederates from the Arkansas River. Hours later, Blunt had three thousand men at his disposal, and he approached at daybreak. Confederate attempts to maintain their position against repeated Federal charges eventually resulted in Cooper's command moved to the safety of the rear. Wet powder hampered

Cooper's troops, and during an attempt to secure new ammunition during a downpour, Cooper discovered Blunt was attempting to turn his left flank. Cooper determined to burn the majority of Confederate supplies rather than see them fall into Federal possession. Cooper failed to secure one artillery piece and a stand of colors, as well as two hundred arms and fifteen wagons. The Federal losses were reported at less than ninety total casualties, while Cooper's troops suffered an estimated one hundred fifty killed, four hundred wounded, and seventy-seven captured. The Federal army had gained control of the Indian Territory north of the Arkansas River.[36]

Always willing to praise his soldiers, Brigadier General Cooper reported, "Too much praise cannot be awarded the troops for the accomplishment of the most difficult of all military movements, an orderly and successful retreat, with little loss of life or property, in the face of a superior number, flushed with victory."[37]

Muriel Wright, a Twentieth Century Cooper biographer, noted that Cooper's soldiers managed to successfully protect the 200-mile long border of Texas and Indian Territory from invasion. Although various military engagements took place from 1863 forward, Cooper's line stood strong until the end of the American Civil War.[38]

In January 1864 Brigadier General Douglas Cooper assumed "command of all the Indian troops in the Trans-Mississippi Department on the borders of Arkansas." That July, the Confederate War Department added, "The Indian Territory west of Arkansas is hereby constituted a separate district of the Trans-Mississippi Department...of which Brig. Gen. D. H. Cooper...is assigned." Although it was delayed until February 1865, Cooper gained full military command of the District of the Indian Territory.[39]

In early May 1865, the news of the Confederate surrender reached Cooper and the other soldiers stationed in Indian Territory. By the end of the month, the Trans-Mississippi Department had surrendered at New Orleans. On June 28, Brigadier General Cooper agreed to the terms of the surrender, making "his old command...the last in the Confederate Army to surrender."[40]

After the war, Cooper and his son-in-law, who had served on his staff the previous four years, operated a store at New Boggy Depot, near Fort

Washita. Cooper's son-in-law, Thornton Heiston, had married Cooper's daughter Elizabeth in 1863. In 1866, Cooper joined Charles Mix in pursing Indian claims. Cooper worked on behalf of the two groups of Native Americans and sued the United States for "failed promises" as old as 1830. On a more personal note, in 1866 Cooper's pardon application was approved after he swore allegiance to the United States.[41]

The major blemish on Cooper's post-war life arose during his attempts to gain funds for the Choctaw and Chickasaw during the proceeds claims battle. Cooper was accused of misappropriation of funds, but a lengthy and expensive legal battle enabled him to clear his name. Evidently a combination of the effects of the Civil War, life on the plains, and the emotional strain of the claims battle took a vicious toll on the former Confederate general.[42]

On April 30, 1879, Cooper died at Fort Washita from the effects of pneumonia. The monument dedicated to him at that location states, "He lies buried on these grounds in an unmarked and unknown grave."[43]

JOSEPH ROBERT DAVIS, C.S.A.
1825-1896

Joseph Robert Davis entered the world at Woodville, Mississippi, on January 12, 1825. Joseph's father, Isaac Williams Davis, a veteran of the War of 1812, and Susannah Gartley Davis, Isaac's mother, later moved from the Wilkinson County, Mississippi town of Woodville to Madison County, Mississippi. Isaac's younger brother, Jefferson, was seventeen when the family moved; the fact that Joseph Robert Davis was the nephew of Jefferson Davis proved beneficial for Joseph Robert when the latter entered the Confederate military. Meanwhile Isaac's older brother, Joseph Emory Davis, a resident of Warren County, Mississippi, had provided Isaac and Susannah with a temporary home while the family was in the process of moving.[1]

The Davis family determined that Joseph Robert Davis would gain a better education in another state. He was initially sent to Nashville, and later to Kentucky. Davis also furthered his education at Oxford, Ohio's Miami University. Following his 1848 graduation from Miami University, Joseph returned to Madison County, Mississippi to establish his career as a lawyer.[2]

In 1848, Davis married Frances H. Peyton. Three years later, he began his legal practice and pursued farming.[3]

In 1860, Davis was elected to the Mississippi State Senate, but put aside that, his profitable legal career, and his personal supervision of his farming business, when Civil War began. Davis helped raise a company of troops from Madison County, and was elected captain. The unit became Company I, the Madison Rifles, of the 10th Mississippi Infantry Regiment.[4]

In March 1861, Joseph Robert Davis and his compatriots gathered in Mobile, Alabama. By mid-April they were in route to Pensacola, Florida, and camped near Fort Barrancas, a Confederate post located a short distance from the Federally-controlled Fort Pickens and Santa Rosa Island. Davis was placed in command of soldiers who were stationed at Fort McRee and was promoted to the rank of lieutenant-colonel on April 12, 1861. On May 20, 1861 Lieutenant-Colonel Davis was ordered to report to Montgomery for a change in assignments.[5]

The reason for the summons was that Davis had been selected to serve on the personal staff of Confederate President Jefferson Davis. The family connection between these two men raised brows when Joseph Robert Davis was appointed to the position of Aide-de-Camp for President Davis. Additional criticism and accusations of nepotism arose from the fact that, on August 31, 1861, Joseph Robert Davis was promoted to the rank of colonel. Colonel Davis moved to Richmond where he would work closely with his uncle.[6]

An evaluation of the duties of Colonel Davis indicates that his ensuing year of service in the Confederate capital was filled with him "assessing military matters and making reports," duties that evidently created boredom for the officer who was now in his late thirties. Perhaps the knowledge of his father's military service during the War of 1812, added to the fact that Samuel Emory Davis, Isaac's father, had served in the American Revolution created a desire to gain a new assignment. Seeking a more visible or active level of participation in the Confederate military, Davis was promoted to brigadier general in September 1862. With further allegations of Davis benefitting from his family connections widely circulating, the promotion was initially rejected, but eventually confirmed when the value of his previous service was made known.[7]

In November 1862, Davis was given command of a brigade that grew to include the 2nd, 11th, 26th, and 42nd Mississippi Regiments, and a group of North Carolina troops. Other units he commanded included the First

Confederate Battalion and the Madison Light Artillery. The highest level of notoriety and a high level of negative comments for Davis and his brigade came as members of Heth's Division of the Third Corps of the Army of Northern Virginia.[8]

On July 1, 1863, Brigadier General Davis led his brigade in an approach to Gettysburg, Pennsylvania. Leaving from their camp near Cashtown, the Mississippi troops followed the members of Brigadier General James Jay Archer's Tennessee Brigade as they advanced along a turnpike that approached Gettysburg. Davis had left the 11th Mississippi behind as the men of that unit were serving guard detail for the division's wagon train.[9]

Davis recalled, "Within 2 miles from town, our artillery was put in position, and opened fire. I was ordered to take position on the left of the turnpike, and...press forward toward the town. About 10:30...a line of battle was formed...skirmishers thrown forward, and the brigade moved forward to the attack."[10] The ensuing battle would be the largest of the war and had devastating effects on the ranks of the brigade of Davis and dozens of similar Confederate units.

Davis continued his recollections of the engagement, "Between us and the town...was a commanding hill in wood, the intervening space being inclosed [sic] fields of grass and grain, and was very broken. On our right was the turnpike and a railroad, with deep cuts and heavy embankments, diverging from the turnpike as it approached the town...the brigade moved forward about 1 mile, driving in the enemy's skirmishers, and came within range of his line of battle...drawn up on a high hill in a field a short distance in front of a railroad cut."[11]

The railroad cut Davis noted was an unfinished extension of the Western Maryland Railroad and the middle of three such recessed areas. The cut was intended to eventually allow Gettysburg to be connected to towns that were east and it ran parallel to the Chambersburg Pike. Unfortunately, the steep sides of the cut made it almost impossible for Davis's Confederates to accurately return fire once they entered the same.[12]

The intensity of the subsequent action is clearly noted in Davis's report of the battle. He stated, "The engagement soon became very warm. After a short contest, the order was given to charge, and promptly obeyed. The enemy made a stubborn resistance, and stood until our men were within a few yards, and then gave way...but rallied near the railroad...

after desperate fighting, with heavy loss on both sides, he fled in great disorder toward the town, leaving us in possession of his commanding position and batteries."[13]

The success of Brigadier General Davis and his Mississippi troops was short-lived, as the Federal troops soon "returned in greater numbers, and the fight was renewed." What Davis referred to as a "greatly superior" number of Federal soldiers caused the Mississippians to, "Give way under the first shock of his attack, many officers and men having been killed or wounded, and all much exhausted by the excessive heat."[14]

The fighting in the railroad cut had not reached a conclusion. Davis noted this fact in composing, "The line was promptly formed, and carried to its former position, and while there engaged, a heavy force was observed moving rapidly toward our right, and soon after opened a heavy fire on our right flank and rear. In this critical condition, I gave the order to retire, which was done in good order, leaving some officers and men in the railroad cut, who were captured, although every effort was made to withdraw all the commands. This was about 1 p. m."[15]

Men from the 2nd and 42nd Mississippi Infantry Regiments, as well as the 55th North Carolina had sought cover from the intense fire of the 6th Wisconsin Infantry Regiment, of Lieutenant-Colonel Rufus Dawes. Soon the members of the retreating 84th and 95th New York rallied and faced north, firing into the members of Davis's Brigade in the railroad bed.[16]

The 6th Wisconsin made an advance upon Davis's troops seeking shelter in the unfinished railroad cut. A report from Lieutenant-Colonel Dawes indicated one hundred sixty of his four hundred fifty Federals fell in the charge upon Davis's Brigade. When the Confederate surrender was sought, the "shocked and exhausted Confederates" of Davis's command complied.[17]

A review of the casualties of the 2nd Mississippi is indicative of the vicious struggle Brigadier General Davis and his troops endured at Gettysburg. The regiment had served on picket duty the night before marching to Gettysburg, and the men had managed to grab a quick breakfast, unbeknownst that a major battle lay ahead. A colonel of the regiment was killed while crossing a fence on the Chambersburg Pike, while Lieutenant A. K. Roberts died in an attempt to capture the flag of the 56th Pennsylvania. All but two of the field officers for the regiment were killed or wounded. In the railroad cut, all members of the color guard were killed or wounded with the regimental flag bearing a dozen piercings and the flagstaff splintered. In addition, seven officers and two hundred twenty-five men of the 2nd Mississippi surrendered in the railroad cut.[18]

Brigadier General Davis and his troops, despite suffering heavy casualties, clearly made their Federal enemies aware of their presence. For example, the 147th New York Volunteers, a regiment that fought with the Mississippians during the action at the railroad cut, had three hundred one of three hundred eighty members killed, wounded, captured, or missing.[19]

On July 2, 1863, the second day of action at Gettysburg, the Mississippians who comprised the majority of the brigade of Davis did not participate in any of the military actions of the day. The men of the 2nd, 11th, and 42nd Mississippi, as well as the 55th North Carolina, were allowed to rest and attempt to recover from the devastating battle of the previous day.[20]

Two modern markers denote the contributions of the members of Davis's Mississippi Brigade at Gettysburg. The first is located west of Gettysburg, along North Reynolds Avenue. The second is southwest of town and is located on West Confederate Avenue.[21]

On July 3, 1863, Brigadier General Davis led his brigade as it participated in the assault known as Pickett's Charge. In the action, the 42nd Mississippi reported a total of thirty-two killed and one hundred seventy wounded. Sixty-two of those wounded were mortal wounds as a respective number passed away in the coming weeks. The 2nd Mississippi listed its casualties as forty killed and one hundred eighty three wounded, while the 11th Mississippi proclaimed thirty-two killed and one hundred seventy wounded.[22] Conflicting reports of the battle note that Davis was among those brigade members who were wounded.

During the retreat from Gettysburg, the men of Davis's Brigade encountered a group of Federal cavalrymen at Williamsport. Casualties for this engagement were slight in number, but those suffered at Falling Waters on July 14 resulted in the 2nd Mississippi to record that the entire Gettysburg Campaign had caused a casualty rate of approximately eighty-five percent.[23]

Brigadier General Davis suffered from typhoid fever in the weeks after Gettysburg and was unable to rejoin his brigade until October 1863. His command fought at Bristoe Station, and endured the bloodbath of the Mine Run Campaign. The brigade entered winter encampment near Orange Court House and remained there through the winter of 1863-1864.[24]

Another bout with poor health plagued Brigadier General Davis in the spring of 1864, and he yielded the command of his brigade to Colonel John Stone of the 2nd Mississippi. Davis was able to return in time to lead his troops in the Overland Campaign during which heavy casualties were inflicted upon his command. During related action, particularly during the second day of the Wilderness, members of Davis's brigade held their ground while others in Heth's Division reportedly abandoned in the face of overwhelming odds. The fortitude of his troops enabled Confederate reinforcements to launch a counterattack. After the battle at the Wilderness, Davis remained with his brigade in the trenches of Petersburg from June until August of 1864.[25]

Brigadier General Joseph Robert Davis was incapacitated during most of August and early September, 1864, as illness once again riddled his body. By late September, he was able to return to his command and joined his brigade as it continued to endure the hardships of the Petersburg trenches. Area action at Jones's Farm and Burgess Mill added to the already staggering casualty numbers the brigade had suffered, as Davis and his troops spent the winter of 1864-1865 in trenches located approximately six miles outside Petersburg. During the stay in the trenches a member of Davis's brigade wrote of the Federal Dictator cannon, "...the enemy frequently shoot very large shells...but the people are getting used to it..."[26]

The spring of 1865 witnessed Brigadier General Davis participating in the action at Hatcher's Run. By late February he had taken command of the division and Colonel A. M. Nelson succeeded Davis as brigade leader. With the end of the war quickly approaching, Davis joined his soldiers in a series of battles of various sizes before surrendering at Appomattox.[27]

After the war Davis settled in Biloxi and resumed his law practice. When his health allowed, Davis also enjoyed a limited amount of farming. Davis divorced his wife Frances in 1878, but married Margaret Carey Green the next year. A majority of his remaining years were spent at *Beauvoir*, the Biloxi home of his uncle, the former Confederate President. On September 15, 1896, Davis passed away in Biloxi and was buried in the local cemetery.[28]

WINFIELD SCOTT FEATHERSTON, C.S.A.
1820?-1891

The youngest of seven children, Winfield Scott Featherston was born to Charles and Lucy Pitts Featherston in Murfreesboro, Tennessee. Sources vary in respect to the exact date of his birth, with some noting August 8, 1820, while another proclaims August 5, 1821 as the day he entered the world. An additional source contains August 8, 1821 as Featherston's birthday; while a different one provides June 9, 1814 as the day Featherston was born. The date of August 8, 1819 is given in another source. Therefore, the placement of complete confidence in any one of the sources that provides a date on which Winfield Scott Featherston was born is fallible.[1]

More certain aspects of Featherston's early years are related to the fact that he spent the early portion of his life four miles outside of Murfreesboro, a growing community in Rutherford County, Tennessee. His parents, who named him for General Winfield Scott, had moved from Virginia to Tennessee in 1815 and settled in Sumner County before relocating to Rutherford County three years later. In addition to Winfield Scott, the Featherston couple had two other sons and four daughters. Evidence indicates that not only did the family lack the ability to attain a suitable level of wealth, but also that Winfield Scott Featherston learned strong work habits and became a strong individual from his exposure to the rigors of the era's agricultural pursuits.[2]

In 1836, Winfield Scott Featherston was attending an academy in Columbus, Georgia when hostilities erupted between Georgians and the Creek Indians. The young man placed his studies on hold and enlisted in a company raised to end the uprising. He was praised for bravery when he volunteered to serve as the company's sentry. The post held a high level of danger, as the Creek regularly targeted the guard detail as the objects of their sniper attacks. The following year, with the Creek reportedly being "subdued," Featherston returned to Rutherford County and received additional education from the locally-renowned educator Samuel P. Black. Featherston seized the opportunity to gain "a thorough knowledge of English, Latin, and Greek."[3]

Completing his studies, Featherston moved to Memphis and secured a job in his brother's mercantile business. Featherston either became disenchanted with the business or the relationship with his brother became strained; he left the store after only nine months. Being a veteran as well as a disenchanted merchant, Featherston moved to Houston, Mississippi, the county seat of Chickasaw County, and began to diligently study law. Within three months, in 1840, his seeming obsession with the legal profession allowed him to enter the bar in Houston.[4]

Featherston's reputation as "an able lawyer" allowed him to, "rise speedily in his profession and [he] soon acquired a lucrative practice." An evaluation of his early years of practice stated that he was, "a hard student, correct reasoner, and profound thinker; he always discovered the fundamental principle involved and rested his cause upon it."[5]

In 1842, Winfield Scott Featherston married Mary Holt Harris, the daughter of Thomas Harris from Columbus, Mississippi. Sadly, Mrs. Featherston passed away a few months later.[6]

Featherston "soon became prominent in official circles," and he heeded the call of the political arena. In 1847, he was nominated to serve as his district's candidate for the Mississippi State Senate. An election analysis said, "He was scarcely eligible to the seat, on account of his youth, without experience and had never been a candidate for any office." He ran against a well-respected duelist, Colonel A. K. McClung, "a man of experience, of talents, an able debater," and a Mexican War veteran. McClung entered the race "upon his crutches, compelled to do so by two bleeding wounds… evidences of his bravery at…Buena Vista." Despite McClung's emotional appeal, Featherston debated him "in every county in the district" and won.[7]

Featherston served as a Democratic member of the state body from 1847 until 1849. He then ran against Judge William Harris. Harris was a Whig whose legal profession, and his "talents, culture, and fine attainments" gained many followers. Somehow, Featherston again arose victoriously. The outcome was different two years later when John A. Wilcox, a Union candidate from Aberdeen, defeated him. As a side-note, all of the candidates who were held a states' rights stance, as did Featherston, were defeated in that year's Mississippi elections.[8]

In 1852, Featherston resumed his full-time legal profession, but he also served as a Franklin Pierce elector that year. The next year, Featherston was offered his party's nomination for the Mississippi Senate, yet he declined. He avoided the political world for most of the next decade and moved to Holly Springs, Mississippi in 1857.[9] He became one of the most prominent lawyers in a town known for its ability to produce the same.

The eve of the American Civil War witnessed Winfield Scott Featherston once again yielding to the call of public service. In December 1860, at the request of Mississippi Governor Pettus, Featherston served as a Mississippi commissioner to Kentucky to discuss the Blue Grass State's plans for secession. The basis of the talks centered upon whether or not Kentucky would join its Southern sister states. His position as an "ambassador" to Kentucky proved unsuccessful in that the effort to convince the state to secede did not achieve the desired effect.[10]

The 1860, Marshall County, Mississippi Census indicated that W. S. Featherstone [sic] was a man of notable wealth. The thirty-eight year old lawyer and his twenty-six year old wife were recorded as caring for four children aged four to ten. The census also revealed that Featherston's real estate was valued at $10,000; his personal property was worth $315,000.[11]

With the onset of war, Featherston took it upon himself to raise a company. The company was assigned to the 17th Mississippi Infantry Regiment and Featherston was given the rank of colonel. The rise in rank occurred on June 4, 1861, with his regiment being mustered into Confederate service at Corinth, Mississippi later that week. The leadership position seemed to fall naturally to Colonel Featherston, a man who stood over six feet tall.[12]

The 17th Mississippi arrived at Manassas Junction, Virginia on June 17, 1861. The regiment was brigaded with the 18th Mississippi and 5th South Carolina Infantry Regiments. The next month, Featherston led his regiment in a battle at Manassas. The regiment "advanced up Rocky Run until forced to retire." At First Manassas, or Bull Run, the 17th Mississippi suffered a total of twelve casualties, with two men killed and ten wounded.[13]

Featherston, nicknamed "Old Swet," also commanded his troops at Leesburg or Ball's Bluff. For a majority of the battle, the 17th Mississippi joined the 8th Virginia and 18th Mississippi Infantry Regiments. When the Virginia Regiment was depleted of ammunition, Featherston led a charge toward a Federal battery. Over three hundred soldiers were captured, and two Federal cannon fell into the hands of Featherston's men. Featherston personally accepted the surrender of the troops and guns, earning the praise of his superiors.[14]

The Confederate victory at Ball's Bluff can be explained in analyzing the casualties of the October 1861 battle. Reported casualties for the Federal forces at Leesburg were two hundred twenty-three killed, two hundred twenty-six wounded, and five hundred fifty-three captured.[15]

Confederate casualties were thirty-six killed and one hundred seventeen wounded. No Confederates were noted as missing; only two fell captive.[16]

Because of his exhibition of gallantry at Ball's Bluff, Colonel Featherston was promoted to brigadier general. With the rank becoming effective on March 4, 1862, Brigadier General Featherston led his brigade into the Seven Days' Battles in the vicinity of Richmond.[17]

At Frazier's Farm, also known as Frayser's Farm or Glendale, the fifth battle of the Seven Days' Campaign, Brigadier General Featherston was wounded. He was fortunate in that his wound was not serious. However, the total casualties for the battle were staggering, with the Confederate tally being six hundred thirty-eight killed, two thousand eight hundred fourteen wounded, and two hundred twenty-one captured. Lower figures, though clearly indicative of the tenacious struggle, were posted for the Federal soldiers. The reported numbers for the men in blue were two hundred ninety-seven killed, one thousand six hundred ninety-six wounded, and one thousand eight hundred four missing. As for a victor, the battle of Frayser's Farm is regularly regarded to have been inconclusive.[18]

In January 1863, Featherston was granted his request to transfer from the Army of Northern Virginia. When the initial Federal appearance in Mississippi had taken place, Featherston had asked to lead troops in an effort to expel the blue-clad soldiers from his state of residence. With General Joseph Johnston asking Confederate President Jefferson Davis for a skilled general to serve in Mississippi, President Davis offered the assignment to Featherston.[19]

Brigadier General Featherston was, by that time, in General William Wing Loring's Division, and he next encountered Federal troops in the Vicksburg Campaign. In that series of battles, Featherston first saw action at Baker's Creek, an engagement also known as Champion Hill. By then, Brigadier General Featherston commanded the Third Brigade of Major General William Loring's Division under the leadership of Lieutenant General John Pemberton. Within Featherston's Brigade were the 3rd, 22nd, 31st, and 33rd Mississippi, the 1st Mississippi Sharpshooter Battalion, and four guns of Company D, 1st Mississippi Light Artillery.[20]

Featherston's participation at Baker Creek is recorded in his official report. Featherston said, "About 8 o'clock on the morning of the 16th, one of the enemy's batteries opened fire on our regiments...My brigade was immediately put in line of battle...About 2 or 3 o'clock in the evening I received an order from General Pemberton...to move my brigade... to the support of Generals Bowen and Stevenson...We traveled through the woods and over very rough ground a distance of about 2 miles before reaching the scene of the conflict. The march was a rapid as possible... we found no one to give us directions or...what to do. General Pemberton was not there, and no one present could tell us where he was...As our army advanced in front, my brigade, with the artillery, was moved to the front and placed in new positions. This was done twice. In our last position the enemy advanced on our rear, as well as on the right and left flanks, and a brisk skirmish ensued, in which they were held completely in check until the brigade and artillery were withdrawn slowly and in good order. During this skirmish, and, in fact, the entire day, my brigade behaved well. All orders were promptly obeyed, and an eagerness to meet the enemy was manifested during the engagement by the whole command."[21]

Casualties for Featherston at Champion Hill were light compared to those of the entire Confederate force. Featherston reported one each for the categories of killed, wounded, and missing. By comparison, overall Confederate figures were recorded as three hundred eighty-one killed, one thousand eighteen wounded, and two thousand four hundred forty-one missing.[22]

Loring's Division was separated from the major wing of General John Pemberton's Army in the latter stages of the Vicksburg Campaign. As a result, Featherston joined the other units in Loring's command as they marched toward General Joseph Johnston's troops in Jackson, Mississippi. The fall of Vicksburg led to Featherston's Brigade, as part of Loring's Division, serving with General Leonidas Polk.[23]

In May 1864, Brigadier General Featherston joined General Johnston in Resaca, Georgia. For the majority of time he was in the Peach State, Featherston commanded a division of Confederate troops. With the death of General Polk, General Loring assumed the role of Corps commander and Featherston replaced Loring. Featherston led the members of Loring's former division as they participated in many of the battles associated with the fall of Atlanta.[24]

During the Atlanta Campaign, Featherston's assigned role was to command the First Brigade. That unit was composed of the 3rd Mississippi, 22nd Mississippi, 31st Mississippi, 33rd Mississippi, and 40th Mississippi. Additionally, the 1st Mississippi Battalion Sharpshooters were under Featherston's leadership. Featherston's Brigade was placed into Major General William Loring's Division, part of Lieutenant General Leonidas Polk's Army of Mississippi.[25]

Featherston's Brigade took part in the battle of New Hope Church in May 1864. In this engagement, the first of the Atlanta Campaign, his troops were hit with a Federal advance and undertook a countercharge. Of the four hundred men from Featherston's command who took part in the movement toward the Federal lines, about one hundred were killed or wounded.[26]

At Kennesaw Mountain, on June 27, 1864, Featherston managed to repel a series of Federal attacks, one of which came within one hundred yards of his position. He wrote, "A brisk fire was kept up on this line during the evening, and...the battalion...acted with great coolness, courage and determination." The next month, at Peachtree Creek, Featherston reported that his command suffered eleven killed, seventy-one wounded, and six missing. From the following day until the Confederate evacuation in early September, Featherston and his men were in the trenches around Atlanta.[27]

In October 1864, Featherston's Brigade joined other commands in a battle near the Chattanooga and Atlanta Railroad. In that series of actions, Featherston's Brigade captured the Federal camp at Big Shanty. They were also involved in the capture of Acworth and played an active part in the destruction of a rail line located between Resaca and Dalton. He then led his command to Gadsden, Alabama and Decatur, where a late October skirmish took place.[28]

Featherston next participated in the battle of Franklin, Tennessee in November 1864. His command at Franklin, as well as in the Nashville Campaign that soon followed, were the 1st, 3rd, 22nd, 31st, 33rd, and 40th Mississippi and the 1st Battalion Mississippi Sharpshooters. While still a brigadier general in Major General William Loring's Division, Featherston was, at Franklin and Nashville, a part of Lieutenant General Alexander Stewart's Corps. Featherston wrote of Franklin, "The color bearers of the Third and Twenty-second planted their colors on the enemy's works and were wounded and captured..." At Franklin, six Confederate generals were killed, eight wounded, and another captured. Total Confederate casualties were six thousand two hundred fifty-two, with almost eighteen hundred killed, and three thousand eight hundred wounded. Figures for Featherston's Brigade were sixteen officers and sixty men killed, twenty-two officers and one hundred enlisted men wounded, and four officers, as well as seventy-two men missing. Federal totals were two thousand four hundred, with a majority of those eleven hundred identified as missing having been captured. While General John Bell Hood's Army hastily abandoned the area of Nashville, Featherston's troops covered the retreat across the Duck River and joined six others in conducting the same activity near Columbia.[29]

In early February 1865, Brigadier General Featherston joined General Joseph Johnston in the Confederate march into North Carolina in a last ditch effort to maintain Confederate hopes for a successful conclusion to the war. During the final campaign in the Carolinas, Featherston led his brigade in battle. In late April 1865, Featherston surrendered with Johnston's Army at Bennett Place near Durham Station, North Carolina.[30]

After his parole, Featherston returned to Holly Springs and resumed his law practice. He remained active in postwar organizations as he served as the Grand Commander of the Mississippi United Confederate Veterans.[31]

In 1876 and 1877, Featherston returned to politics as a member of the Mississippi State Legislature. An early project of his tenure sought the removal of Adelbert Ames, a Maine native and a reported carpetbagger, as Governor of Mississippi. Ames resigned in exchange for all charges being dropped. Among Featherston's personal accomplishments was the manner in which he forced a large number of scalawags and carpetbaggers from Jackson, Mississippi.[32]

His personal life was tragically altered during the yellow fever outbreak that struck North Mississippi and West Tennessee in 1878. Having remarried after the death of his first wife, he took Lizzie McEwen, the daughter of Alexander McEwen, a leading member of society in Holly Springs, as his second wife. The couple had eight children, but two of them, boys named Charles and Lucius, died in infancy. Yellow fever not only killed two more of his children, a son and a daughter named Joseph and Georgia, but it also took the life of Lizzie McEwen Featherston. She passed away September 17, 1878.[33] Featherston remained a bachelor the rest of his life.

The 1880 Marshall County, Mississippi Census reported that Winfield Scott Featherston, whose age was then recorded as sixty, was raising his four remaining children, aged thirteen, eleven, eight, and three. In addition to caring for his children, Featherston was providing a home for his seventy-three year-old mother-in-law, Eliza McEwen. While enjoying the role of a devoted father, Featherston returned to the Mississippi Legislature in 1880 and was assigned to be the chairman of the Judiciary Committee that wrote the state's new code. That same year, he served as a delegate to the Democratic National Convention in Cincinnati, Ohio. Two years later, Featherston was appointed judge of the Second Judiciary Circuit for Mississippi.[34]

Politics summoned Featherston again in 1889, when a large number of his friends and supporters urged him to run for governor. Featherston yielded to their calls and sought the gubernatorial office as a Democrat, the party he had served for decades. Unfortunately, Featherston failed to earn his party's nomination. A period commentary stated, "Too honest to stoop to the tricks of the ordinary managers, he was defeated…but was all the more honored and beloved by the people on that account." Showing no hard feelings toward those who chose another man, and never one to shed his political obligations, Winfield Scott Featherston served as a member of the Mississippi State Constitutional Convention in 1890.[35]

After briefly suffering from paralysis, Featherston passed away at his Holly Springs home on May 28, 1891. One source reported a week after Featherston's death that the former Confederate general had passed away in Columbus on May 29. However, the location of Holly Springs is the correct site of his passing. His family members, as well as his "sorrowing friends," were at his side when he died. He was buried in Hillcrest Cemetery.[36]

Perhaps the best praise for Featherston was written in the *Biographical and Historical Memoirs of Mississippi*. The notation declared, "General Featherston filled every trust to which he [was] called with marked ability and fidelity…He never sought office, and only accepted when tendered him. His integrity was never questioned. No charge of corruption…was ever made…He lived and died an honest man that no money or position could buy…"[37]

SAMUEL WRAGG FERGUSON, C.S.A.
1834-1917

Samuel Wragg Ferguson was born in Charleston, South Carolina on November 3, 1834. His formative years were spent there, and he left Charleston to attend West Point. Little additional information exists in regard to other aspects of Ferguson's youth.[1]

Cadet Ferguson graduated from the United States Military Academy in 1857. Ferguson was ranked nineteenth in his class of thirty-eight cadets. Among Ferguson's classmates were two other future brigadier generals, Edward Porter Alexander and Robert Huston Anderson, as well as George Crockett Strong and John Sappington Marmaduke, who both became major generals. The cadet who ranked immediately behind Ferguson was Marcus Reno, the man who would gain notoriety and become the subject of controversy with Custer at Little Big Horn.[2]

While holding the rank of lieutenant in the dragoons, Ferguson joined Albert Sidney Johnston in the Utah expedition from the time of his graduation through 1858. The venture into Utah, conducted under the orders of President James Buchanan, pitted members of the United States military against Mormons determined to defend themselves against what they viewed as a government initiative against the Mormon way of life.

Following his exploits in Utah, Lieutenant Ferguson served at Fort Walla Walla, Washington and remained there through 1860.[3]

The results of the 1860 Presidential election had serious results for Ferguson's military career. Reportedly, as soon as he heard the news that Abraham Lincoln had been elected, Ferguson resigned his commission with the United States and offered his services to the newly-formed Confederate States of America.[4]

Ferguson's offer to the Confederacy was apparently well-received. In March 1861, a short time after he resigned, he was promoted to captain in the Provisional Confederate Army.[5]

An early claim to fame for Ferguson was his attendance at the bombardment of Fort Sumter located in the harbor of his boyhood home of Charleston. He was in the group in that accepted Major Robert Anderson's surrender and witnessed the raising of the Confederate flag over Sumter. Captain Ferguson also assisted in the posting of the Confederate guard. Ferguson was ordered to the Confederate capital in Montgomery, Alabama for the purpose of presenting the Confederate Congress with the Confederate flag that had flown over Fort Moultrie. That standard was the first to be struck with Federal fire during the battle for control of Fort Sumter.[6]

Colonel A. R. Chisolm recalled his interaction with Ferguson, "Having visited Fort Sumter five times under a flag of truce, and once after the surrender, I became...acquainted... with Captain Samuel W. Ferguson, the officers jokingly complained of being short of cigars and like luxuries... the next time duty called us to the fort, we presented them with several cases of claret and boxes of cigars."[7]

Captain Ferguson served as aide-de-camp to General P. G. T. Beauregard, and was a member of the general's staff since Sumter. In that capacity Ferguson became one of thousands of men to hold the honor of participating in the April 6-7, 1862 battle of Shiloh, Tennessee.[8]

A Louisiana brigade at Shiloh was reportedly missing a commander. The twenty-seven year-old Ferguson was sent to the vicinity of Tilghman Branch in order to take leadership of the group. General Hardee ordered Colonel Ferguson to capture a Federal battery that had been firing into the Confederate position. The missing officer associated with the Louisiana soldiers was a Colonel Pond who returned from a reconnaissance operation at almost the exact time Ferguson reached the brigade. The two officers exchanged heated words, but Pond eventually agreed to the assault, though under protest.[9]

Dead and dying Confederates littered the area of the Federal battery as Ferguson made it within forty paces of the battery's position. The Confederates lost approximately ninety of the one hundred fifty men Ferguson had at his disposal. Ferguson recorded, "Those that were unhurt had to tell all about how near they came to being killed…I quit them in despair."[10]

Ferguson also saw action at the battle of Farmington. There, he was again on duty with General Beauregard. That battle was Ferguson's first with the rank of lieutenant-colonel. In that action Ferguson commanded the 28th Mississippi Cavalry.[11]

Evidence also indicates that Ferguson was appointed colonel of the Fifth South Carolina Cavalry Regiment, but he never joined the regiment. This 1863 failure on Ferguson's part was partially corrected when Lieutenant-Colonel Robert Josiah Jeffords assumed temporary command of the Fifth South Carolina.[12]

Ferguson also saw action in the Vicksburg Campaign where he participated in halting the attacks of Admiral David Porter and troops of General William Sherman as they approached from Deer Creek. Ferguson also supervised several of the pickets in the Vicksburg area. Ferguson's cavalrymen were also active in the Yazoo River Delta where Ferguson led them against cavalry and artillery that were positioned in the advance of the Federal transports.[13]

Ferguson received a promotion to brigadier general from rank on July 23, 1863, with his commission also assigning him to a cavalry unit. In a short period of time, an additional promotion to major general was proposed. Stern objections from Major General Joe Wheeler, the highly-respected Confederate cavalryman, eliminated the escalation in rank from taking place.[14]

Brigadier General Ferguson led men in engagements during the Atlanta Campaign. His force of Alabama and Mississippi cavalry harassed the flanks of Sherman's Federal troops during Sherman's March to the Sea. Ferguson's cavalry joined two other Confederate brigades to form the cavalry of the Army of Mississippi. Operating on the left wing of General

Joseph Johnston's army, Ferguson's brigade was in a regiment that was under the command of General W. H. Jackson. Ferguson also managed to defeat the famous Federal Lighting Brigade.[15]

Comments related to Ferguson in the Atlanta area battles came from General Joseph Johnston. The Confederate commander said in the May 28, 1864 battle at Dallas, one he termed as "a very small affair," that the Confederate losses were approximately three hundred while "the Union troops must have lost more than ten times as many." Johnston noted that "this was an assault made upon troops of the Fifteenth Corps...supported by Smith's brigade of Bate's division and Ferguson's and Ross's brigades of Jackson's cavalry."[16]

Ferguson was also active in assisting in the evacuation of Savannah, Georgia. When Ferguson neared Savannah, he abandoned his horses, leaving them on the South Carolina side of the river. His cavalrymen swam the river and entered Savannah as approximately one thousand dismounted cavalry. In that capacity, Brigadier General Ferguson's troops served as the rear guard for General Hardee's army as it exited the confines of Savannah. During his remaining time in Georgia, Ferguson led his brigade in their "display of gallantry on every field."[17]

An order was issued regarding Brigadier General Ferguson making a move toward Danville, Georgia. Before he was able to arrive in Danville, Ferguson received additional orders to go to Charlotte, North Carolina. There, Ferguson was to meet with President Davis.[18]

Arguably, the highlight of Ferguson's Confederate military career was serving on the escort for President Jefferson Davis. As Davis fled the safety of Charlotte, North Carolina and moved into Georgia, Ferguson remained an advisor to the leader of the dying Confederacy.[19]

In Abbeville, South Carolina, the final meeting of the Confederate States Cabinet took place on May 2, 1865. The members of cabinet included President Jefferson Davis, Secretary of State Benjamin, Secretary of Navy Mallory, and John H. Reagan, the Confederate Post Master General. Brigadier General Ferguson was among the general officers who "decided after mature deliberation and discussion that it was useless to continue the war longer and that the government should be disbanded." Other generals who took part in the meeting were W. C. Breckinridge, George Dibrell, Basil W. Duke, J. C. Vaughn, and Braxton Bragg.[20]

W. L. Wittich, an individual who served under Ferguson on the Presidential escort, recalled some of the incidents involved with the series of events. Wittich wrote, "Ferguson's… brigade…had a Mississippi regiment, and General Ferguson was a Mississippian, but the majority of the brigade was composed of Texans and Alabamians."[21]

As his notations continued, Wittich elaborated, "Mr. Davis left…in the early morning, and at sunrise we followed him, being from time to time in sight in his rear…continued several days until 6 p.m. May 8, when we were captured, our company numbering at that time thirteen men… Mr. Davis was taken prisoner next day a few miles from where we were captured…"[22]

Wittich concluded his thoughts, "The morning of the day we surrendered we had a brush with a squad of Yankees, and had one man wounded…The Federals seemed very glad to capture us, and told us… we were about the last armed Rebels at large. The officer in command gave us an order on any United States quartermaster we might meet for supplies."[23]

Ferguson stated in an article published in 1908, "I reached Abbeville… and reported to…Breckinridge…He told me that the President expected to remain in Abbeville for two days. I remonstrated, stating that it would certainly result in his capture, and I told him what I knew of the movements of the enemy. He then determined to assume command…of the cavalry…"[24]

In regard to the last meeting of the Cabinet, Ferguson wrote, "The council met at 4:30 at the house of Colonel Burt…Each brigade commander, beginning with the junior in rank, was in turn questioned as to the temper and disposition of his command and of the willingness of the men to escort the President to and across the Mississippi River. Each commander unhesitatingly answered in substance that his men would go to the end of the earth with their chieftain."[25]

In adding insight into the final days of the Confederacy, Ferguson said, "The constant stream of paroled soldiers returning to their homes was sure to have a depressing effect …the command was too small to contend with the thousands which…surrounded us and too large for a swift and rapid flight…I marched at 2 a.m…Breckinridge with me. We crossed the river about sunrise…I went…where the other brigades had already camped. ...specie was distributed in bulk to the several commands. I did not pay my men until we reached Washington..."[26]

Ferguson continued, "I reached Washington at 1 p.m. May 5... The next morning General Breckinridge directed me to discharge my command, that they might return to their homes...I never doubted...that the men I had so often seen tried in battle would fight as gallantly as they had always done, but I doubted what effect the approach to homes and dear ones from whom they had been so long parted might have when they saw comrades free to go where they would, and I thought it but due to the President to say so frankly...The temptation to turn off for a glimpse of home might prove too strong..."[27]

L. C. McAllister, a member of the 2nd Alabama Cavalry of Ferguson's Brigade, recalled the units represented in the surrender that occurred in early May 1865. He noted that, in addition to the 2nd Alabama Cavalry, the various commands included the 56th Alabama Volunteers, the 12th Mississippi Cavalry, Muldrove's regiment, the 9th Mississippi, and members of both the 40th Alabama Infantry and the 4th Texas Infantry.[28]

Samuel Wragg Ferguson moved to Greenville, Mississippi when the American Civil War ended. There, the former brigadier general, after being admitted to the bar and successfully completing his requirements, practiced law.[29] The connection between Ferguson and Jefferson Davis extended into their post-war years as both resided in the state of Mississippi.

Ferguson married Catherine Lee Ferguson, seven years his junior. Catherine's parents were Eleanor Percy Lee and William Henry Lee, cousins of Robert D. Lee. The couple produced two children, James DuGue Ferguson and Percy Ferguson. Although the marriage seemingly appeared to be a happy one, there are indications it was far from peaceful. Catherine or Kate, as she was also called, was known to entertain men while Samuel was away on business. In 1886, Kate portrayed a young Indian maiden, while dressed in "very inadequate clothing, her kirtie only coming down to the knees on one side" with her arms, legs, and other body parts bared, and her ankles adorned with massive bracelets. She also published the novel *Cliquot* in 1888. The scandalous nature of the book included passages in which scantily-clad females exhibited their affections toward males in ways which past generations would have avoided completely.[30]

The Ferguson couple's home was located next to LeRoy Percy and became known as the societal center of Greenville. Percy was an extremely influential individual, and he helped Ferguson gain employment in the treasury department. Ferguson was eventually appointed treasurer of the Delta Levee Board.[31]

Ferguson became a member of the United States River Commission in 1883. The additional appointment as the president of the Mississippi River Commission was a directive of President Chester Arthur.[32] The administrative position associated with LeRoy Percy consumed the majority of Ferguson's time, but controversy also lay ahead.

In 1894, Ferguson returned to Charleston. The general consensus regarding the reason for Ferguson making a sudden move centers on allegations that he had embezzled as much as $59,000 from the Delta Levee Board. In an effort to avoid facing the charges and the possibility of a related prison term, Ferguson left the United States for Tambillo, Ecuador. He returned to Charleston after years of hiding and began practicing civil engineering.[33]

Ferguson's absence lent Kate the ability to additionally exhibit her "risqué life." She was regularly witnessed spending time with groups of males, attending "all-male feasts in a high class 'colored' salon for white southerners, drinking, joking, and smoking cigars" as many of the males of the era did."[34]

When the Spanish-American war erupted in the late 1800s, Ferguson offered his services to the United States. By then, the former Confederate brigadier general was in his mid-sixties, and his generosity was declined. Ferguson began spending the remaining years of his life between Charleston and Jackson, Mississippi.[35]

Ferguson passed away on February 3, 1917. A discrepancy exists regarding the death of his controversial wife, Catherine or Kate. One account notes that, in a state of financial destitution, she died in 1907. Another avoids the monetary issues and states that she passed away in 1928. Samuel Wragg Ferguson was buried in Greenwood Cemetery in Jackson, Mississippi.[36]

JOHN CALVIN FISER, C.S.A.

1838-1876

Although he was born and buried in Tennessee, John Calvin Fiser spent many years in Mississippi, serving with the state's Confederate troops. Another interesting aspect of his life took place in his final decade. At that point, John Calvin Fiser changed the spelling of his surname to Fizer, a more phonetically correct presentation, in his opinion. Despite an intriguing set of circumstances and situations related to his life, Fiser proved his physical endurance and willingness to undergo personal sacrifice in that he survived a total of five combat wounds.

John Calvin Fiser was born on May 4, 1838 in Dyer County, Tennessee. The town of Dyersburg is usually regarded as the location of his birth, but the name of Fiser's mother is unrecorded. John's father was Matthew Day Fiser, an early resident of the county and a man who served on the county court. Despite the apparent success the family experienced in Dyersburg, they moved to Panola County, Mississippi in 1848.[1]

The time the Fisers spent in the Panola County town of Batesville was short-lived. The year after the family's exodus from Tennessee, John Calvin's mother passed away from an undisclosed cause. Three years later, in 1852, Matthew Fiser died. The orphaned John Fiser moved into the home of his uncle, John B. Fiser, a merchant and political figure in Panola County, and a person who was considered to be one of Mississippi's prominent citizens.[2]

At the age of fifteen John Calvin Fiser moved to Lafayette County, Mississippi and obtained employment near the Tallahatchie River. He took a job as a clerk in a small store and worked in that capacity for two years. In 1855, the young Fiser relocated again, moving to his birth state and settling in Memphis. From a financial standpoint, Fiser was rather successful, as he dealt in both the mercantile and cotton merchant sectors of the economy.[3]

John Calvin Fiser returned to Mississippi in the days following the April 1861 attack on Fort Sumter. He then helped raise a regiment that became the 17th Mississippi Infantry Regiment. Fiser was elected to the rank of lieutenant of Company H which also held the designation of the Panola Vindicators. Another future brigadier general, Winfield Scott Featherston, was the first colonel of the regiment that Fiser assisted in forming.[4]

In the period prior to the June 1861 battle at Manassas, Virginia, John Calvin Fiser was promoted the regimental adjutant for the 17th Mississippi. In that capacity, he also participated in the Battle of Ball's Bluff. Fiser received praise for his conduct in the action at Ball's Bluff; he offered what was termed a "most important and effective service." Another promotion for Fiser took place immediately after the battle of First Manassas. At that point he was given the task of serving as the adjutant for the brigade of Brigadier General William Barksdale.[5]

The 17th Mississippi underwent a major reorganization on April 26, 1862. The event was beneficial for Fiser in that he received another promotion. For some time in the future, the former brigade adjutant would serve as Lieutenant-Colonel John Calvin Fiser.[6]

Additional combat confronted Fiser in July 1862. A record of the event recorded that the action at Malvern Hill, during the Peninsula Campaign, resulted in the wounding of Colonel Holder of the 17th Mississippi Infantry Regiment. The account said that at approximately six o'clock on the evening of July 1, 1862 the 17th Mississippi made a charge against the Federal position at Malvern Hill. The attack was made, "under a terrible fire of shell, grape, canister and Minie balls, but without success." With Holder wounded in the charge, Lieutenant-Colonel Fiser took over leadership of the regiment.[7]

On September 17, 1862, Lieutenant-Colonel Fiser led the 17th Mississippi at Antietam. In the battle, the day in which more Americans were killed or wounded than in any other day in history, the 17th Mississippi was in the brigade of Brigadier General William Barksdale. The 13th, 18th, and 21st Mississippi Infantry Regiments rounded out Barksdale's command which suffered heavily in the action at Antietam. Total casualties for the brigade were thirty-five killed, two hundred seventy-two wounded, and four missing.[8]

At the battle of Fredericksburg, Virginia, in 1862, Lieutenant-Colonel John Fiser suffered a wound on the afternoon of December 11. Major-General Lafayette McLaws reported that he received a message from General William Barksdale that a dense fog had negated an effective analysis, but sounds from the Rappahannock River bank opposite his position caused Barksdale to believe Federals were constructing a pontoon bridge as a means of reaching the Confederate position. McLaws replied that allowing the Federals to pursue their task would put them within range of the Confederate sharpshooters.[9] Fortunately, Fiser soon recovered from his wound.

McLaws recorded the progress of the bridge's construction and the conduct of the troops under Fiser's leadership in writing, "With the sound of the cannon was mingled the rattle of the rifles of the Mississippi men, who opened a concentrated fire from the rifle-pits and swept the bridge, now crowded with the construction parties."[10]

Colonel Fiser's detachment of Mississippi troops managed to thwart an estimated nine Federal attempts to complete the pontoon bridge. It was said that "such [a] heavy loss" encountered on the part of the men in blue caused a construction delay that lasted until just before noon. The reply was "the tremendous array of the Federal artillery" that McLaws stated, "Opened fire from the heights above the city."[11]

The complimentary remarks regarding Fiser's command comprised a large portion of the post-battle report from Major-General McLaws. The general wrote, "It is impossible fitly to describe the effect of this iron hail hurled against the small band of defenders...The roar of the cannon, the bursting shells, the falling of walls and chimneys, and the flying bricks and other material dislodged from the houses...made a scene of indescribable confusion..."[12]

McLaws continued, "Under cover…the Federals renewed their efforts to construct the bridge, but the little band of Mississippians in the rifle-pits under Lieutenant-Colonel John C. Fiser, 17th Mississippi…10 sharpshooters from the 13th Mississippi, and 3 companies of the 18th Mississippi…held their posts, and successfully repelled every attempt."[13]

By 4:30, Fiser and his men were receiving heavy cannon fire. It was noted, "The concentrated fire from all arms, directed against…men in the rifle-pits, became so severe that it was impossible for them to use their rifles with effect." A portion of a falling wall knocked Fiser down and temporarily stunned him. In a display of physical tenacity, Fiser managed to regain consciousness, "held his post, and cheered on his men."[14]

Additional praise for the conduct of Fiser and his troops came from a veteran of the battle of Fredericksburg. In an 1899 article, Major Alfred Edwards wrote, "McLaws was in command of the portion of the line… that included Fredericksburg…and the defense made by Col. Fiser and his gallant regiment…won them a fame that will last as long as time."[15]

Fiser then received orders to move his command into the city. An estimated thirty to forty of Fiser's troops did not hear the order and fell captive to the Federals who managed to cross the river.[16]

Barksdale's Brigade joined those of Brigadier Generals Joseph Kershaw, Thomas Cobb, and Paul Semmes to form McLaws Division. The casualties for the brigade at Fredericksburg were twenty-nine killed, one hundred fifty-one wounded, and sixty-two missing, for a total of two hundred forty-two.[17]

At Chancellorsville, in May 1863, the composition of Barksdale's Brigade was similar to that at Fredericksburg. However, there were some minor changes in the brigades that compiled McLaws Division. Brigadier General Barksdale continued to command Fiser and the 17th Mississippi, but other brigades of the division belonged to Brigadier Generals W. T. Wofford, Paul Semmes, and Joseph Kershaw. The losses of the brigade were heavy, as Fiser and his fellow Confederates of Barksdale's Brigade endured five hundred and ninety-two casualties, with three hundred forty-one missing, two hundred eight wounded, and forty-three killed.[18]

Having seen Colonel W. D. Holder replace him as commander of the 17th Mississippi at Chancellorsville, Lieutenant-Colonel John Fiser shared command of the regiment at Gettysburg in July 1863. In addition to the

17th Mississippi, the remaining regiments of Brigadier General William Barksdale's Brigade were the 13th, 18th, and 21st Mississippi Infantry Regiments. In the ensuing battle, Barksdale was mortally wounded, and command of the brigade went to Colonel Benjamin Humphreys. Colonel Humphreys combined with the brigades of Brigadier Generals Kershaw, Semmes, and Wofford to complete those in Major-General Lafayette McLaws' Division. Semmes also suffered a mortal wound at Gettysburg, and Lieutenant-Colonel John Calvin Fiser received another painful battle injury.[19]

During some of the most heated fighting at Gettysburg, Fiser suffered a series of serious wounds. He was initially shot in the cheek, but continued to fight. Additional suffering lay ahead, as two shots to his leg completed Fiser's participation in the battle of Gettysburg.[20]

In addition to Lieutenant-Colonel Fiser's wound, three of the four men who commanded the 17th Mississippi at Gettysburg received battle injuries of varying severity. Colonel William Holder was wounded on the same day as Fiser. Acting Major Andrew Pulliam was also seriously wounded during the battle. Acting Major Richard Jones was also killed at Gettysburg, and the regiment's command fell to Captain Gwen Cherry.[21]

Fiser recovered from his wounds and led the 17th Mississippi at Chickamauga. On November 29, 1863, he also saw action at Fort Sanders during the battle at Knoxville, Tennessee. While approaching the Federal stronghold of Fort Sanders, Lieutenant-Colonel Fiser suffered what was arguably his most severe wound of the war.

General McLaws had informed General James Longstreet that Lieutenant-Colonel Fiser was one of two regimental commanders from the entire division who McLaws felt confident could make a successful advance against Fort Sanders. McLaws reportedly stated that he was "of the opinion they could take the work, and I would put them at it if an assault should be made." Fiser clipped his hatchet to his sword belt and intended to use the weapon to cut down the pole from which the United States flag flew inside the fort.[22]

As members of the Confederate advance party attempted to scale the slippery slopes of Fort Sanders, a heavy exchange of fire riddled those making the onslaught. An almost complete cessation of fire from within the fort allowed color bearers to plant battle flags on the parapet. Renewed fire from within Fort Sanders trapped many of the Confederates in an area where neither advance nor retreat was possible.[23]

Colonel H. P. Thomas of the 18th Georgia and Colonel Kennon McElroy of the 13th Mississippi were killed in the apparent quagmire. Lieutenant-Colonel Fiser was shot in the right arm while fighting against the Federals. The point-blank shot apparently came from a member of the 79th New York Cameron Highlanders who had been given the task of guarding the flag pole on the southwest side of the fort. The critically-wounded Fiser refused to abandon his post until his men were able to safely evacuate the confines of Fort Sanders. The severity of Fiser's wound, his fifth of the American Civil War, necessitated the amputation of his injured limb.[24]

In an 1893 account of the battle, a former captain of the 18th Mississippi noted the lack of leadership in the Confederate attack against Fort Sanders. W. Gart Johnson reported in *Confederate Veteran* that, "The assaulting force was composed of regiments of different brigades with no general officer in immediate command."[25]

The inability of Fiser's wound to completely heal caused him to resign from his February 1864 promotion to colonel. His June 1864 resignation lasted until the winter, when Major-General Lafayette McLaws requested Fiser's return to the Confederate service. Colonel Fiser was assigned to the command of a Georgia brigade who was to join in the fight against Federal troops under Major-General William T. Sherman.[26]

In April 1865, as the American Civil War was reaching its conclusion, Fiser's command was combined with a senior officer, Colonel George Harrison. That consolidation relegated Fiser to the leadership of a regiment rather than the entire brigade. In addition, Fiser was soon promoted to the rank of brigadier general, but there is no evidence to support the Confederate Congress acting upon the recommendation.[27] However, given the fact that he helped raise a regiment in Mississippi, his leadership experience with Mississippi and Georgia troops, as well as the filing of the promotion to brigadier general, Fiser is included in this list of generals from the state of Mississippi.

Fiser's last military action was at Bentonville, after which he was given command of a post in Savannah, Georgia. At the latter location he received his parole and embarked upon his return to Tennessee. Passing through

Georgia, Fiser encountered a starving group of recently-paroled soldiers who were attempting to maintain possession of army supplies. Local homes and businesses were being robbed in the process, and Fiser managed to gather enough soldiers to successfully disperse what had become a riotous crowd.[28]

After the war, Fiser returned to the business world and settled in Memphis, Tennessee. He was eventually made president of the Office Security Building and Loan Association. In addition to holding an executive position in the professional portion of his life, Fiser also took it upon himself to serve his fellow Confederate Veterans. In 1871, he was elected president of the Confederate Historical and Relief Association. Fiser also allotted a great deal of his public service time to local Memphis politics, where he was active in the Democratic Party.[29]

Fiser also married Hayes Dunn and changed the spelling of his last name to Fizer. Hayes, or Hays as she sometimes spelled her name, and John Calvin Fizer eventually had three daughters. A large portion of his time was also devoted to working in the cotton brokerage firm, Estes, Fizer, and Company, where John Calvin was a partner. By most reports the business endeavor was financially successfully.[30]

In 1871, the thirty-eight year-old John Calvin Fizer succumbed to a bout with dysentery and passed away on June 14. A large number of former Confederate soldiers, dressed in their uniforms, participated in the funeral, reportedly the largest in Memphis to that time. The Confederate veteran was buried in Elmwood Cemetery in Memphis. His widow lived until 1911 and passed away in her mid-sixties.[31]

SAMUEL JAMESON GHOLSON, C. S. A.

1808-1883

Samuel Jameson Gholson was born in the Madison County, Kentucky town of Richmond on May 19, 1808. Indications are that the names of his parents were Francis and Susana Brown Gholson. Francis, a native of Spotsylvania County, Virginia, usually went by the name of Frank and was a veteran of the French and Indian War as well as the American Revolution.[1]

Samuel joined his parents in their 1819 move to Alabama. After finishing his requirements for completion of his education in local schools, Gholson moved to Russellville, Alabama. There, he began his private study of law and earned admission to the bar in 1829.[2]

In 1830, Samuel Gholson moved to Athens, Mississippi. He was one of the early settlers in Aberdeen, the county seat of Monroe County. Named for President James Monroe, the area once belonged to the Alabama Territory and became part of Mississippi in the early 1820s. He became active in politics and served in the Mississippi State Legislature from 1833 to 1836.[3]

A Democrat, Samuel Gholson was elected to fill a Congressional vacancy in 1837. A special election held months later enabled him to assume the same seat in his own right. A heated dispute regarding the election resulted in his dismissal, and his opponent received the position. His two terms as U. S. Representative from Mississippi ran from 1836 to 1837 and from 1837 to 1838. Gholson was also a member of the Mississippi State House of Representatives in 1839.[4]

A January 30, 1838 letter from W. B. Campbell to Adam Ferguson noted the part Congress played in the scandal involving Samuel Jameson Gholson and J. F. H. Claiborne. In short, Campbell stated, "We are engaged in the House...on the Mississippi election, and hope to have the vote taken upon it tomorrow. I calculated that the party in power will retain Gholson and Claiborne, contrary to the decision of the people of Mississippi at their regular election. This...will be one of the most flagrant acts of corruption ever perpetrated by...assembly."[5]

A compatriot of Gholson's recalled the entry of Gholson onto the national political scene. M. L. Vesey, was a member of Company I, 14th Mississippi, during the war and served under Gholson's command. Vesey wrote, "Judge Gholson came into national prominence...as one of the principals in the celebrated election contest case between Gholson and Word on one side and Prentiss and Claiborne on the other. S. S. Prentiss's speech before Congress in this case gave him a national reputation as an orator, but was of no avail, as Gholson and Word were seated."[6]

Gholson also entered into an argument with Virginia politician Henry A. Wise. The disagreement became so heated that Gholson and Wise intended to settle it with a duel. Only the intervention of associates of the two men, including the powerful John C. Calhoun, led to a peaceful solution of the seemingly-pointless kerfuffle. While Gholson eventually served as a Confederate general, Wise later became the governor of Virginia.[7]

On February 9, 1839, President Martin Van Buren nominated Samuel Gholson the U. S. Judge for the Districts of North and South Mississippi. Gholson received Senate confirmation on February 13, 1839. Judge Gholson served in that capacity for the next twenty-two years. No major controversies evidently arose during his lengthy term, and only the arrival of the American Civil War ended Gholson's tenure in the position. In 1846, approximately a decade into his term as District Judge, Gholson served as a Mississippi State Militia Lieutenant.[8]

Known as a States-rights advocate, Gholson was a Mississippi delegate to the 1860 Democratic Convention. With his reputation as a supporter for secession, Judge Gholson was a delegate for the Mississippi Secession Convention in 1861. Gholson cast his vote for the state to secede; the secession articles passed on January 9, 1861. A vote of eighty-four to fifteen led Mississippi to become the second state to sever its ties with the United States.[9]

The secession of Mississippi touched Gholson to the extent that he resigned his position of what has been termed "a prominent judgeship" on January 10, 1861. He then enlisted in a locally-raised company that initially offered its services to the state of Mississippi. Private Gholson and fellow company members became part of the 14th Mississippi Infantry Regiment.[10]

Company I of the 14th Mississippi, raised in Monroe, County, Mississippi, was named the Monroe Volunteers. It was one of ten companies in the 14th Mississippi. With an aggregate enrollment of 1,034 enlisted men and officers, the 14th Mississippi moved to Corinth, Mississippi and was sworn into Confederate service for twelve months, beginning in late May of 1861.[11]

Gholson was soon elected captain. He was soon promoted to colonel and then to brigadier general, both in the service of Mississippi. Gholson commanded the Mississippi State Troops as they readied for action in the Fort Donelson and Fort Henry locations.[12]

In February 1862, Gholson participated in the battle of Fort Donelson, Tennessee. Gholson and the 14th Mississippi were under the command of Major Washington Doss. The 14th Mississippi also joined the 2nd Kentucky and 41st Tennessee to compile the 2nd Brigade of Brigadier General Simon Buckner's Division. The 2nd Brigade was attached to Colonel John Brown's 3rd Brigade at Fort Donelson.[13]

Frank Rogers, captain of Company E in the 14th Mississippi, had, like Gholson, been a judge before the war. The Aberdeen, Mississippi lawyer was regarded one of the "distinguished men" in leadership roles of the 14th Mississippi. Sadly, he was killed during a Confederate charge at Fort Donelson.[14]

At Fort Donelson, Gholson, commanding Company I of the 14th Mississippi, was also wounded as a bullet passed through his right lung.

Gholson was one of eighty-five members of the 14th Mississippi wounded at Fort Donelson. Another seventeen regimental members were killed and ten missing. The subsequent Confederate surrender at Fort Donelson resulted in approximately six hundred fifty members of the 14th Mississippi becoming prisoners.[15]

Gholson was a prisoner for a short period of time, with his injury negating him having to endure some of the horrible conditions many of his fellow Confederates faced. At least one record indicates that Gholson managed to escape from the military hospital, as did Andrew Jackson Lowry, another wounded member of the 14th Mississippi. After Gholson recovered from his wound received at Fort Donelson, he saw action at Iuka, Mississippi in September 1862.[16]

In October 1862, Gholson was engaged in Corinth, Mississippi and was wounded for the second time in the war.[17] The wound apparently was not deemed as serious, for there is no indication of Gholson missing roll calls during the period following the injury.

On April 18, 1863, Samuel Gholson received another promotion in the state forces of Mississippi. That elevation in rank provided Gholson with the title of Major-General Gholson.[18]

Gholson used his rank as a means of expressing his opinion about those who held subordinate ranks. An April 1863 correspondence with Brigadier General Daniel Ruggles, camped in Columbus, Mississippi, concerned the command of troops in the First Military District. Gholson wrote from Verona, Mississippi and informed Ruggles that Captain J. F. White would be a superior leader to Major Inge, who was leading the area's troops at the time.[19]

On November 3, 1863, General Gholson raised a two hundred seventy member force that included a battalion of men of Major Thomas Ham's Battalion. Working in conjunction with Colonel Neely, Gholson left his camp at Knight's Mill on a reconnaissance mission. In turn, Gholson's troops burned three railroad trestles. The largest accomplishment of Gholson was to burn the railroad depot, the Federal barracks, and stockade at Middleton, Tennessee.[20]

A Federal officer reported that in February 1864 he encountered Gholson at Houston, Mississippi. The officer noted that he had managed to push aside the "rabble" of Gholson's state troops and proceeded to set as many as two million bushels of corn on fire. The resulting inferno allegedly created "a line of fire from place to place." Another report involved interaction with Gholson's six hundred men at Pontotoc. Along the Houlka River, Federals under General Sooy Smith struck Gholson's location and "drove [them] pell-mell across the swamp."[21]

After battles near West Point and Okolona, his command was used to pursue retreating Federals. The success of General Gholson's troops was apparent as it was stated, "When last heard from [they were] still driving the enemy, capturing horses and prisoners."[22]

Although it meant a reduction in rank, Gholson was commissioned as a brigadier general in the Provisional Confederate military on May 6, 1864. Gholson was given the command of a cavalry brigade that saw action in Mississippi, Alabama, Tennessee, and eastern Louisiana.[23]

Brigadier General Gholson had been assigned the command of General James Chalmers's First Division, a unit in the cavalry of Nathan Bedford Forrest. The transfer of Gholson's troops to the Confederate States took on May 1, 1864 at the directive of the State of Mississippi. By May, Chalmers's Division and Gholson's Brigade were detached from Forrest's command and sent to Alabama to lessen the Federal threat of Georgia-based raids. In due time, Gholson's Brigade was placed in Wirt Adams's Central Mississippi unit.[24]

On May 13, 1864, Brigadier General Gholson received an order from General Stephen Dill Lee. Lee had information that the Federal army had gained control of a position on the Mississippi Central Railroad. Lee and Forrest sent Gholson on a forced march toward Benton, Mississippi, where Gholson would report to General Wirt Adams. There was also an agreement that if Gholson ran short on weapons, Forrest was to "send at least two good regiments" to the aid of Gholson. Changes in strategy caused Gholson to stop in Aberdeen to replenish horse feed. The stopover also enabled sergeants to drill men termed as "green and imperfectly armed."[25]

Supply shortages continued to hamper Gholson during his early tenure with Forrest. Lee's plans recalled Gholson from Aberdeen to join General Adams, in defense of South Mississippi, as soon as Gholson's men gained armaments and were accoutered. By May 22, the only shortage for Gholson's Mississippians was a baggage train and cooking utensils. A directive was issued for those to be gained in Alabama, but a May 26 order redirected Gholson to Canton where he arrived on June 2.[26]

Gholson received another wound near Jackson, Mississippi. At the time General Lee's command had an approximate strength of nine thousand five hundred. General Gholson's portion of the Confederate effort at that time were recorded with those of Neely and a battalion under Beltzhoover and amounted to some two thousand one hundred cavalrymen.[27]

At the July 1864 battle of Tupelo, Mississippi, Gholson served under Brigadier General Hylan Lyon, whose brigade of Kentuckians was under the leadership of Colonel Ed Crossland. Gholson was then redirected to Central Mississippi[28] and then Atlanta.

During the Atlanta Campaign, Gholson was praised for the service of his brigade. Gholson also joined the Confederate cavalry in actions in Tennessee. The end of the Tennessee Campaign resulted in Gholson engaging in a series of battles and skirmishes in Mississippi.

In December 1864, one of Gholson fought at Egypt, Mississippi, a Mobile and Ohio Railroad stop located approximately eight miles south of Okolona. Egypt Station pitted Gholson's against the 4th and 11th Illinois Cavalry Regiments, the 7th Indiana Cavalry, one company from the 2nd Iowa Cavalry Regiment, as well as the 3rd and 4th Iowa Cavalry Regiments. Other men in blue included the 4th and 10th Missouri Cavalry, the 1st Mississippi Mounted Rifles, the 3rd U. S. Colored Cavalry, and the 2nd New Jersey Cavalry Regiment.[29]

Facing the Federal troops which numbered approximately three thousand six hundred, Brigadier General Gholson managed to gather some two hundred fifty stragglers and "a camp of dispersed cavalry collected to be returned to the front. Other Confederate forces included Lieutenant-Colonel Michael Burke's Regiment of five hundred men, as well as dismounted members of Ferguson's Cavalry Brigade and Lieutenant-Colonel William Wier's five hundred men of the 1st Confederate Veterans Infantry. A battery under Captain Houston King and arrivals from Captain J. C. Shoup's Cavalry pushed the number to almost one thousand five hundred.[30]

Brigadier General Ben Grierson's Federal Cavalry were determined to destroy the Mobile and Ohio Railroad, and left Memphis on December 21, 1864 for that purpose. Gholson was between Grierson and the railroad, but there was no ammunition within the ranks of Gholson's command. Seventeen boxes of .58 caliber ammunition reached Gholson, but his men were armed with .54 caliber weapons.[31] The stage was set for a one-sided confrontation.

During the fighting at Egypt, Mississippi, Brigadier General Gholson was hit in the left arm. The severity of the wound caused the attending surgeon to amputate the officer's arm, resulting in a slow recovery period. In turn, Gholson's combat duty had come to an end.[32]

Grierson noted in his official report that Gholson was killed at Egypt. A similar, but distinctly different analysis came from Colonel Joseph Karge, a member of a regiment under Grierson's command. Karge stated that Gholson had been mortally wounded.[33]

Federal casualties at Egypt Station were twenty-two killed, fourteen wounded, and fifty-three wounded; an additional thirty-four Federal wounded fell captive. The Confederate totals were reported as two mortally wounded and five wounded. However, an additional five hundred Confederates, according to a Federal report of the battle, fell captive to Colonel Joseph Karge. Few of Gholson's men were captured, and Colonel Osband of the Illinois Cavalry recalled that his command drove Gholson's cavalry from the field.[34]

Recovering, Gholson returned to Aberdeen and his law practice. He was reelected to the Mississippi Legislature in 1865 and became Speaker of the House. Gholson's opposition to the Reconstruction policies cost him his position, and he left the legislature in 1867.[35]

The former Confederate brigadier general returned to his law practice in Aberdeen in 1866. His service in the legal profession endured for the next seventeen years and was briefly interrupted with a one-year term in the Mississippi State House of Representatives in 1878.[36]

On October 16, 1883, Samuel Jameson Gholson passed away at his home in Abedeen. His body was interred in the city's Old Fellows Cemetery.[37]

Accolades for Samuel Jameson Gholson were widespread. Perhaps no better of the same were offered in a paragraph that contained the words, "He was an earnest and gallant soldier...an able, brave, and generous gentleman." An Aberdeen camp of the Sons of Confederate Veterans also honored Gholson by having his surname as the camp's namesake.[38]

HENRY GRAY, JR., C.S.A.
1816-1892

Henry Gray, Jr. came from a family whose patriarchs were clearly identified with military tradition. His father had been a captain in the War of 1812. Fredrick Gray, the grandfather of the future Civil War general, was an American Revolution captain.[1] The stage was set for Henry Gray, Jr. to serve in the military should a war erupt in his lifetime.

Born to Elvira Flanagan Gray and her husband on January 19, 1816, Henry Gray, Jr. spent the early years of his life in South Carolina. From his birth in Laurens District through his early legal training, Henry Gray, Jr. made his home in South Carolina. In 1834 he graduated from South Carolina College, now known as the University of South Carolina. He was admitted to the bar soon afterward and left the state of his youth.[2]

Henry Gray, as he was called from that point forward, determined that his new place of residence was to be Winston County, Mississippi, with Louisville as the county seat. In 1841 Gray married Eleanora Ann Howard. In the meantime Gray served as the district attorney for Winston County from 1839 to 1845. In the process, Gray became well-known for his legal prowess as well as his oratorical and political skills.[3]

Gray was elected to the Mississippi Legislature in 1846. He only served one term in that capacity, but ran for the United States Congress in 1850. Gray's bid for a national seat was unsuccessful as he lost the election as a Whig candidate.[4] The failure to secure the Congressional post evidently soured Gray on additional tasks for Mississippi, at least for the time being.

In 1850 Gray purchased a tract of land in Bienville Parish, Louisiana. Gray's three hundred thirty-two acre parcel was situated near Brushy Valley, Louisiana. The community had been settled some twenty-seven years earlier and became a location for entertainment. Gray and his wife contributed to the area's reputation when he and others began racing horses.[5]

The political life summoned Henry Gray again and he became a Democratic elector for James Buchanan in the 1856 Presidential election. In the process, he traveled much of Louisiana with Senator Judah Philip Benjamin who, like Gray, was destined to serve the Confederate States of America in the near future. While Gray's service was to be on the battlefield, Benjamin's would be as a member of the Confederate Cabinet, where he held the position of Attorney General before becoming the Secretary of War. Gray was also elected to the Louisiana State Legislature in 1860. Interestingly, Gray ran against Benjamin that same year, with Gray attempting to defeat Benjamin in the latter's bid for reelection. Benjamin defeated Gray, with the Louisiana State Legislature determining the results by only one vote.[6]

The arrival of the American Civil War caused Gray to abandon his plantation, his legal practice, and his family, as he returned to his former home state of Mississippi and enlisted in a regiment being raised in the Magnolia State. Jefferson Davis, an "intimate friend" of Gray's and a fellow Mississippian, contacted Gray to determine the possibility of Gray raising a regiment in Louisiana. After being recalled and approached with the strong suggestion, Gray consented.[7]

The unit organized at the order of the Confederate President eventually became the 28th Louisiana Infantry Regiment. In the spring of 1862 the regiment was raised at Camp Bisland, Louisiana. The recruits of the 28th Louisiana Infantry Regiment came from a variety of parishes across the state including Jackson, Bienville, Winn, Claiborne, Ouachita, and Calcasieu. Henry Gray was elected colonel of the regiment, and the 28th Louisiana entered into Confederate service on May 2, 1862. The 28th Louisiana was assigned to the Trans-Mississippi Department.[8]

It was noted about Colonel Henry Gray, "Through the first months of his service he had no opportunity for distinction." That situation changed when the Federal troops based in New Orleans began making attempts to spread "their conquests in the southwest."[9] The resulting battle that had serious ramifications for Gray came to be known as the battle of Bayou Teche.

The battle at Bayou Teche, Louisiana pitted Federal forces of General Nathaniel Banks against Confederates who were under the leadership of Richard Taylor, the son of the former United States President Zachary Taylor. In the course of the April 14, 1863 action, Henry Gray was seriously wounded.[10] In a short time, Gray managed to recover and returned to his regiment.

A report on a portion of the early action was featured in an article in *Harper's Weekly*. The article, in part, stated, "An artillery duel commenced between our gun-boats [Federal] and the gun-boat *Cotton* and the rebel batteries...our land forces were by no means idle...at once attacked the rebels in the rear of their rifle-pits...killed several, took forty prisoners..."[11]

During April 1863, Gray received a nomination from Edmund Kirby Smith for Henry Gray's promotion to brigadier general. For some reason the Confederate Congress did not approve Smith's recommendation for Gray. However, Gray gained command of a brigade in French-born General Camille Armand Jules Marie, Prince de Polignac's Division.[12]

Colonel Henry Gray continued to gain combat experience as he led his brigade in various engagements around Vicksburg and in Louisiana. During the Red River Campaign Gray joined his fellow members of the 28th Louisiana Infantry Regiment and the Consolidated Crescent Regiment as they followed orders from General Richard Taylor. One of Taylor's requests sent the above-noted units as the lead soldiers against Federal troops of General Nathaniel Banks.[13]

Gray was in charge of the brigade consisted of the 18th, 24th, and 28th Louisiana Infantry Regiments. These units were particularly active at Mansfield and Pleasant Hill. When General Alfred Mouton was mortally wounded during a charge at Mansfield, Colonel Henry Gray assumed the leadership of Mouton's command and was commended for the skill of doing so.[14]

An evaluation of Gray's performance in battle stated, "Gen. Gray was not famous for his expertness as a commander of troops, but was brave and fearless as a lion and distinguished himself for boldness and fearlessness in the bloody charge…at Mansfield."[15]

Although Gray was generally regarded as a small man who was "not prepossessing in appearance," he held a high level of respect among his troops. He was often referred to as a "baby on a monument" due to his appearance when he entered battles while atop his horse. It was noted that Gray was known to grumble when situations required him to wear a full uniform, "he was averse to everything in the way of display." However, his kindness and the manner in which he treated his soldiers and was "attentive to their wants…possessed a…keen, black eye that would dance when he got his anger aroused"[16] were traits those who served with him and knew him well remembered about him.

A major shift in Henry Gray's contribution to the Confederacy occurred soon after the Red River Campaign. Although he neither sought the position nor was he aware of his consideration for the post, Gray was elected, in absence, to serve as the Northwestern Louisiana Congressional District's representative in the Second Confederate Congress. Gray left his compatriots in Camden, Arkansas and established his residence in Richmond.[17]

Another alteration in Gray's leadership occurred on March 17, 1865. On that date, Gray received a promotion to brigadier general, based primarily upon his performance during the previous year's battle at Mansfield. Brigadier General Henry Gray returned to Polignac's Division and served there to the end of the American Civil War. Like many of his fellow Confederates, Gray never received a United States parole.[18]

The American Civil War ended approximately one month after Gray's elevation in rank to brigadier general. At that point he returned to Louisiana and served one term in the post-war Louisiana State Senate. Gray was involved in a long-term battle to recover his financial status he held before the war and reportedly spent a great deal of time in seclusion. Having lost his only son in 1864, Gray also suffered the death of his wife in the years after the Civil War.[19]

It was said that the losses of his son and wife negatively affected the former soldier a great deal. A fellow Confederate said that the deaths of the two Grays, "weighed heavy on the old man's mind and removed from him all the charms of life."[20]

Henry Gray was at his daughter's Coushatta, Louisiana home on December 11, 1892. Recently suffering from poor health, the seventy-six year-old Gray passed away on that date and was buried in Springville Cemetery in Coushatta. As such, his remains lie near the Red River, where he attained his military glory in 1864. His memory was preserved when a Sons of Confederate Veterans Camp in Louisiana used Gray as their namesake as did the Shreveport, Louisiana-based Henry Gray Chapter of the Military Order of the Stars and Bars.[21]

RICHARD GRIFFITH, C. S. A.
1814-1862

Richard Griffith was in Philadelphia, Pennsylvania on January 11, 1814. Richard's father died when Richard was just a boy. As a result of the family patriarch, the youngster and his mother relocated from the northeastern part of the nation to what was then the northwestern edge of major settlement. Richard's mother determined that a better life awaited them elsewhere and moved to Ohio. After Griffith completed his early education, Griffith entered Ohio University located in Athens, Ohio. In a few years he graduated with high honors from the institution.[1]

After graduating from Ohio University, Richard Griffith moved to Vicksburg, Mississippi and became a school teacher. He served the Vicksburg community in that capacity until the advent of the Mexican War.[2] At that point Griffith left the educational sector and volunteered to fight against Santa Anna and the military members of Mexico.

During the Mexican conflict, Griffith was a member of the 1st Mississippi Rifles. He also held the position of adjutant for the unit and served the entire war in that capacity. Perhaps most significant to his future military rank was the fact that, during the war, Griffith became close friends with a specific higher-ranking officer. That individual was

Colonel Jefferson Davis,[3] the future President of the Confederate States of America.

With the rank of lieutenant, Richard Griffith spent a great deal of time with Colonel Jefferson Davis. Lieutenant Griffith gained a great deal of combat experience and received accolades for his performance in battle. Colonel Davis praised Griffith for his gallantry,[4] a fact that undoubtedly contributed to Griffith's quick rise in rank in the war to erupt a decade later.

Griffith returned to Vicksburg when the Mexican War concluded and entered the banking profession. Seeming to find a vocational area that satisfied his quest for adventure, Griffith entered politics, a popular arena for the era's men who wanted to serve their fellow man. Another position Griffith held was that of Mississippi State Treasurer, a title that his banking background greatly aided him in securing. Griffith managed to hold the job of State Treasurer for two terms in the Antebellum Era. Reportedly a man who possessed a powerful physique, Griffith was also appointed United States Marshal for the Mississippi Southern District.[5]

Experimenting with the above-noted vocations, Griffith also managed to find time to delve into other ventures as well. Additionally, Griffith tried was the fruit tree business. He and a partner managed a nursery that was based in Jackson, Mississippi and grew a variety of trees.[6]

Griffith married, and the couple eventually had five children. One of his sons later served in the Confederate Army with Griffith. The family attended First Baptist Church were reportedly regular worshippers at the congregation. Financially, Griffith appeared to have been rather successful. He was, according to the 1860 Census, the owner of thirty-six slaves.[7]

The onset of the American Civil War resulted in quick and decisive action on the part of Richard Griffith. He utilized his past military experience and a portion of the wealth he had attained to form what was arguably the first volunteer unit from Mississippi. Griffith raised a company from Raymond, a town in Hinds County, Mississippi, located near Vicksburg.[8]

The company Griffith led the formation of was named the Raymond Fencibles, a group that was created only five days after the firing on Fort Sumter. One historian of the Fencibles wrote, "The men of the company dressed in their new uniforms of gray made by the patriotic ladies of Raymond assembled in the presence of a multitude of spectators to receive the beautiful flag of the company likewise made by the ladies of Raymond."[9]

Within two weeks of the Raymond Fencibles being raised, the company's members traveled by train to Bolton and Jackson and became one of the earliest, if not the first, Confederate unit to arrive at the Confederate base in Corinth, Mississippi. While in Corinth Griffith and the men of the Raymond Fencibles joined other companies such as the Sardis Blues, Vicksburg Sharpshooters, Pettus Relief, Claiborne Guards, Lawrence Rifles, and Satartia Rifles to form what became 12th Mississippi Infantry Regiment. Griffith was elected colonel.[10]

A history of the regiment said, "At Union City this regiment was organized with Richard Griffith as colonel, W. H. Taylor, lieutenant colonel, and John Dinkins as major. Private Inge was made adjutant…he had spent some time at West Point, and was most efficient for the position." During most of 1861 the 12th Mississippi Infantry Regiment was in and around Leesburg, Virginia.[11]

A former member of the regiment noted, "The Twelfth Regiment reached Manassas…President Davis was at Manassas Junction, and rode to the front with Col. Griffith." The writer of that statement also proclaimed, "Col. Griffith was adjutant of Col. Jefferson Davis's Regiment in the Mexican War." It was proposed that this relationship played a major role in the quick elevation in rank that Colonel Richard Griffith received.[12]

The notation was made, "Griffith afterwards was promoted to brigadier general." In fact, Griffith's promotion took place on November 2, 1861. In turn, he was placed in charge of four Mississippi regiments and assigned to the division of Major General John Magruder.[13]

The first significant battle for the 12th Mississippi Infantry Regiment, with Griffith as brigadier general, was at Seven Pines. The May 31 and June 1, 1862 engagement allowed the one thousand thirteen members of the regiment to display its prowess in combat. One of the largest regiments at Seven Pines, the 12th Mississippi Infantry Regiment suffered forty-one killed and one hundred fifty-two wounded. The tenacity of the battle in which Brigadier General Griffith and those of the brigade took part is evident in the brigade's casualty totals of two hundred forty-one killed and eight hundred fifty-three wounded.[14]

During the summer of 1862 General George McClellan, with over one hundred thousand Federal troops, marched toward Richmond, Virginia. The intent of the excursion was to attack the Confederate capital in an attempt to end the war. The series of battles became known as the Seven Days Battles; the fourth day took place at Savage Station. At Savage Station Brigadier General Richard Griffith joined Major General John Magruder in leading the Confederate forces who were determined to stop the Federal approach. Griffith's 12th Mississippi Infantry Regiment combined with the 13th, 17th, 18th Mississippi Infantry Regiments and the recently-arrived 21st Mississippi Infantry Regiment to form the Third Brigade of Magruder's Division.[15]

Tragedy struck the Griffith family during the June 29, 1862 action at Savage Station. The troops of Brigadier General Griffith's command were engaged in the pursuit of federal soldiers who were retreating along the Nine Mile Road when they encountered Federal reinforcements from Major General Edwin Vose Summer's Second Corps. Griffith, acting under orders from Magruder, took two regiments to support Brigadier General Kershaw's troops, while the others of Griffith's command were to remain in reserve.[16]

Heavy Federal artillery fire was directed toward Griffith's position, a fact that soon proved devastating. During the ensuing bombardment a shell fragment hit Brigadier General Richard Griffith's left thigh. The mortally wounded Griffith fell from his horse.[17]

An 1893 recollection noted, "Gen. Griffith, of Jackson, Miss., commanded the brigade. On the morning of the battle of Savage Station, while we were driving the enemy before us along the railroad track, he was struck by a shell from one of the enemy's guns. [He] fell from his horse and died in a few hours."[18]

Reportedly, Colonel Inge was with Griffith when the mortal wound occurred. An account stated, "The General fell, mortally wounded...In that crisis Col. Inge sprang from his horse and took the general in his arms as he fell. Asking the nature of his wound..." Brigadier General Richard Griffith was informed that the wound was fatal.[19]

Griffith, in response to the disclosure of the severity of his wound, was said to have uttered, "If I only have led my brigade through this battle, I would have died satisfied." One account held to the decree that all members of Griffith's staff, with the exception of Colonel Inge, were with Griffith at the time of his death. A different record of Brigadier General Griffith's passing declared that President Davis, a friend of Griffith's for a decade and a half, was with Griffith when the officer died.[20]

Another story recalled, "A shell struck the railroad section house just in front of the troops and exploded; a fragment was distinctly seen passing overhead before it struck Griffith." The account continued, "Borne off the field by members of his staff, he was transported to the home of a banker in Richmond, where he died that night."[21]

A summary of the battle at Savage Station, focusing on the magnitude of Brigadier General Griffith's death, was given in the words of Confederate President Jefferson Davis. In his book, *The Rise and Fall of the Confederate Government,* Davis wrote, "Our loss was small in numbers, but great in value. Among others who could ill be spared, here fell the gallant soldier, the useful citizen, the true friend and Christian gentleman, Brigadier General Richard Griffith. He had served with distinction in foreign war, and, when the South was invaded, was among the first to take up arms in defense of our rights."[22]

The body of the forty-eight year-old general was transferred to Jackson, Mississippi. Eight days after his death, Richard Griffith was interred in Greenwood Cemetery.[23]

A favorable evaluation of Brigadier General Richard Griffith's impression among his troops was written in a post-war memoir. A sentence from the manuscript stated of Griffith that he was, "A good man, a true patriot, and a gallant officer."[24]

In addition, a group of soldiers who once served under Griffith became known as "The McLaws Minstrels," a designation associated with their later assignment to the brigade of General Lafayette McLaws. At Fredericksburg the individuals performed at a theater and charged an admission fee for those who attended. The money raised in the effort was used to construct a monument for Griffith.[25]

NATHANIEL HARRISON HARRIS, C.S.A.
1834-1900

Nathaniel Harrison Harris was born in Natchez, Mississippi on August 22, 1834. Little is known about his younger years, other than the fact that Harris attended and graduated from the University of Louisiana Law School. Upon his completion of law school, Harris entered into legal practice in Vicksburg, Mississippi, a town near his hometown of Natchez.[1]

On June 1, 1861, Harris and the company he organized were enlisted into Confederate service in Richmond, Virginia. Harris had been the catalyst for the formation of the Warren Rifles, a company raised in Warren County, Mississippi. Additional companies that joined the Warren Rifles came from the counties of Noxubee, Jefferson, Lafayette, Panola, Marshall, Tippah, Itawamba, and Tishomingo. These formed the 19th Mississippi Infantry Regiment.[2]

The Warren Rifles was designated as Company C of the 19th Mississippi Infantry Regiment, and Harris was elected captain of the company. The regiment, under the command of Colonel Christopher Mott, was "ordered to rendezvous at Oxford, Miss...proceed to Richmond...and report to Major-General Lee."[3]

On July 4, 1861, the 19th Mississippi left Richmond and joined other units assigned to General E. Kirby Smith. Captain Nathaniel Harrison Harris advanced to Manassas, but arrived after the conclusion of the battle. The 19th Mississippi entered winter quarters near Centreville.[4]

Captain Harris first saw action at Seven Pines. During that battle, Harris was serving on the staff of Brigadier General Cadmus Wilcox. Harris received complimentary remarks in Wilcox's report, warranting serious consideration for a promotion.[5]

The next action for Captain Harris was the March 5, 1862 battle of Williamsburg, during the Peninsula Campaign. Captain Harris was wounded during the battle. Colonel Mott was also killed "directly in front of the fence" where Federal troops were positioned, an event that led to Lieutenant-Colonel L. Q. C. Lamar gaining command of the 19th Mississippi. Lamar acknowledged Harris in writing, "To Capt. N. H. Harris of Company C special praise is due, not only for his gallant bearing on the field, but for his unremitting attention to his command."[6]

After recovering from the wound received at Williamsburg, Harris received another increase in rank and became a major. The promotion was effective to the date of the battle at Williamsburg.[7]

Additional military engagements awaited Major Harris at locations such as Glendale or Frazier's Farm. It was said, "The brigade went into battle at five in the evening and sustained the attack of a large force." In the struggle at Frazier's Farm, Harris received another wound. He was one of two hundred sixty-four regimental members wounded at Frazier's Farm. While Major Harris recovered from that particular setback, he was able to join his fellow Confederates in time to participate in the fighting at Bull Run.[8]

During the action at Second Manassas, on August 30, 1862, Major Harris was reported as being "severely wounded." His third battle injury necessitated a lengthy recovery period for the otherwise healthy Harris. Again, the brigade to which the 19th Mississippi Infantry Regiment belonged was dealt a high number of casualties, with the total approaching one hundred seventy. Harris's return to the 19th Mississippi Infantry Regiment did not take place until October 5, 1862. On November 24, 1862, Harris was promoted to the rank of Lieutenant Colonel.[9]

On April 2, 1863, Lieutenant Colonel Harris was given command of the 19th Mississippi Infantry Regiment. In a rather rapid progression, he also received a promotion to colonel on that date. Colonel Harris led his beloved group of soldiers into the battles of Chancellorsville and Gettysburg in May and July 1863, respectively.[10]

A report on the role Colonel Harris played at Chancellorsville stated, "...they advanced to the furnace, capturing many prisoners...the Nineteenth leading, and charged the Federal breastworks. Col. N. H. Harris led the attack...in spite of murderous fire...the Mississippians took the intrenched line." The casualties for the 19th Mississippi Infantry Regiment at Chancellorsville was six killed, thirty-nine wounded, and six were captured.[11]

In his report of the battle at Gettysburg, Brigadier General Carnot Posey mentioned Colonel Harris's performance of July 2, 1863. Posey wrote, "I received an order from the Major-General to advance but two of my regiments, and deploy them closely as skirmishers. I had then a thin line of skirmishers in front and at once sent out the Forty-eighth and Nineteenth Regiments, Colonel Jayne and Colonel Harris commanding." In the related action, the 19th Mississippi Infantry Regiment had four men killed and another twenty-three wounded.[12]

Sickness riddled Colonel Harris during the early fall of 1863. Therefore, he was absent from his regiment most of September and October 1863. However, the events of mid-October had serious implications on his military service. The death of Brigadier General Posey, on October 14, 1863, resulted in Harris being given command of Posey's Brigade. On January 20, 1864 Harris received a promotion to the rank of brigadier general. The regiments of Brigadier General Harris included the 12th, 16th, 19th, and 48th Mississippi Infantry Regiments, the ranks of which were filled with men from his home state. Brigadier General Harris and his brigade were part of the division that belonged to General R. H. Anderson's Division. In time, the brigade joined General William Mahone's Division in the 3rd Corps of the Army of Northern Division.[13]

Brigadier General Harris took part in the action at Spotsylvania. Harris led his brigade in a strong Confederate counterattack in the infamous Mule Shoe Salient. It was stated, "Harris and his Mississippians...rushed through the blinding storm of lead to fill the gap on Ramseur's right." His activities earned recognition for his gallantry in battle.[14]

Major General Evander Law recalled Harris's actions in writing,

"Rodes's right being still hard pressed, Harris's and McGowan's brigades were ordered forward and rushed through the blinding storm into the works on Ramseur's right...All day long and until far into the night the battle raged with unceasing fury..."[15]

It was also recorded that at Spotsylvania Court House, Brigadier General Harris encountered General Robert E. Lee as Lee rode at the head of Harris's brigade and shouted orders for the group to advance. A witness wrote, "Lee was present dictating notes and orders in the midst of his guns. At one time he rode at the head of Harris's Mississippi brigade, which by his orders I was guiding down in column to the assistance of Rodes...the protesting shouts of 'Go back, General Lee,' and the same promises to do their duty."[16]

Harris soon found his line of soldiers exposed to Federal fire that struck his command. In turn, Harris's brigade, "for...twenty hours... were exposed to a constant and destructive musketry fire, both from front and flank..." At the conclusion of the action at Spotsylvania, Brigadier General Nathaniel Harrison Harris reported that just within the 19th Mississippi Infantry Regiment the casualties were twenty-two killed, fifty-five wounded, and forty-five missing.[17]

During the August 21, 1864 battle of Globe Tavern, in the Petersburg Campaign, half of the members of Brigadier General Harris's brigade were casualties. Other activities during the Siege of Petersburg involved skirmishes and battles near the Weldon Railroad. At Fort Gregg Harris, displayed more leadership skills and yielded praise from his superiors. At Fort Gregg, Harris's troops composed approximately two hundred fifty men who able to "so long and stoutly" avoid falling to any of the three assaults from Federal troops under General Gibbon.[18]

Throughout the final months of the Civil War, Brigadier General Harris was responsible for overseeing a portion of the defenses of Richmond, Virginia. By April 1865, Harris commanded Mahone's Division. In that capacity, Brigadier General Harris surrendered his soldiers at Appomattox, Virginia. Harris's brigade stacked approximately one hundred fifty guns from its once mighty ranks while thirty-three officers and three hundred thirty-nine enlisted men were surrendered with Harris. Harris's parole took place on October 19, 1865.[19]

In his post-Civil War life, Nathaniel Harris renewed his law practice in Vicksburg. Future vents and situations led to his exodus to other parts of the United States and into different vocations. He served as president of the Mississippi Valley and Ship Island Railroad. He also became the registrar for the Aberdeen, South Dakota United States Land Office. From 1890 until his death, Harris made his home in California where he entered into a mining partnership.[20]

On August 23, 1900, Nathaniel Harrison Harris was on a business trip in England. While visiting in Malvern, England, Harris died. Single his entire life, Harris had requested that he be cremated. His request was carried out, and his ashes were buried in Green Wood Cemetery in Brooklyn, New York. His grave is located in section 185 of lot 21229.[21]

THOMAS CARMICHAEL HINDMAN, JR. C.S.A.
1828-1868

Knoxville, Tennessee was the location for the January 28, 1828 birth of Thomas Carmichael Hindman, Jr. The newborn's father was Thomas Carmichael Hindman, a planter and federal agent who dealt with Indian affairs in the state. His mother was Sallie Holt Hindman, and she bore six children, with the younger Thomas being the fifth offspring. Two boys and four girls eventually compiled the make-up of the Thomas and Sallie Holt Hindman children.[1]

The Thomas, Sr. and Sallie Holt Hindman family moved from Knoxville in the early 1830s and soon made their home in Ripley, Mississippi, where the patriarch had invested in a plantation. After the younger Thomas Hindman completed classes in area schools, he enrolled at the Classical Institute in Lawrenceville, New Jersey. He graduated with honors, as the salutatorian, on September 25, 1843.[2]

At the age of seventeen, Thomas Carmichael Hindman, Jr. was attending Princeton with his brother Robert when news of the onset of the Mexican War reached them. In turn, the brothers left Princeton and joined the army. Thomas enlisted as a second lieutenant, while Robert held the rank of private. The majority of Second Lieutenant Hindman's tenure with the 2nd Mississippi Volunteer Infantry was relegated to garrison duty, but his writing skills eventually enabled him to be assigned to serve as the regiment's adjutant. By the end of the war Thomas Carmichael Hindman had managed to hold the rank of lieutenant.[3] From that point forward he appears to have abandoned any other use of the suffix Junior from his name and became known by the same name as his father.

Robert Hindman completed his service in the Mexican War when he was discharged while suffering from smallpox. He then became engaged in a violent argument with another man. The source of contention was an individual named William Falkner. Falkner stood against Robert in a gunfight, but after Robert's gun misfired, Falkner stabbed Thomas Hindman's brother to death. The jury in the resulting trial determined that Falkner was innocent through his use of self-defense. A Hindman family friend soon fell victim to Falkner, but the subsequent trial again acquitted the victor. Eventually, Thomas Hindman battled Falkner in a gunfight, but neither of the combatants was wounded.[4]

Upon the conclusion of the Mexican War, younger Thomas Hindman returned to Ripley, Mississippi and studied sufficiently enough to pass the bar exam. He also served as the recording secretary for the Sons of Temperance. In 1854, the young Democrat was elected to the Mississippi legislature as Tippah County representative and became immersed in the state's politics. However, the high level of competition resulting from the large number of people seeking to gain elected offices in Mississippi created Hindman's disenchantment with the political arena. In addition, he gained a reputation for engaging in duels and fights, during which he was forced to "defend his honor" against slurs that arose from his political career. Those aspects combined to lead Hindman to seek greener pastures in another Southern state when the legislature adjourned in early 1854.[5]

In March 1854, Thomas Hindman was a resident of Helena, Arkansas and entered into a law partnership with John Palmer. Evidence indicates that Hindman's initial endeavor into the practice of law was financially unsuccessful. After a period of increasing activism in local politics and civic affairs, Hindman determined to run for Congress. The race pitted Hindman, a States' Rights advocate, against Dorsey Rice. During the campaign, Hindman and Patrick Cleburne, his roommate and a fellow Democrat, were attacked. The culprits in the incident were Rice, John

Rice, and James Marryatt, a brother-in-law of Hindman's opponent. Both Hindman, who was wounded in his left side, and Cleburne, who survived a shot that went completely through his body, were fortunate in the ambush. The Rice brothers fled the scene, while Marryatt was shot dead during the melee. Thomas Hindman was by then also serving as the editor of the *Helena States-Rights Democrat*, and arose victorious in the political campaign and assumed his seat in 1857. He eventually served two terms in the United States House of Representatives.[6]

In the meantime, Hindman began dating Mary Watkins Biscoe, the daughter of a wealthy planter. Also known as Mollie, Miss Biscoe continued to date the young politician despite her parents' objections. On November 11, 1856, Hindman and Mollie married, with Patrick Cleburne serving as their best man. The marriage not only improved Hindman's financial condition, but his new father-in-law's political connections added to the former Mississippi resident's ambitions. On a more personal note, in time, Thomas and Mollie had five children.[7]

Hindman and Cleburne had also been law partners in Helena and created a firm that was duly named Hindman and Cleburne. Hindman's business venture with Cleburne was more lucrative than his partnership with John Palmer. It was stated of the firm, "They were successful, and in…1858 Hindman and Cleburne dissolved [their] partnership."[8]

Hindman's political life included his battle against a powerful Democratic faction known as "The Family." The Family endorsed candidates who ran against Hindman, including William Sebastian, Hindman's 1858 opponent. There was also an attempt on the part of Governor Elias Conway to gain control of the assets of individuals who were indebted to the state's bank. One such individual was Hindman's father-in-law. Such developments led Hindman to declare himself an independent. In 1860, Hindman supported Henry Rector in Rector's bid for governor. In that election, Rector defeated Richard H. Johnson, a brother of Senator Robert Johnson.[9]

Hindman and Senator Johnson soon made amends, and the two held the common belief that Arkansas was unable to remain in the United States. The 1861 secession of Arkansas, of which he was a major proponent, resulted in Thomas Hindman resigning his United States Congressional post in an effort to serve the Confederate States of America. The thirty-one year-old failed in his quest to gain a seat in the Confederate Congress and used Helena as the location to raise a group of soldiers that became known as Hindman's Legion. Hindman managed to raise ten companies by June 1861, with four of them based in Pine Bluff and the remainder stationed at Helena. Thomas Carmichael Hindman was elected colonel of the unit that also used the designation of the Second Arkansas Infantry.[10]

When Hindman's Legion reached Bowling Green, Kentucky, Hindman was promoted to brigadier general by September 1861. Brigadier General Hindman was assigned to the Army of Mississippi and made his way to Corinth, Mississippi.[11]

Brigadier General Hindman took part in the April 1862 battle of Shiloh. A veteran of the battle recalled that during the first day's fighting he witnessed Confederate General Albert Sidney Johnston and his staff ride past. At that time, "Gen. Hindman passed in front of us...His horse was at full gallop, his long hair streaming out behind him, and he was waving his cap...and cheering the men on. I shall never forget what a picture of daring and courage he was."[12]

In the early hours of the battle, "Hindman's whole division moved on, following the ridge and drifting and drifting to the right, and drove in the grand guards and outposts until they struck Prentiss's camps. Into these they burst, overthrowing all before them."[13]

While leading a division during the carnage of the first day's fight, Thomas Hindman was seriously wounded. At the time Brigadier General Hindman was wearing an oilcloth poncho as he joined Brigadier General A. P. Stewart in guiding a regiment of Tennesseans into position. Hindman was reported to have been "whooping like a Commanche...with his horse on a dead run" as he rode along the Confederate line. A Federal Howitzer fired in Hindman's direction, and the shell slammed into the general's horse's front quarters. One account stated that the general's horse was blown apart, and Hindman sailed an estimated ten feet into the air. Another record of the event said that Brigadier General Hindman was pinned beneath the dead animal. Hindman attempted to regain his composure and stood, telling the Tennessee troops, "Take that battery." Hindman then fell and was carried from the scene.[14]

Colonel William Price, a staff member for General John Marmaduke, recalled his interaction with Hindman. Price wrote, "He and I were wounded...the same day...I shall never forget his kindness in having me taken to his tent to have my wounds dressed during the night."[15]

Sadly, for the men of Thomas Hindman's command who were still engaged in battle, the area that came to be known as the Hornet's Nest proved disastrous for the leaderless group. It was stated, "Hindman's brigades, which earlier had swept everything before them, were reduced to fragments, and paralyzed for the remainder of the day."[16]

In recognition of his "good conduct" and leadership at Shiloh, Brigadier General Hindman was promoted to major-general one week after the bloodbath at Shiloh. His May 31, 1862 assignment carried Hindman to the Trans-Mississippi District, formerly under the command of General Earl Van Dorn, where he was responsible for organizing and obtaining equipment for a massive number of soldiers. The Trans-Mississippi District comprised "the States of Missouri and Arkansas and that part of Louisiana north of the Red River and the Indian Territory." Arkansas was to be used for a base from which the Confederates would launch a campaign to establish control of Missouri. Highly-exaggerated rumors soon circulated that Hindman "was at the head of from 40,000 to 70,000 men." In actuality, his August 24, 1862 personnel numbers were "between 9,000 and 10,000 men, of whom about 3,000 were Indians."[17]

In a short time, Major-General Thomas Hindman managed to improve the state of his army, although doing so had been enabled through his confiscation of shoes, ammunition, blankets, and medical supplies from his Helena stockpiles. He had also raided Memphis, where he managed to seize one million dollars from banks in the city, as well as a minor amount of medical and military supplies. More controversial actions of Hindman included his declaration of martial law and burning cotton to prevent it falling into Federal hands. Hindman allegedly proclaimed, "I have come to drive out the invaders or perish in the attempt." As historian William Shea stated, Hindman, "during his brief period of command...demonstrated what fanaticism and a complete disregard for constitutional rights could accomplish."[18]

While Helena, Major-General Hindman's adopted hometown, had fallen to the Federals in July 1862, Hindman entered Missouri in September and established an outpost near Springfield. From there he received orders from General Theophilus Holmes to return to Little

Rock "in order to organize the troops in that neighborhood for his expedition."[19]

Along the trek, Hindman made a decision to fight for control of Arkansas. As a result, action for Major-General Hindman took place at Prairie Grove, Arkansas, a battle in which Hindman commanded Confederate forces. Although the Federal troops held the numerical advantage, Hindman managed to achieve a moral victory. One historian noted, "Hindman...was badly defeated." Another account stated, "...the Federals...were defeated and demoralized..."[20]

A summary of Prairie Grove said, "...the bloody battle...December 2, 1862, in which about twelve thousand Confederates...[fought] about sixteen thousand Federals...raged all day, and it is said the dead literally covered the field."[21]

A reference to Prairie Grove was in a Twentieth Century *Confederate Veteran* article. A town resident stated, "This village was the scene of a spirited and hotly contested engagement between...Gen. Thomas C. Hindman and...Herron, reinforced by Blunt...Hindman carried the day, his men acquitting themselves with great credit." The citizen concluded, "Although they took up their march southward during the succeeding night, they withdrew leisurely, and their adversaries showed no the slightest disposition to risk the hazard of pursuit."[22]

A final statement on Prairie Grove came from Colonel Thomas Snead. He stated, "Hindman had then to confront the united army, which was not only stronger than his own in numbers, but very much stronger in organization, arms, artillery, and leadership...Hindman's loss in killed wounded, and missing was 1,317" while those of the Federals were reported as "1,251, of which 918 belonged to...two divisions, which bore the brunt of the battle."[23]

A highly-slanted evaluation of Major-General Hindman's leadership skills came from an admiring fellow officer who wrote, "...if...Hindman had been given command of all the troops west of the Mississippi...and allowed full sway for his military genius and executive talents he would have made Missouri the battle ground in the West...and the chances for the success of the Confederacy would have been made more favorable."[24]

Not all individuals affected during Hindman's tenure in Arkansas were as impressed. This fact would have likely been due to the general's directive to "destroy every pound of meat and flour, every ear of corn and stack of fodder, oats and wheat that can fall into his hands; fell trees as thickly as rafts, in all roads before him, burn every bridge and block up the fords."[25]

A March 1863 letter from the Confederate Secretary of War indicated that the state of affairs in Arkansas was far from ideal. The letter stated, "General Hindman…has rendered himself by alleged acts of violence and tyranny perfectly odious. The consequences as depicted are fearful. The army is stated to have dwindled by desertion, sickness, and death…the people are…in a state of consternation, multitudes suffering for means of sustenance…"[26]

In the aftermath of a "strategic defeat" at Prairie Grove, Hindman ventured to Little Rock and asked to be reassigned. His request was quickly granted, and Hindman was removed from command of the District of Arkansas. He was then assigned to a Mississippi Court of Inquiry.[27]

Thomas Hindman returned to a more active military role in July 1863. At that point he was assigned to a divisional leadership role in the Army of Tennessee. Major-General Hindman found that the new assignment was to an officer corps that was divided in loyalty. Hindman aligned himself with General William Hardee, while a group of other officers yielded their support to General Braxton Bragg, the commander of the Army of Tennessee.[28]

Major-General Hindman's next opportunity to lead a division in battle arose at Chickamauga. Hindman suffered a severe wound at Chickamauga, one that required several months of recovery before he was able to return to the command of his division.[29]

Prior to being wounded, Hindman played a significant role in the death of a Federal officer. A witness reported, "…Hindman was moving up…under a terrific fire…The leader of a Federal infantry division… cheered on his men…Hindman knew his danger, and he knew the remedy. In his flanks was a company of skirmishers armed with…Whitworth rifles…a lieutenant of this company was operating with a dozen marksmen. Hindman called him up, ordered him to fire upon the Federal commander, and kill him if possible, well knowing the effect of his death upon his men…Twelve rifles cracked simultaneously. Rider and steed went down together, and the black mane of the horse waved over [Major General William H.] Lytle."[30]

At Chickamauga, General James Longstreet was in command of the Confederate left. One of the divisions in his corps was that of Thomas Hindman. At the time Major-General Hindman's division consisted of the brigades of Brigadier Generals Manigault, Patton Anderson, and Deas. It was reported, "Hindman had advanced a little later than the center, and had met great and immediate success."[31]

Major-General Hindman, conversing with General John Bell Hood, reportedly made a statement that had serious ramifications on Hindman's career. Confederate J. C. Higdon recalled, "Stephenson's Division...part of Hindman's, had a sharp engagement with the enemy, in which we accomplished nothing and lost several good men...Gen. Hood, with part of his staff, rode up and saluted Gen. Hindman." Hood was said to have pointed to a hill and uttered to Hindman, "When you see the enemy crown that eminence, take your division and charge them off."[32]

Hindman proclaimed, "Let me take my division and post them there, and the enemy will not crown that eminence." An angered Hood asked, "Gen. Hindman, why is it that I can never give an order but that you have some suggestion to make?" Hindman replied, "Because you never give me an order with any sense." A period historian noted, "This ended Hindman's career with the Army of Tennessee. His old division regretted to lose him very much."[33]

A "broad, high, long ridge" was located on the west side of Crawfish Spring Road at Chickamauga. A post-battle sketch, written in 1893, added that it was that location "over which Hindman's men drove General Sheridan, and on which Hindman halted, and from which his troops moved...to the east and joined Bushrod Johnson in the assault on Snodgrass Ridge."[34]

West Point, Mississippi resident A. M. Chandler was a member of the 44th Mississippi at Chickamauga and served in Brigadier General Patton Anderson's brigade of Major-General Hindman's Division. Chandler recalled, "In this charge...our brigade led by General Hindman, broke the Federal line and drove them nearly one mile...we were recalled and reformed, and marched back to the old field...literally covered with dead and wounded Yankees."[35]

Chandler remarked that at that point he encountered Major-General Hindman. Chandler wrote, "General Hindman stopped his horse in rear of our company...I said to him, 'General, we are the boys to move them!' He replied, 'You are, sir'."[36]

In February 1864, after recovering from his wound received at Chickamauga, Major-General Hindman took a stand on issues that were facing the Confederate army. For example, on February 2, Hindman addressed the practice of placing problematic soldiers on guard duty. He ordered, "Putting men on extra guard duty as a punishment is prohibited. Standing guard is the most honorable duty of a soldier, except fighting, and must not be degraded." Four days later he stated, "Slaves may be employed to cook and wash for the enlisted men at the rate of four to each company, receiving the pay of soldiers, with rations, and being reported as 'laundresses'."[37]

In the June 1864 battle at Kennesaw Mountain, Georgia, Major-General Hindman was one of two division commanders who "were repulsed, in an assault on the Union line, with a loss of one thousand men...Their loss was but nine percent, while that of the troops of the Army of the Cumberland...was 17 percent."[38]

Kennesaw Mountain was Major-General Thomas Carmichael Hindman's final battle of the American Civil War. While involved in the struggle, Hindman was wounded again, and was partially blinded. Due to the severity of his injury, Hindman left the army and moved to Texas to rejoin his family who had fled eastern Arkansas when the Federals invaded the area.[39]

With the end of the war, Thomas Hindman and his family sought exile in Carolota, Mexico and remained there for approximately three years. W. H. Bradley was a member of a fifty-two person group who also made their way to Mexico in an attempt to seek asylum. Hindman apparently served as an ambassador of sorts as Bradley commented, "At Monterrey Gen. T. C. Hindman...made us a very patriotic speech, praising our brigade for the part we had taken in behalf of the Confederate cause..."[40]

While in Mexico, Hindman attempted to practice law, but his efforts were far from successful. Additional limited income came from his involvement in a coffee plantation.[41]

Thomas Carmichael Hindman eventually returned to Helena, Arkansas in 1868 with the intention of protecting the people of Arkansas from the carpetbaggers in the state. The former soldier retained his earlier tendency to use combative methods to get his points and beliefs across, a fact that alienated him from many of his fellow statesmen. He also urged Arkansans to take the oath of allegiance in order to vote against the state's Republican candidates. This practice contributed to further animosity toward Hindman.[42]

On September 27, 1868, Thomas Carmichael Hindman's life was affected in a highly negative manner. The controversial man, who had gained a large number of enemies through his political and military activities, obviously created one or more enemies with a strong tendency toward violence. Known for his promotion of conservative politics and African American suffrage, he had managed to offend many of his fellow Southerners. As Hindman read in his parlor that evening, one or more individuals fired deadly shots through the window, striking Hindman's face, neck, chest, and hands. The murderer or murderers were never arrested.[43]

A record of the burial of Thomas Carmichel Hindman noted the location of his internment in Helena's Maple Hill Cemetery was near that of his former law partner Patrick Cleburne. The article proclaimed, "The burial places of...Hindman and...Cleburne, devoted friends and distinguished generals from Arkansas, are in the city of Helena, where they resided prior to the war."[44]

BENJAMIN GRUBB HUMPHREYS, C.S.A.

1808-1882

George and Agnes Wilson Humphreys welcomed their son, Benjamin Grubbs Humphreys, into the world on August 26, 1808. The child was born at the couple's Claiborne County, Mississippi plantation home that was named *Hermitage*. The Humphreys had once been New England residents, but the recent parents of Welsh descent had come to consider Mississippi their home.[1]

Agnes Wilson Humphreys passed away when Benjamin Grubb Humphreys was a child, and the youngster followed his father's request that the boy to move to Kentucky. While in the Bluegrass State, young Benjamin lived with his grandfather and received his early education in area schools. In 1821 teenager Benjamin moved to New Jersey, primarily for the purpose of furthering his education. He remained in New Jersey three years, at which time George Humphreys requested that the young man return to Mississippi.[2]

At the age of sixteen Benjamin Grubb Humphreys secured employment as a clerk in a Port Gibson, Mississippi store. His time in that particular vocation was short-lived, as he gained an appointment to the United States Military Academy in 1825.[3] The cadet's early life at West Point was largely uneventful, but that changed approximately one and a half years after his entry into the prestigious institution.

Cadet Benjamin Grubb Humphreys was a member of the West Point class that included other future Civil War generals such as Joseph Johnston and Robert Edward Lee. It had become somewhat of a tradition for the cadets to make eggnog during the Christmas holidays, add alcohol, and temporarily escape the "grueling regimen" of West Point life. However, Colonel Sylvanus Thayer, the Superintendent of West Point at the time, held a strict set of rules that included cadets avoiding the consumption of alcohol.[4]

An estimated seventy students joined in participating in a West Point Christmas celebration of unequaled proportions. In the process some of the drunken cadets smashed windows, heavily damaged the North Barracks, and assaulted two officers. A December 26, 1826 directive titled Order No. 98 placed twenty-two cadets on restrictions. An entire month of inquiries then began, with the decision being reached to court-martial nineteen of the cadets. Individuals such as Robert E. Lee testified on behalf of the individuals, but to no avail. Benjamin Grubb Humphreys and ten other accused cadets were banned from wearing the traditional gray uniforms of West Point; in March they were dismissed from the academy. The Christmas 1826 incident at the United States Military Academy became sarcastically known as the Eggnog Riot.[5]

Having apparently recovered fully from the embarrassment of his dismissal from West Point, Benjamin Grubb Humphreys began a studying law. He also made a major decision in regard to his personal life in 1832 when, on March 15 of that year, the dismissed cadet married Mary McLaughlin. The newlyweds initially made their home in the Big Black River region of Claiborne County. Three years later Mary died, leaving two children behind. One of the children, Thomas McLaughlin Humphreys, passed away at the age of four. However, Mary Douglass Humphreys, the daughter of Mary and Benjamin, survived.[6]

Four years after Mary McLaughlin Humphreys passed away Benjamin Humphreys made his entry into the crowded and highly-competitive world of Mississippi politics. He managed to secure a position in the Mississippi House of Representatives. As a member of the Whig Party, Humphreys began his elected service to the citizens of the Magnolia State.[7]

The widower Benjamin Grubb Humphreys remarried in 1839, the year after he entered Mississippi politics. The new Senator's second wife, Mildred Hickman Maury, supported her husband as he served his constituents until 1844. At that point of his life Humphreys and Mildred returned to their Mississippi plantation. They moved to Sunflower County in 1846 and formed a new plantation that they named *Itta Bena.*[8]

During the ensuing years Benjamin and Mildred Humphreys significantly expanded their family. Four children were born to the Benjamin and Mildred Humphreys union, with one daughter and three sons gracing the halls of the couple's home. The children of the second marriage for Benjamin Humphreys were given the names of Mildred Maury, John Barnes, David Smith, and Benjamin George Humphreys. However, an almost entirely different set of the five Humphreys children's names are noted as Julian Maury, Sarah Smith, James Maury, Benjamin George, and Elizabeth Fontaine in another Humphreys record.[9]

The arrival of the American Civil War resulted in Mississippi forming a large number of companies with the purpose of serving the Confederate States of America. Although Benjamin Grubb Humphreys was originally a secession opponent, he eventually raised a company known as the Sunflower Guards and offered the group's services to the Confederate cause. Humphreys received his commission as captain on May 18, 1861. The Guards soon gained the designation of Company I in the 21st Mississippi Infantry Regiment. Humphreys was elected to the rank of colonel in September, an event that took place after the 21st Mississippi Infantry Regiment joined other Mississippi-raised companies in Virginia.[10]

The 21st Mississippi Infantry Regiment was assigned to the Seventh Brigade, under the command of General Joseph Johnston. As such, the regiment, along with the 13th, 17th, and 18th Mississippi Infantry Regiments combined to form the components of the brigade. Colonel Benjamin Grubbs Humphreys and the soldiers of the aforementioned units remained in Leesburg, Virginia until March 9, 1862.[11]

During the Seven Days Battles of June and July 1862 the 21st Mississippi Infantry Regiment, then part of the brigade that was then under the leadership of Brigadier General William Barksdale, lost thirty-two men killed and one hundred nineteen wounded. Battles in which Colonel Benjamin Grubb Humphreys and the regiment participated included

Savage Station and Malvern Hill. The brigade's casualties were heavy, with twenty-three killed and eighty-three wounded.[12]

Colonel Benjamin Grubb Humphreys saw action in the battle of Antietam in September 1862. During what became the bloodiest single day in the American Civil War, Humphreys tendered unequaled service to the 21st Mississippi Infantry Regiment and the brigade to which it belonged. It was recorded, "Captain Sims commanded in the battle, but Colonel Humphreys arrived near the close of the fight and his timely presence cheered and animated the whole brigade." Colonel Humphreys and the 21st Mississippi Infantry Regiment managed to push the Federal troops from the woods that stood at their front and chased the blue-clad warriors into an open field. The casualties for the 21st Mississippi Infantry Regiment at Antietam were six killed and fifty-six wounded from the eighteen officers and one hundred eighty-two enlisted men who participated.[13]

During the December 1862 battle at Fredericksburg, Virginia, Colonel Benjamin Grubb Humphreys commanded the 21st Mississippi Infantry Regiment in Brigadier General William Barksdale's Brigade while his regiment endured eleven men wounded. The casualties for the December 13, 1862 battle were far less than many of the other units involved in the action at Fredericksburg battle. It was stated, "The Twenty-first had an honorable part in the remarkable performance of Barksdale's brigade…"A second battle at the same location, usually referred to as the battle of Chancellorsville, took place in May, 1863. Colonel Humphreys led the 21st Mississippi at Chancellorsville, while the unit's casualties totaled three men killed and twenty-five wounded. In addition, the total losses for Barksdale's Brigade were forty-three killed, two hundred eight wounded, and three hundred forty-one missing.[14]

A Federal recollection noted the part Colonel Benjamin Grubb Humphreys and the 21st Mississippi played in the July 1863 battle of Gettysburg. The writer proclaimed, "When all that was left of Bigelow's battery was withdrawn, it was closely pressed by Humphrey's Twenty-first Mississippi…His men had entered the battery and fought hand-to-hand with the cannoneers…"[15]

At Gettysburg Colonel Benjamin Humphreys remained in command of the 21st Mississippi Infantry Regiment and had four hundred and twenty-four men at his disposal. On July 2, 1863, the 21st Mississippi Infantry Regiment joined the remainder of Brigadier General Barksdale's Brigade as they advanced to Plum Run. Brigadier General William Barksdale was mortally wounded during the 21st Mississippi Infantry Regiment's assault on the Federal position in the Peach Orchard, south of Gettysburg. Of the one thousand six hundred men Barksdale's Brigade placed on the field at Gettysburg, one hundred five were killed, five hundred fifty were wounded, and ninety-two missing, for a total casualty number of seven hundred forty-seven.[16] The tragic series of events provided an opportunity for an increase in rank for Humphreys.

On August 18, 1863 an announcement centering upon the military career of Colonel Benjamin Grubb Humphreys was made. The proclamation stated that Humphreys had been promoted to the rank of brigadier general six days earlier. A fellow officer said of General Humphreys, "He is a...very fine officer. The boys are delighted with his promotion."[17]

The next major engagement for Brigadier General Benjamin Grubb Humphreys was the bloodbath at Chickamauga. At that significant engagement Humphreys commanded a brigade that included the 13th, 17th, 18th, and 21st Mississippi Infantry Regiments. It was recorded that Humphreys's Brigade took part in "a gallant attack" at the Snodgrass House, but a lack of troops led to a failed assault. Humphreys reported that during the day his brigade captured over four hundred prisoners in addition to five stands of colors and approximately one thousand two hundred weapons. The losses for the 21st Mississippi Infantry Regiment were seven killed and forty-three wounded. Brigade losses were twenty killed with one hundred thirty-two wounded.[18]

Another comment on the action at Chickamauga said, "Humphreys's brigade was on the right of Anderson and was to cooperate in the movement. It began at 3:30 p.m. A terrific contest ensued. The bayonet was used, and men were killed and wounded with clubbed muskets. A little after 4, the enemy was reinforced, and advanced..."[19]

During November 1863 Brigadier General Humphreys and his brigade attacked the Federal position at Fort Sanders in Knoxville, Tennessee. General McLaws reported, "My special thanks are due to Brigadier-General B. G. Humphreys, who commanded the assaulting column... for his zeal, courage and coolness in conducting that assault, and for his activity, energy and earnestness in the performance of all his duties on every occasion. I take pleasure in recommending him for promotion."[20]

The May 1864 battle of the Wilderness dealt Brigadier General Benjamin Humphreys and his command a total loss of twenty-seven killed, eighty-five wounded, and one missing. A report of the action at the Wilderness stated, "Humphreys brigade shared in one of the most memorable exploits of Longstreet's corps."[21]

In late September 1864, Brigadier General Benjamin Grubb Humphreys led his troops during the battle of Berryville, Virginia. Unfortunately, the brigadier general was wounded during the course of the action and the severity of his injury rendered Humphreys disabled. A subsequent January 5, 1865 medical certificate recommended that Humphreys's furlough be extended due to medical reasons. Humphreys never again saw military action.[22]

In his autobiography, Humphreys evaluated the impact of the American Civil War. Humphreys said, "It is my philosophy that though the South lost all but honor to save that honor, it was better to have fought and lost than not to fight at all."[23]

The former Confederate brigadier general gained a unique spot in Mississippi history when he became the state's first elected post-Civil War governor. Benjamin Grubb Humphreys, unpardoned at the time of his gubernatorial campaign, took it upon himself to be inaugurated, but the act was carried out in the absence of approval from the President. A petition of the same time period contained signatures of a large number of Mississippi citizens who sought the restoration of Humphreys's civil rights. In turn, a May 22, 1865 pardon from President Andrew Johnson enabled Humphreys to legally hold the position of governor. Taking office in October 1865 Humphreys remained in power until June 15, 1868. Serving during the early stages of Reconstruction, Humphreys managed to gain the release of Confederate President Jefferson Davis. In the time of his tenure Humphreys and the residents of Mississippi witnessed the enactment of the Black Codes and the Military Reconstruction Act.[24]

Governor Humphreys was quoted, "It has been reported in some quarters that our people are insincere and the spirit of revolt is rampant...if an unflinching fidelity in war gives evidence of a reliable fidelity in peace; if the unvarying professions that spring from private and public sources furnish any evidence of truth, it is sufficiently demonstrated that the people of the South, who so long and against such terrible odds maintained the mightiest conflict of modern ages, may be safely trusted when they profess more than a willingness to return to their allegiance."[25]

In 1868 Benjamin Grubb Humphreys was reelected as the governor of Mississippi. The earlier passage of the Military Reconstruction Act led to his eventual removal from office, a feat that was achieved only with the intervention of federal military authorities. Strong opposition Humphreys held toward the Radical Republicans was a major catalyst for his dismissal. Governor Humphreys and his family were literally marched from the governor's mansion in Jackson, Mississippi at the points of bayonets. In turn, Massachusetts resident Adelbert Ames replaced Humphreys as the governor of Mississippi, ending Humphreys's political career.[26]

Benjamin Grubbs Humphreys became an insurance agent after his tenure as Mississippi's governor ended. Working for the New York Life Insurance Company, he maintained offices in the Mississippi towns of Jackson and Vicksburg. Following his 1877 retirement from the insurance business, Humphreys returned to his Leflore County plantation and farmed.[27]

The beloved former Confederate officer, successful insurance agent, and controversial Mississippi governor passed away on December 20, 1882. Benjamin Grubb Humphreys, seventy-four years of age, was buried in the Wintergreen Cemetery in Port Gibson, Mississippi. As a tribute to the beloved Confederate officer, Humphreys County, Mississippi was named in his honor. Additionally, his memory was further preserved with the 1993 formation of the Brigadier General Benjamin G. Humphreys Sons of Confederate Veterans Camp 1625 in Indianola, Mississippi.[28]

MARK PERRIN LOWREY, C.S.A.

1828-1885

McNairy County, Tennessee couple Adam and Margaret Doss Lowrey experienced the birth of a child on December 20, 1828. Mark Perrin Lowrey was the youngest of their five sons, and he eventually had two younger sisters. Tragedy struck the family when Adam Lowrey passed away during a trip to New Orleans while on a trek undertaken in the company of neighbors attempting to carry produce to the river city's market. Adam was struck with cholera, and the effects of the disease robbed nine-year old Mark Lowrey of his father. The loss was made stronger with the fact that Ada, Lowrcy was buried in an unmarked grave.[1]

The death of Adam Lowrey affected the family in many ways. Among those was the educational perspective of Mark Perrin Lowrey. For the ensuing years of his life the youngster sacrificed his education and assisted his widowed mother in securing the funds necessary for the survival of the large family. As for the situation surrounding the death of his father, Mark Perrin Lowrey recalled, "Leaving my mother…with a large family of children to raise with but little means," Lowrey felt strongly compelled to seek work. He later wrote, "My mother was not able to give me a good education, and as the first resolution of any importance that I ever formed was to make a fortune." Lowrey added, "I neglected the cultivation of my mind…"[2]

During Mark Lowrey's fifteenth year his family moved from McNairy County, Tennessee to Farmington, Mississippi. The "little village" in Tishomingo County, Mississippi was located a short distance of some four miles from Corinth. Farmington served as the home for the Lowrey family for years to come. Lowrey indulged upon learning a trade in Farmington and gained a solid reputation as an accomplished bricklayer.[3]

At the age of eighteen, Mark Lowrey volunteered to serve the state of Mississippi in the Mexican War. The company he joined failed to fully organize, but another established the following year enabled him to travel to Mexico. In his autobiography Lowrey remarked, "The regiment was well-drilled, and was kept under good discipline; and here I formed a taste for military discipline and tactics." Private Lowrey was in Captain Alex Jackson's Company that belonged to a regiment under Colonel Charles Clark, a future Confederate brigadier general and Mississippi governor. During his time in Mexico, Lowery never experienced battle, but he remained a member of the Second Mississippi Volunteers until July 1848. He then made his way to Vicksburg where he was relieved of duty after serving nine months.[4]

A significant aspect of Lowrey's life took place when he was seventeen. Lowrey noted, "I had professed the Christian religion…and became a member of the Baptist Church." Four years later another major change in Lowrey's life occurred when he married fellow-Tishomingo County resident Sarah Holmes. The Holmes family had moved to Lincoln County, Tennessee years after Sarah's 1828 South Carolina birth. The family then moved to Tishomingo County. He noted Sarah was the "daughter of Isham Holmes, a thrifty farmer who lived near Rienzi."[5]

Additional praises for Sarah Lowrey proclaimed that she was full of patience and wisdom and held a high work ethic. Most significant was her possession of a strong Christian character. The latter trait likely played a major role in Lowrey stating that Sarah was responsible for half of the successes he attained in his lifetime. Another set of accolades said, "Her distinguished husband had great confidence in her judgment. He was heard to say…that he never departed from her advice without afterward coming to see she was right."[6]

At the age of twenty-four, Lowrey concluded what he termed an "almost unconquerable resolution to become rich." He described the heart-sought decision in writing, "In my 24th year...I yielded to the call of my church, began the work of the gospel ministry, and devoted my whole time to the pursuit of knowledge and to other duties of my profession." In 1853, Farmington Baptist Church ordained Lowrey to the ministry of Jesus Christ.[7]

It was recorded that when Mark Lowrey informed Sarah of his calling to preach, she was extremely supportive. Sarah Lowrey reportedly said, "Well, if you are going to preach, I don't want you to be a half-way preacher. Go to your books and I'll take care of the family."[8]

In contrast to his early education, Lowrey's adult pursuit of the same was extensive and effective. His eldest son, Dr. W. T. Lowrey, stated, "My father was a very close observer and an excellent listener...always on the lookout for a chance to learn...not an extensive reader...the King James Version... had more influence on his English than any other score of books."[9]

In presenting the gospel, as well as in his future military leadership roles, it is likely that Lowrey's physical appearance was a factor in his delivery of both sermons and orders. Lowrey was described as being over six feet tall and standing extremely straight. In addition, "He had a keen eagle eye and a commanding appearance."[10]

Mark Perrin Lowrey's service to God and the churches to which Lowrey ministered was extremely successful. The preacher recalled his early years of his pastoral duties in noting, "I received great encouragement, both from the church and from the world. I was favored with large and attentive congregations, and my first labors were crowned with encouraging success. I was soon called to positions that opened my way to usefulness, gave me a support for my family, opportunities to improve my education, and to give my wholly to my profession."[11]

As the tensions that eventually led to the American Civil War increased, Lowrey focused on his religious studies and largely ignored the political turmoil. The majority of Lowrey's ministry, by the early 1860s, was directed toward the people in the area of Kossuth, Mississippi. That town was located "nine miles southwest of Corinth." Lowrey remarked, "I did not think it became a minister of the gospel to engage in the heated discussion that then prevailed..."[12]

Lowrey felt responsible to provide guidance to those around him. He recorded, "...our people were all aroused, and were, to a man, for the Confederacy. My feelings ran in the same channel, and there was no neutral ground to occupy. I was called out in several public meetings, and gave free expression to my sentiments."[13]

Parishioners and fellow residents of North Mississippi regularly urged Lowrey to assume command of groups volunteering for military service. Despite his Mexican War service and his interaction with many enlistees, Lowrey managed to avoid taking the leadership role of any military unit. He wrote, "...more than once [I]...was urged to do so, but positively declined."[14]

With the Mississippi Legislature's passage of a fall 1861 act, Lowrey acted. The action called for ten thousand men to serve for sixty days and be equipped and armed for an emergency. Lowrey penned, "My neighbors raised a company...elected me captain... urging that I could go with them for sixty days and that it was my duty to do so. I could not refuse."[14]

Within a few days, Lowrey and his company were in Corinth. They were placed into a regiment of which Lowrey "was almost unanimously elected colonel." The group was established as the Fourth Regiment and moved to Bowling Green, Kentucky. There, the unit was placed under the command of General Reuben Davis.[16]

The sixty-day term in Bowling Green, Kentucky proved physically devastating to the men of Lowrey's command. Colonel Lowrey recalled, "My men having left comfortable homes in cold winter, and being unused to camp life, nearly all got sick. Measles and pneumonia prevailed to an alarming extent, and many good men died. At the close of our term we were discharged, and I felt that my military career was at an end." Lowrey returned home and readily resumed "...to take care of my Christian congregations."[17]

The February 1862 fall of Fort Donelson created a clamor in relation to the fervor of enlistment for Lowrey's church flock and community. Men who had served the sixty days with Lowrey pleaded with him to return with them and serve the Confederate military. Lowrey stated, "Old ladies and old gentlemen...entreated me to go with their sons. Tishomingo County had lost a regiment at Fort Donelson...our people resolved to put another in its place, and I was selected to organize it. Our state was threatened with invasion, and Tishomingo County was the threatened point."[18] With this assignment acknowledged and accepted, Lowrey began a much longer tenure in the service of the Confederate States of America.

Lowrey remarked, "I was restless and my blood was hot within me. The thought of sitting still until the enemy would overrun my home and family was more than I could bear...I raised and organized the 32nd Mississippi [Infantry] Regiment in a little less time than any other regiment was raised and organized in North Mississippi." Lowrey was unanimously elected colonel of the unit. The regiment was organized in Corinth in early April 1862.[19]

Although the 32nd Mississippi was not involved in the fighting at Shiloh, Lowrey and his colleagues gained experience in the aftermath. The fact that neither equipment nor arms had been issued to the men of the regiment negated their combat participation. Procurement of abandoned and captured weapons allowed the 32nd Mississippi to play an important role as they, "...received prisoners and captured property, and accompanied prisoners to the interior."[20]

After Shiloh Lowrey's regiment was assigned to the brigade of Brigadier General Sterling Alexander Martin Wood in Hardee's division. The brigade was often without a present brigadier general, necessitating Lowrey to assume the role of brigade commander.[21]

Aside from the participation in skirmishes around Corinth, the first military engagement for Colonel Lowrey took place at Perryville, Kentucky. Lowrey commanded the 32nd Mississippi, but a shell wounded Brigadier General Wood and Colonel Lowrey gained command of the Fourth Brigade of Major General Simon Buckner's Division.[22]

Colonel Lowrey was responsible for troops of the 16th and 33rd Alabama Infantry Regiments as well as a detachment of the 3rd Georgia Cavalry. The 15th Mississippi Sharpshooters Battalion, Semple's Alabama Battery, and the 3rd Confederate were also at his disposal. Infantry units from the Magnolia State that served under Lowrey at Perryville included the 32nd and 45th Mississippi and the 15th Mississippi Sharpshooters Battalion.[23]

Lowrey recalled the dichotomy of his assignment at Perryville, "I commanded a brigade in the first battle I was ever engaged in. But I was soon painfully wounded in my left arm, by which I was disabled about eight weeks."[24]

Lowrey was unable to return to his home for the period of recuperation as his Kossuth home was near a Federal camp. Instead, he went to Ripley, Mississippi, the hometown of his brother Calvin. The plan Mark and Calvin Lowrey devised called for Calvin to make a visit to Sarah Lowrey and her children and assist the family in moving to the Ripley area cabin the duo had rented from Captain J. J. Guyton.[25]

The Lowrey family eventually managed to reach Lowrey. He briefly visited with them before returning to the front. The three-room cabin served as the Lowrey residence for three years, as Sarah and the children relied upon the help of other area citizens.[26]

Colonel Mark Lowrey recovered in time to join the 32nd Mississippi at Murfreesboro. The regiment did not participate in the first day's fight. However, Lowrey noted that the unit took part in the skirmishing that occurred afterward and that he was responsible for leading the 32nd Mississippi as it "brought off the brigade in the retreat from that place."[27]

The 45th Mississippi Infantry was consolidated with the 32nd Mississippi at Tullahoma, Tennessee in early 1863. Colonel Lowrey was given command of the regiments and spent the majority of the spring of 1863 drilling. Lowrey recalled that little time had been devoted to the task prior to Tullahoma. The endeavor was profitable as Lowrey wrote, "In an inspection by Gen. Hardee...my regiment was pronounced by him the best drilled regiment of the brigade."[28]

It was the September 1863 battle of Chickamauga where Colonel Mark Perrin Lowrey would experience what he termed, "the next regular battle in which I was engaged." Lowrey was assigned to the division of General Patrick Cleburne. Lowrey noted, "We drove the enemy from a strong position...my regiment charged gallantly through an open field on the most exposed part of the line. Gen. Cleburne complimented me personally, but the gallantry displayed was not mine, but that of my men." The mutual admiration of Lowrey and Cleburne was epitomized in Cleburne's declaration that Lowrey was "the bravest man in the Confederate Army."[29]

Mark Lowrey continued to praise his troops in writing, "In the engagement the next morning, when we charged the enemy's works and were repulsed with heavy loss, my regiment was...in the most exposed part of the line, but held its position until all the troops had retreated...and then was the first regiment to rally and form for another onset."[30]

Lowrey received additional praise from Cleburne in the general's official report of the battle. Lowrey was promoted to brigadier general on October 4, 1863. Lieutenant General Daniel Harvey Hill explained his approval of the new title of Brigadier General Lowrey and stated, "... Lowrey has been deservedly promoted and a worthier object could not have been selected."[31]

Brigadier General Mark Lowrey saw additional action at Ringgold or Taylor's Ridge as he commanded the Alabama-Mississippi Brigade. There, he received an order from General Cleburne to move from his reserve position and "Go upon that hill and see they don't turn my right." Lowrey moved his troops along the difficult terrain and "...found the 1st Arkansas standing alone against a large force of the enemy, who had already reached the summit."[32]

Lowrey recalled that he "...got my horse up the hill with much difficulty, but my field officers all left their horses and went up on foot. On reaching the top of the hill, I heard firing on the right about a quarter of a mile ahead of me...I went full speed to see what the firing meant." Discovering the 1st Arkansas, Lowrey encouraged the members by notifying them that reinforcements from his brigade were nearby. Lowrey added, "They gathered courage and held their ground. I dashed back in full speed...threw forward a regiment at a time, leading each regiment in person, and...drove the enemy from the top of the hill."[33]

Regarding the November 1863 action at Ringgold, Lowrey concluded, "The victory was ours, and the enemy was gone down the hill in perfect confusion. And there is nothing more certain than that the tardy movements would have resulted in not only the loss of that position, but the defeat of the entire division."[34]

The admiration Brigadier General Lowrey held for his troops, and the affection those men returned to him, were exceeded only in Lowrey's sense of devotion to Jesus Christ. It was regularly noted that it was a frequent practice of Lowrey's to preach while his armies were encamped. In the spring of 1864, Lowrey led a series of sermons that resulted in a spiritual revival. Within a period of two weeks he had baptized fifty of the men in his command. For this and other such actions, Lowrey was given the designation as the Preacher General.[35]

Dr. William W. Bennett provided a high level of praise for Brigadier

General Lowrey's sincere care for the well-being of others when he said, "He takes great interest in the soldiers' religious welfare, often preaches to them, and feels that the ministry is still his high and holy calling. I wish I had the space to...speak of this noble and pious officer as he deserves."[36]

Additional words came from S. M. Cherry, a Confederate chaplain, "...in Lowrey's Brigade...last night about 140 penitents came forward for prayer, 53 have joined the Church; the general assists in the labors of the pulpit and alter...baptized a dozen of his own soldiers."[37]

Another soldier expressed his respect for Lowrey in proclaiming, "He is a Christian, a soldier and a zealous preacher, and his influence is great. It was truly a beautiful sight to see a general baptizing his men. He preaches for our brigade next Sabbath."[38]

In 1864, Brigadier General Lowrey engaged the Federals at Dalton, Georgia. Lowrey recalled, "General Granbury...had nothing but a few cavalry on his right, and these were rapidly giving way...Gen. Cleburne... told me to move rapidly...and... 'Secure Granbury's right'." Lowrey joined Colonel Sam Adams and managed to save the situation for the Confederates. Lowrey stated, "I went to his assistance when he was in the midst of...a terrible fire...I dashed into their midst on old Rebel, my favorite horse, and the position was held."[39]

At Cobb's Mill, in July 1864, Lowrey's brigade was "cut to pieces." Half of the men in the ranks were lost. Lowrey noted that his brigade's movements were hampered in that another Confederate brigade was slow in making its advance. Not usually one to point fingers, Lowrey noted that Brigadier General Hugh Mercer's brigade, as well as Brigadier General George Maney, "was forming to make the movement...I could not move on without running over his line...But I would not like for anything in my personal history to reflect upon another officer."[40]

Lowrey recorded, "I never saw a greater display of gallantry, but they failed to take the works, simply because the thing attempted was impossible for a thin line of exhausted men to accomplish...a direct attack by exhausted men against double their numbers, behind strong breastworks...To add to the difficulties, my men had had neither sleep nor rest for two days and nights...and under the oppressive heat many good men fell completely exhausted..."[41]

Lowrey wrote, "On the 31ˢᵗ I made an attack with the division on the enemy's right flank and drove the dismounted cavalry from their works...the only success achieved by our forces that day...The next day... we fought...five or six to one and held him in check all day...We retired... to Lovejoy Station, and I continued in command of the division for about a week...".[42]

While in the division camp at Jonesboro, Georgia, Lowrey led another series of sermons. September 16, 1864 was a date Confederate President Jefferson Davis had set aside for prayer and fasting. With that decree, Lowrey preached from Psalm 50:15, an event recorded in a Montgomery newspaper that stated, "Brigadier General Lowery...a member of the clerical profession...a man of superior acquirements... always heard with increasing interest. A faithful soldier of the cross, as well as of his country, devout and brave, he unites, more than any living man, perhaps, those cardinal virtues of mind and heart which combine to make the noble, true, conscientious Christian warrior."[43]

In November 1864, Lowrey moved his brigade toward Spring Hill, Tennessee to assist General Nathan Bedford Forrest's attack upon the Federals. Lowrey recalled, "I saw Cleburne on the field, dashed up to him and told him the enemy was about to charge me...With his right hand raised...and in a tone that manifested unusual excitement, he exclaimed, 'I'll charge them'...".[44]

The subsequent Federal stand at Franklin, Tennessee on November 30, 1864 was a literal bloodbath. Lowrey's brigade was in the second line advancing toward the strong position of Federal troops centered at the Carter House. During the action, General Cleburne fell.

Lowrey recalled, "I brought up my brigade under the most destructive fire I ever witnessed. I threw my brigade into the outside ditch of his massive works, and my men fought across the parapet...half my men had fallen, and the balance could not scale the works. It would have been certain death or capture to every one of them. I went...within 30 feet of the works...I saw nothing else could be done I went to the rear, and began the work of gathering up the fragments of our division."[45]

It was noted that while Lowrey led his brigade in the later fight at Nashville, the unit "handsomely repulsed several severe assaults of the enemy." On the second day, Lowrey led General Benjamin Cheatham's division as Cheatham commanded the corps. Lowrey wrote, "The division was in line of battle when I was ordered to take command."[46]

Having previously ordered a brigade to leave the works and move to his left, Lowrey used one of his brigades to reinforce a hill to his rear, a movement that left only one brigade to defend the Confederate works. He noted the brigade was "thinly scattered along the works." Lowrey recalled, "...the enemy poured through by thousands in my rear...my line was soon thrown back, the enemy surrounding me in the shape of a horseshoe..."[47]

Lowrey recalled, "I saw no chance for myself or any considerable portion of my division to escape capture...at the point where escape might be rendered possible...a few men rallied, who held the enemy in check until most of my men passed out and joined our discomforted masses in their inglorious retreat."[48]

Lowrey then lost his horse. Lowrey lamented, "Rebel, my favorite war steed, was killed. I had ridden him in all engagements... except two, and he had been wounded four times."[49]

Lowrey remained in command of Cheatham's division for the next four months. He accompanied his command to their camp at Chesterfield, South Carolina. The outcome of the war became painfully clear to Lowrey; he requested and received a leave of absence to go to Richmond. Lowrey tendered his resignation; the offer was accepted on March 14, 1865.[50]

Using three points to explain his resignation, Lowrey began with the view that the Confederate cause was lost. His second point rested in the fact he had "been separated from the men and officers with whom [he] had borne the burden and heat of the day." Lowrey explained with the Confederate Congress calling for a reorganization of the armies, he felt compelled "to leave the offices to those who were more ambitious for military honor and position."[51]

The Confederate military stated, "After the Tennessee Campaign, from ill health, caused by long service and exposure, that able faithful Christian soldier General Lowrey resigned."[52]

Lowrey's post-war decisions were discussed in a history of the Baptist church in Mississippi, "When the war closed General Lowrey had little money, a big reputation and a big family. Two questions presented themselves:...how can I build up my down-trodden country?...how can I educate my children?"[53]

Mark Lowrey and his family moved to nearby Tippah County, Mississippi. Lowrey continued to preach. He also entered a long-time venture as a contributing writer for *The Christian Index*, an Atlanta-based publication. Lowrey also served as president of the Mississippi Baptist Convention from 1868 to 1877.[54]

An admirer recalled, "Bro. Lowrey is…a noble man. He loves Mississippi, and the interests of the Baptist churches in Mississippi, with all his heart. No man has more influence among Mississippi Baptists… his sound judgment, force of character, and earnest devoutness, could be present every year in the Southern Baptist Convention…he has confined himself almost entirely to his association and State Convention."[55]

Lowrey also founded Blue Mountain College in Blue Mountain, Mississippi. Originally named Blue Mountain Female Institute, the institution was formed in 1873. Lowrey purchased land from the Brougher estate four years earlier, and the tendency of the Brougher family to note the blue haze that clung to the pine trees on the mountain led to the name. An association with William C. Falkner, a railroad executive, enabled Lowrey to secure a rail line that ran near the college, located a few miles south of Ripley, Mississippi. The college grew into a successful location for training and educating.[56]

Mark Lowrey's initial vision to provide an education for women in a means of improving the South began with a personal commitment on his part. Lowrey and two of his daughters, Margaret and Modena, served as the original faculty for the fifty students who graced the halls of Blue Mountain College. In 1873, Modena became vice president of the college and served in that position until 1934, a period of sixty-one years. Two of Lowrey's sons, Dr. B. G. Lowrey and Dr. W. T. Lowrey, served as presidents. Additionally, Dr. Lawrence T. Lowrey, a grandson of Mark Lowrey, completed the tenure of Blue Mountain's Lowrey presidents.[57]

From *History of Mississippi Baptists*, "…Gen. Lowrey's large popularity as a soldier, citizen, and preacher…the popularity and extensive acquaintance of his two daughters."[58]

Another explanation of the respect Lowrey held said his students, "… looked upon him as one of the greatest teachers of his time, so clear were his interpretations, so logical his conclusions, and so broad his sympathy and understanding."[59]

In the midst of his time spent teaching and preaching, Mark Lowrey was approached with requests to run for a political office. He respectfully declined, noting that he had a far greater calling to preach the gospel.[60]

Despite health issues that had become more apparent, Lowrey continued to teach classes at Blue Mountain College. In 1882 his doctors diagnosed Lowrey as possessing a weak heart. Even that diagnosis failed to deter Lowrey's determination to serve God and his fellow man. On February 27, 1885, Lowrey was accompanying a group from Blue Mountain College as they prepared to take a trip to New Orleans. Standing at the train station in Middleton, Tennessee, Lowrey was in the process of making a ticket purchase for the female students when he turned to those around him, gasped, and fell. He had succumbed to a heart attack.[61]

Lowrey's body lay in state at Blue Mountain College; he was buried at Old Macedonia Cemetery in Blue Mountain. The loved and respected general, preacher, and teacher left his widow Sarah Lowrey, their five daughters, and six sons. Sarah passed away in December 1898.[62]

Praise for Lowrey appeared in an 1899 issue of *Confederate Veteran*. The author said, "...a Baptist preacher of singular earnestness and power, and no braver man ever followed the flag of the Confederacy...never forgot that he was called to preach the gospel, and during seasons of rest from active campaigning would preach to his command with zeal and power.[63]

Other words directed to the memory of Lowrey stated, "Lowrey... packed into little more than half a century more constructive Christian living, more shining inspiration, more lasting service to God and mankind than can be accredited to many great Southerners who lived for decades longer and who faced not half so many barriers..."[64]

ROBERT GADEN HAYES LOWRY, C. S.A.

1829-1910

Robert Gaden Hayes Lowry was born March 10, 1829 in Chesterfield, South Carolina. As with many individuals of the time, there are discrepancies regarding the precise year of Lowry's birth. The later dates range from March 10, 1830 to March 10, 1831. With the majority of sources agreeing on March 10, 1829, that date will be emphasized in this discussion.[1]

The infant's parents were Robert, the child's namesake, and Jemimah Rushing Lowry. At the age of two Robert Gaden Hayes Lowry joined his parents when they moved to Perry County, Tennessee. Prior to his tenth birthday Robert Lowry and his family again changed their place of residence and settled in Tishomingo County, Mississippi. It has been noted that the frequent moving limited Robert Gaden Hayes Lowry's education that was largely attained in South Carolina and Mississippi common schools.[2]

At the young age of thirteen Robert Lowry moved to Raleigh, Mississippi, but did so without his parents. While in the Smith County town, Lowry lived with his uncle, Judge James Lowry, and eventually engaged in the mercantile business. Using the knowledge he gained from observing Judge Lowry's business practices, Robert moved to Brandon,

Mississippi and continued the mercantile business in the county seat of Rankin County.[3]

In a few years the seemingly-transient Robert Gaden Hayes Lowry moved to Arkansas and he remained a participant in the mercantile business. Having been in Arkansas for a few years, Lowry returned to Brandon, Mississippi. In due time, he began studying law and was eventually admitted to the bar in 1859. A major catalyst for his practice of the legal profession took place when he entered into a partnership with A. G. Mayers.[4]

In 1849 Robert Gaden Hayes Lowry married Maria Gamage, a Jasper County, Mississippi resident. Robert and Maria eventually had eleven children, seven of whom outlived the couple. The Lowry children included Maria, John Waddell, Eudora, Belle, Mary Gammage, Patrick, Robert, Ela, Lela, Rose, and Ada. Maria passed away in 1873.[5]

With the onset of the American Civil War Robert Lowry enlisted as a private in a company that was raised in Lowry's home county of Rankin County. The company of which Lowry was a member became Company B of the 6th Mississippi Infantry Regiment. As an indication of the faith his fellow company members held in him and the level of respect he commanded, Lowry was elected major of the regiment at the time of its organization.[6]

During the severe level of bloodshed at Shiloh in April 1862, Major Robert Lowry and his fellow regimental members suffered as heavily as any other group at the battle. Of its four hundred and twenty-five troops who reported for duty at Shiloh, the 6th Mississippi Infantry Regiment had a casualty total of three hundred and ten men. Among the wounded was Major Robert Lowry, who endured two wounds. As a sign of the respect and admiration the regiment gained in enduring the casualty rate of seventy-three percent, it was given "the proud soubriquet of the Bloody Sixth."[7]

The 6th Mississippi Infantry Regiment was reorganized shortly after the battle of Shiloh, and Robert Lowry was elected as the regiment's colonel and replaced the wounded Colonel Thornton. Colonel Robert Lowry held that rank while his regiment participated in the battles of Corinth, Port Hudson, Port Gibson, Baker's Creek, and Jackson, Mississippi. He also served as the regiment's primary commander. More battle experience was gained when Lowry joined his regiment in Georgia, serving under General Joseph Johnston "from Resaca to Atlanta."[8]

Perhaps the highest wartime praise given to Lowry came from General Martin Green following the action at Port Gibson. Green wrote in his report, "Col. Robert Lowry...deserves the highest commendation for his coolness and promptness in executing every order."[9]

A May 1864 letter, reportedly from a representative of a group of "concerned citizens of Jones County," Mississippi detailed the exploits of Colonel Robert Lowry during what had to be an unpleasant mission. Lowry was assigned the task of seeking out and bringing justice to Confederate deserters in Smith and Jones Counties in Mississippi. Among the words of the letter were, "My reg't composes part of a detachment of Loring's Division now engaged in arresting and returning deserters to their commands." The author explained that he was "under the command of Col. Robt Lowry of the 6th Miss."[10]

The operation's success was also noted. The writer said, "We have been at this duty since the 23rd March and in that time...we have arrested... about 500 men. Several hundred more have eluded us or reported to their commands rather than be charged and sent under arrest."[11]

Sadly, the dangers and tragedies of the expedition were clearly disclosed, "A small party...of the 6th Miss was fired into and one man was killed...At Knights Mill, Jones Co. four men...were found guilty of desertion and of armed resistance to the civil and military law and were sentenced to death by hanging...This made ten who have forfeited their lives for treason."[12]

Colonel Robert Lowry continued his service with the 6th Mississippi Infantry Regiment as it made its way to Franklin, Tennessee. During that November 1864 engagement the regiment's "brigade commander, the gallant and lamented Gen. John Adams, was killed leading his brigade of Mississippians." As a result, Colonel Lowry "assumed command of the brigade." At that time, the brigade Lowry gained leadership of consisted of the remnants of the 6th, 14th, 15th, 20th, 23rd, and 43rd Mississippi Infantry Regiments.[13]

An article on the life of Robert Lowry stated, "He commanded the brigade on [the] retreat...into Mississippi, and later reported with it to General Johnston in North Carolina." Colonel Lowry's ability to exhibit his leadership skills paid off when, near the war's end, "He was commissioned brigadier general in February, 1865."[14]

Brigadier General Robert Lowry was with General Johnston at the Confederate surrender at Greensboro in April 1865.[15] With his service completed, Lowry returned to civilian life.

Robert Lowry's first act as a productive member of post-war Mississippi society was to restore his legal practice. A. G. Mayers and Lowry resumed their practice that continued until Mayers was appointed circuit judge. With the new position for Mayers, Lowry gained an association of a law practice with Senator Anselm McLaurin.[16]

Lowry also entered the political arena and eventually served in both the State Senate and House of Representatives. Originally elected to represent his fellow county residents in the Senate, he was soon voted to the same designation for his district. His time in those posts was brief, as his years of service only ranged from 1865 to 1866. Reportedly against his will, Robert Lowry was nominated as the State Attorney General during the Democratic Convention of 1869. With the 1881 election that determined the next Mississippi governor, Lowry soundly defeated Republican Governor Benjamin King with a tally of 77,727 to 52,009.[17]

In the 1881 election, Robert Lowry, as a Democrat, was elected as the thirty-second Governor of Mississippi and went on to serve two terms as the state's executive. Inaugurated on January 9, 1882, Lowry's tenure as governor ended on January 13, 1890. Having been in office for those years, Lowry became the first Mississippi Governor to hold the post for two consecutive four-year terms. Several accomplishments took place while Lowry was governor. Among those was the fact that more miles of rail lines were laid under his leadership than had taken place in the combined administrations of all of his predecessors. It was duly recorded that more miles of tracks were laid in Mississippi in 1893 than in any other state. Additionally, a host of organizations were created, including the state's railroad commission, the East Mississippi Insane Asylum, and the Industrial College for Girls. The latter holds the distinction of being the first of its kind in the United States to be state supported. Other accomplishments for Governor Lowry included increases in state college funding and state revenues.[18]

In keeping in touch with his Confederate military background,

Governor Robert Lowry hosted former Confederate President Jefferson Davis and First Lady Varina Howell Davis at a formal state dinner. The Governor's Mansion was the setting for the meal and came twenty years after Lowry sought to gain the release of Davis from Fort Monroe where the former Confederate Chief Executive had been incarcerated for charges of treason. The formal event took place in Lowry's first term and served as one of the final public appearances for Jefferson Davis.[19]

A less successful effort for Lowry came in his attempt to move the state capital from the city of Jackson to Meridian. The growth of Meridian was attributed to the Southern and Mobile and Ohio Railroads; Meridian was located at the junction of these routes. In 1890 the Mississippi Constitution established Jackson as the capital for the duration of the state's existence.[20]

A change of direction in Lowry's contributions to his fellow citizens of the state of Mississippi took place in 1891. That year Robert Lowry worked in conjunction with William H. McCardle, a former editor of the *Vicksburg Times*, to author *A History of Mississippi*. It was stated that the work was "a most excellent" recollection of the events that took place in Mississippi from the exploration of DeSoto through the death of Mississippi resident and Confederate President Jefferson Davis. The duo of McCardle and Lowry also created a shorter version of the text for use in Mississippi's schools.[21]

In 1901 Robert Lowry ran for a seat in the United States Senate. In contrast to his earlier political successes, Lowry lost his quest for the first post-governor election in which he took part. In turn, he ended his pursuit of any additional political positions and entered a phase of the life that was largely composed of solitude.[22]

A quote from the *Confederate Military History* proclaimed, "General Lowry is one of the most highly esteemed citizens of Mississippi, to whose interests he has always been true in war and peace."[23]

On January 19, 1910 Robert Gaden Hayes Lowry passed away at his home. The dedicated servant of Mississippi was buried in Brandon, Mississippi's City Cemetery.[24]

An obituary for the one-time general and governor proclaimed that Robert Gaden Hayes Lowry succeeded former Confederate general Stephen Dill Lee as the commander of the Mississippi Division of the Sons of Confederate Veterans and was "continuously reelected…"[25]

A tribute to Lowry appeared in a 1910 issue of *Confederate Veteran* and stated, "Throughout his eventful life he was devoted to the service of her state. Whether serving her on the tented field, in the halls of legislation, as her Chief Executive, or as her historian, his highest ambition was to do his full duty…As a soldier there were no truer or braver, as a lawyer he was in the front rank of his profession, as Governor of his State his administration was able and without a blemish, as a statesman his ideals were high and his purposes noble, as a historian he had a keen perception of truth and performed services of inestimable value to his State, and as a citizen he was loved and esteemed by all who came in contact with his splendid personality…"[26]

WILLIAM THOMPSON MARTIN, C.S.A.
1823-1910

William Thompson Martin was born in Glasgow, Kentucky on March 25, 1823 to John Henderson Martin and Emily Monroe Kerr Martin. As a young boy William Thompson Martin moved with his family to Vicksburg, Mississippi and spent his formative years in the river city. He returned to Kentucky and entered Centre College in Danville. Martin graduated in 1844.[1]

A well-circulated story exists concerning the years soon after Martin's post-college years. William Martin was allegedly in route to New Orleans, where he would seek employment. The steamboat on which he was a passenger stopped at Natchez, Mississippi, and Martin seized the opportunity to tour the town. A Natchez planter and attorney, John P. Walworth, met Martin and was highly impressed with the Centre College graduate's intelligence. Martin was hired to tutor the Walworth children, and he was able to study law. Martin eventually established a Natchez law practice. At the age of twenty-two William Thompson Martin was elected district attorney.[2]

Martin and his wife, Margaret Dunlop Conner Martin, had a large family during the course of their marriage. Their children included

Margaret Spencer, Emily Monroe, Jane Gustine, Mary Conner, William Conner, Ellie Lee, Lewis Randolph, and Spencer Wood. Three more offspring were Farar Conner, Caroline Kerr, and John Henderson.[3]

As the sectional tensions increased, William Martin made it clear he was a Unionist. However, with the onset of the Civil War, he shifted his support to the Confederacy. As a show of his sincere support, Martin provided the support necessary to raise the Adams County Cavalry Company. Martin was elected captain of the cavalry unit.[4]

Captain led the men of the Adams County Cavalry Company as they made their way to Manassas, Virginia. In October 1861, the group joined two other Mississippi companies and one from Alabama to form the 2nd Mississippi Cavalry Battalion. On November 14, 1861, Martin was promoted to the rank of major of the 2nd Mississippi Cavalry Battalion. In January 1862, the battalion became a unit in the Jeff Davis Cavalry Legion.[5]

On February 13, 1862, Major Martin was promoted to lieutenant colonel and fought at Yorktown and Williamsburg. In June 1862, Lieutenant Colonel Martin participated in Jeb Stuart's infamous circling maneuver against George McClellan's Army of the Potomac.[6]

In reporting on the effectiveness of the Confederate cavalry raids against McClellan, an incident that yielded the men in gray a large number of prisoners, weapons, and information regarding Federal positions, General William Averell praised Martin. The Federal general wrote, "It was appointed with excellent judgment and was conducted with superb address. Stuart pursued the line of least resistance, which was the unexpected. His subordinate commanders were Colonels Fitz Lee, W. H. F. Lee, and W. T. Martin, all intrepid cavalrymen."[7]

During the Seven Days Campaign, Martin served as the commander of the Jeff Davis Cavalry Legion and the 4th Mississippi Cavalry. Following his later participation in the action at South Mountain, Martin served as an aide to General Robert E. Lee at Antietam.[8]

Lieutenant Colonel William Thompson Martin received another promotion December 2, 1862. On that date, Martin became a brigadier general and remained a member of General Lee's staff until March 1863. Martin was then sent westward to Tennessee, where he eventually commanded a division in General Joseph Wheeler's Cavalry Corps. The division under Martin's leadership consisted of brigades of Brigadier Generals George Blake Cosby and Phillip Roddey. Serving with the outspoken Wheeler, Brigadier General Martin saw action in the campaigns of Tullahoma and Chickamauga as well as the March 1863 battle of Spring Hill, Tennessee.[9]

On November 10, 1863, Martin was promoted to major general and, while attached to the command of General James Longstreet, participated in engagements in the Knoxville, Tennessee area. With a reassignment in the subsequent months, Major General Martin led a division in the Atlanta Campaign.[10] Unfortunately, the action in Georgia would have serious effects upon Martin's level of participation in the remaining months of the war.

On August 14, 1864, General Wheeler made an assault on the Federal garrison at Dalton, Georgia. Major General Martin refused to provide the assistance Wheeler requested, and a major argument resulted. In turn, General Wheeler relieved Major General Martin of his command. Martin was then placed in charge of the District of Northwest Mississippi. In that post, Martin, "was employed until the close of the struggle, protecting the people against raiding bands as far as his resources would permit."[11]

William Martin's life after the American Civil War was active. He entered the Mississippi political arena and was a member of the Mississippi State Legislature for over a decade. Martin also served as president of the Natchez, Jackson, and Columbus Railroad. As another indication of William Martin's varied post-war life, he was a trustee of both Jefferson College in Washington, Mississippi and the University of Mississippi in Oxford. Martin was a delegate to the Democratic National Conventions in 1868, 1872, 1876, and 1880.[12]

On March 16, 1910, William Thompson Martin died in Natchez, Mississippi. Martin was buried in the Natchez City Cemetery in the heart of Adams County, Mississippi, the area he served so proficiently in times of war and peace.[13]

EVANDER MCNAIR, C.S.A.

1820-1902

Evander McNair spent the majority of his years of Civil War military service commanding troops from Arkansas, where he also lived for a period of his life. However, his ties to Mississippi during his formative and adult years, as well as his connections to the facts that he died and is buried in the Magnolia State make him a viable Mississippi-based general.

McNair was born in the Laurel Hill, Richmond County, North Carolina area on April 15, 1820. The next year McNair's parents moved the family to Wayne County, Mississippi. That location, as well as Simpson County, where the McNair family later relocated, served as the locations of Evander McNair's youthful experiences.[1]

At twenty-two Evander McNair moved to Jackson, Mississippi, the state's capital. McNair established a mercantile business and remained in that vocation and location for several years.[2] However, the beginning of the Mexican War altered his pursuits and provided the interest in the military that would later lead to his participation in the American Civil War.

Evander McNair's 1846 decision to join his fellow statesmen in fighting against Mexico created a strong connection that proved profitable for his future military endeavors. McNair volunteered as a member of the group that became Company E of the First Mississippi Rifles. Future Confederate President Jefferson Davis was the regiment's colonel, while McNair rose to the rank of orderly sergeant prior to the end of the war. Regarding this rank, it was written, "In such a regiment and in an army as limited as that was as to numbers this was no small compliment." Among the battles in which McNair took part was the victory at Buena Vista.[3]

Upon the conclusion of the war with Mexico, McNair returned to Jackson, Mississippi and resumed his participation in the mercantile business. In 1856 he moved to Washington, Arkansas and continued his years-old profession. Washington, Arkansas was described as, "A community of wealth, culture, and refinement." As for McNair's reception in the town, an Arkansas native wrote, "He...soon gained the confidence and esteem of...elegant people."[4]

Evander McNair not only enjoyed the wealth and prestige associated with his Washington, Arkansas mercantile business, but he also found a wife in the community. On August 11, 1859 McNair married Hannah Merrill, a New York native and a Southern transplant. A recollection of Hannah proclaimed that she was, "a woman of rare culture."[5]

The outbreak of war changed McNair's personal and professional life once again. As he did in the earlier conflict, Evander McNair readily volunteered for service in the Civil War. Two distinct differences were initially noticeable, as in the American Civil War McNair's personal wealth immediately came into play. Secondly, the rank he achieved in the course of the war would be much higher than McNair managed to gain in the entire time of the war with Mexico.

As for Evander McNair's willingness to serve and his ability to support his fellow troops, a post-war article stated, "He promptly raised and organized a battalion of seven companies of infantry, and immediately set out for Southwest Missouri to join Brig. Gen. McCulloch, then in command of the Confederates in that military district." The recruits for the unit McNair established came from the Arkansas counties of Hempstead, Lafayette, Calhoun, Pike, Montgomery, and Polk. In August, 1861, McNair's battalion arrived in Fayetteville, Arkansas, located in the northwest portion of the state.[6]

Evander McNair's command remained in Fayetteville while waiting for the arrival of another company of some one hundred men from Calhoun

County, located in the south-central portion of Arkansas. The officer in charge of the company McNair awaited was Captain J. B. McCulloch, a brother to the military district's commander. A unit history stated, "Two other companies from South Arkansas were added in a few months so as to form a full regiment of ten companies, which was then named the Southwestern Arkansas Regiment." That designation remained the unit's identification until it was mustered into Confederate service, at which time it was officially designated as the 4th Arkansas Infantry Regiment.[7]

A description of Evander McNair's appearance at the time stated, "He was then about forty years old, in manhood's prime, tall and straight, with light auburn hair and dark eyes, neat in his person, dignified in manner, and yet one of the most companionable of men. He was the soul of honor, and could little tolerate smallness or meanness in others...he was in the most optimistic spirit, and expressed himself as happy in all his surroundings."[8]

Evander McNair and his troops arrived in Mt. Vernon a short time after the battle of Wilson Creek. Meeting Brigadier General McCulloch's division at that location, McNair was mustered into Confederate service on August 17, 1861and given the rank of colonel.[9]

During the battle of Elk Horn Tavern or Pea Ridge, Arkansas, Colonel Evander McNair was given the opportunity to prove his leadership skills. A commentary on McNair's participation in the engagement, one of the earliest in the war, stated, "He commanded his regiment in the battle... and when McCulloch and McIntosh had fallen, and Col. Louis Hebert... the senior colonel, had been captured in the early stages of the battle, he commanded the infantry of the division, and repulsed the enemy in front of the Confederate right." The casualties for McNair's command at Pea Ridge totaled fifty-four, with sixteen killed and thirty-eight wounded. In his report of the battle, written six months later, Colonel McNair added information about his soldiers at Pea Ridge in stating, "Some 40 were found missing after the battle, but all except 5 or 6 have since then rejoined the regiment."[10]

The low number of casualties at Richmond is interesting when taking into account the tenacity of the fighting Colonel McNair's troops encountered. He stated, "Ordering a charge, my men obeyed with alacrity and cheerfulness; but after advancing some 200 yards they were, owing to the nature of the ground and obstacles in the way, thrown into disorder and were halted...The enemy...immediately opened upon us a heavy fire of shell grape. In a few minutes the order was given to renew the charge... We attacked the whole body and repulsed them again; but, rallying upon their reserves, they made a stand, but were soon driven back again by our brave troops. In this last charge one of the enemy's batteries, at a distance of 200 yards, opened on us, but we charged and took it in a very short time...the loss of the enemy was very great."[11]

Arriving at Corinth, Mississippi after missing the nearby battle of Shiloh, Colonel Evander McNair made his way to Tupelo, Mississippi. A report of the ensuing events elaborated, "The brigade of which the Fourth Arkansas formed a part, together with what was afterwards known as Ector's Brigade, and another division under Brig. Gen. Pat Cleburne, were detached from that army and sent to Chattanooga, thence to Knoxville... and...over the Cumberland Mountains into Southeastern Kentucky."[12]

On August 30, 1862, Colonel McNair saw action at Richmond, Kentucky. It was said of the Federal Army at Richmond, "This army, variously estimated at 10,000 or 12,000 men, was attacked on its right center...by McNair, then in command of the brigade..." Colonel McNair's attack was successful, and the total number of casualties for his regiment at Richmond was twenty-three.[13] This successful action of the part of McNair would not go unwarranted.

An article on the life of Evander McNair noted the series of events that transpired in relation to his achievements at Richmond, Kentucky. The commentary said, "For the excellent management of his brigade...as well as for the gallant manner in which his troops broke the line of the Federals and put their whole force to the rout...Gen. Kirby Smith, who had been an eyewitness, promoted Col. McNair on the battlefield to a brigadier generalship, which was accordingly was fully accomplished by the War Department shortly afterwards."[14]

Brigadier General Evander McNair was assigned to command the brigade to which his old regiment belonged. At Murfreesboro, Tennessee, in late December, 1862, McNair led his troops into battle, this time in command of one of three brigades "in the division of Maj. Gen. John P. McCown, in the corps of Lieut. Gen. W. J. Hardee." At McNair's disposal at Murfreesboro were the 1st and 2nd Arkansas Mounted Rifles, the 4th and 30th Arkansas Infantry Regiments, the 4th Arkansas Battalion and Humphreys Arkansas Battery. The group endured seventy-nine casualties in the battle. It is noteworthy that poor health limited the amount of time McNair spent with his troops at Murfreesboro.[15]

In the summer of 1863, Brigadier General McNair joined General Joseph Johnston "in his efforts to relieve the beleaguered city of Vicksburg, Mississippi. As such, McNair participated to varying degrees in some of the battles around Vicksburg and Jackson, Mississippi.[16]

Additional combat experience for Brigadier General McNair took place "in the great battle of Chickamauga." McNair was in command of a brigade of one thousand two hundred seven troops of the 1st and 2nd Arkansas Mounted Rifles, the 4th, 25th and 31st Arkansas Infantry Regiments, the 39th North Carolina Infantry Regiment, and a total of twelve guns from three batteries. McNair, "took an active part...received a painful flesh wound in the thigh, which... incapacitated him for service in the field for a long time." McNair's wound was far from unique as twenty-four percent of his three hundred eighty-five troops engaged became casualties.[17]

J. C. Moore wrote of McNair, "It was McNair's Brigade, all Arkansas troops, that did the heavy fighting on Snodgrass Hill...I would not pluck one laurel from gallant sons of any of the thirteen states, but...want it known that McNair's brigade was composed of Arkansans only..."[18]

A turn-of-the-century article recalled the strong relationship the troops of McNair maintained with those of Ector's Brigade. The author wrote, "Every man in these brigades remembers the time down on Big Black, in Mississippi, when Gen. Walker separated Ector's and McNair's Brigades. At the time he had a poor opinion of us. He said we had no discipline and ought to be discharged. Both Ector and McNair resented his remarks, and talked with him about it. After the two days' fighting at Chickamauga, Gen. Walker apologized for what he said, and complimented both brigades very highly."[19]

In addition, McNair's Brigade was recognized for its valor, although the Confederates eventually retired from the battlefield. Having held their position on the Confederate left, the unit received the designation as "The Star Brigade of Chickamauga."[20]

During his recovery period Brigadier General McNair was transferred to the Trans-Mississippi Department, a reassignment that took place near Christmas, 1863. Afterwards, "upon recovering from his wound, he was assigned to the command of one of the four brigades in Gen. Churchill's division...composed entirely of infantry." A report on the remaining months of the American Civil War noted that the division that was McNair's new assignment "was not engaged in any important battle after the assignment of Gen. McNair to it."[21]

An exception to the lack of important action was McNair's participation in what became known as the "Missouri Raid." The raid was conducted under the leadership of General Sterling Price in 1864. During that series of events, McNair and the remainder of Price's Confederates took part in an estimated forty-three battles and traversed some one thousand four hundred miles in September and October. A pure indication of the Confederate failure during this expedition is that Price returned to Arkansas with only six thousand of the estimated sixteen to twenty thousand soldiers who began the raid into Missouri.[22]

The conclusion of the war enabled Evander McNair to return to his home in Washington, Arkansas, but he only remained there a short time. In the meantime, the one-time Confederate officer received an official pardon on December 12, 1865. McNair left Washington, where the poor post-war Southern economy had led to the failure of his once lucrative mercantile business, and moved to New Orleans. The rationale for this transfer, proposed one account of McNair's life was, "like all Confederate soldiers, in search for a business that promised support to him and those dependent upon him, while he should watch with the natural anxiety growing out of such a situation the changing scenes about him."[23]

The Evander McNair family returned to Mississippi, making their home in Magnolia. Sadly, Hannah Merrill McNair died in 1878 and was buried in that location. Evander survived his wife and was left to preserve her memory with their three children Edward Fletcher, Myra Conway, and Maggie Merrill.[24]

Widower McNair eventually moved to Hattiesburg, Mississippi where his two daughters "married and prospered." His son settled in the nearby town of Chatawa, Mississippi while one daughter married S. C. Eaton and the other was wed to Dan Fairly.[25]

Evander McNair passed away at the Dan Fairly family home in

Hattiesburg, while family surrounded his deathbed. Following his death on November 13, 1902, McNair's body was taken to Magnolia, Mississippi. He was buried next to his beloved wife Hannah.[26]

An outstanding eulogy for McNair came from a former soldier who was familiar with the former general "socially and officially, from the commencement of the war...until the close of the year 1863." That individual stated he took, "pleasure in bearing testimony to his noble character as a man and soldier." Among the many expressions of praise the one-time compatriot offered for McNair were the words, "He was public spirited in a high degree, and a Christian with the broadest charity of feeling toward other...Christians. He was consequently beloved by all, and all freely advised and conferred with him in all great moral and religious movements. He thus lived and died, loved and respected, the friend of all who knew him. An honorable, Christian life, and a death befitting such a life, in an epitaph that can be written on the tomb of only the very best..."[27]

CHRISTOPHER "KIT" HAYNES MOTT, C.S.A.
1826-1862

Christopher Haynes Mott was born on June 23, 1826 in Livingston County, Kentucky. At a young age he moved with his family to Holly Springs, Mississippi. The majority of what is known about the ensuing years of Mott's life center upon the facts that his education was received at St. Thomas Hall in Holly Springs, and that he eventually studied law under the leadership of Roger Barton.[1]

Often known by his nickname of "Kit," Mott entered the legal profession and practiced with such renowned Mississippi attorneys as James Autry and Lucius Quintus Cincinnatus Lamar. These associations allowed Mott to serve in many of the areas in and around Marshall County, Mississippi,[2] a district of which Holly Springs served as the county seat.

Kit Mott briefly abandoned his law practice in order to serve in the Mexican War. Like many men from his hometown, Mott joined the Marshall Guards, a local group destined to participate in the acquisition of land from Mexico. As a member of what became Company I of the 1st Mississippi Infantry he rose to the rank of lieutenant before the war concluded in 1848.[3]

In 1853 Christopher Haynes "Kit" Mott married Sally Govan, eight years his junior and a resident of Fayette County, Tennessee. Sally was also considered to be an extremely beautiful lady. The newlyweds traveled to New York City where they boarded a steamer for Mexico. The purpose of the trip was to eventually end up in California, where Kit Mott's job as an employee of the United States Government would be exercised. The couple managed to make a successful trip to Mexico and walked across the country where they boarded another vessel that took them to their destination. In turn, Kit and Sally Mott landed in San Francisco and briefly made the states of California and Oregon their homes before returning to Mississippi.[4]

Christopher Mott's governmentally-assigned task was to work as a special commissioner for the United States. In that capacity he investigated Federal officials in Oregon and California in order to determine if misconduct existed. This experience, combined with his time in Mississippi as a probate court judge and one term in the Mississippi State Legislature, made Mott a well-respected and trusted member of society in the minds of many.[5]

The American Civil War brought about changes for the Mott family. Mott used the arrival of the war as an opportunity to establish the Jeff Davis Rifles with the intention of serving the Confederate States of America. In a short time his association with the Jeff Davis Rifles came to an abrupt end when Mott was offered the distinction of being one of four brigadier generals in charge of troops serving Mississippi.[6]

Brigadier General Christopher Mott was placed in command of the 9th and 10th Mississippi Infantry Regiments, but he reportedly found a great deal of dissatisfaction with that state-appointed position. As a result, he resigned his commission as a general with Mississippi and became a colonel in the 19th Mississippi Infantry Regiment. Interestingly, Mott's direct commander in the 19th Mississippi Infantry Regiment was Lieutenant Colonel L. Q. C. Lamar, one of the men with whom he had practiced law prior to the American Civil War.[7]

Christopher Mott's decision to vacate his rank of brigadier general and become a colonel in another regiment apparently aggravated area residents. The law shingle that notified the public of the location of the Autry, Lamar, and Mott Law Practice was torn from the Holly Springs post and was found floating in the Mississippi River. The sign's modern whereabouts are unknown.[8]

On May 5, 1862, Colonel Mott, who had been recommended for a promotion to brigadier general in the Confederate Army, participated in the Battle of Williamsburg, Virginia. The engagement at Williamsburg would become the first such action in what came to be known as the Peninsula Campaign. The May 5 battle took place during a pouring rain, with Confederate soldiers being shot down as they crossed a muddy field.

Colonel Christopher Haynes "Kit" Mott was among the one thousand five hundred sixty casualties from the battle of Williamsburg. Fifteen of the men who filled the ranks of the 19th Mississippi Infantry Regiment were killed, with another eighty-five being wounded from the approximately five hundred who saw action at Williamsburg. Mott was killed in the struggle.[9]

In an attempt to be near her husband, Sally Mott was in Virginia during the fighting at Williamsburg. Mott's servant was the colonel at the time of his death and carried Mott's body from the place of his death.[10] It is unknown as to whether or not Mott was aware of the recommendation of his promotion in rank.

Mott was buried on the field at Williamsburg, but in the years after the war concluded, he was reinterred in the Hillcrest Cemetery in Holly Springs. His widow ultimately remarried, becoming the wife of widower John Marshall Billups. Sally remained with Billups until his death, having shared in the responsibility of raising four children. She is buried near Mott.[11]

The memory of Christopher "Kit" Mott was preserved in a method related to his time in the Confederate military spent serving the country he died defending. The Christopher "Kit" Mott Camp 1379 of the Sons of Confederate Veterans was formed in Mott's hometown of Holly Springs, Mississippi and remains active to the current day.

CARNOT POSEY, C.S.A.

1818-1863

On August 5, 1818 Carnot Posey was born in the Wilkinson County, Mississippi town of Woodville. He was the fourth of eight children of John Brooke and Elizabeth Screven Posey, a Mississippi planter couple. His early schooling also took place in Woodville.[1]

Following his attainment of a college education in Jackson, Mississippi, Posey began to study law at the University of Virginia. Once he fulfilled his studies in Virginia he returned to Mississippi and established a law practice in Woodville. In addition to his pursuit of a successful legal career, Carnot Posey ventured into farming and became a planter.[2]

The following decade would be one of mixed emotions for Carnot Posey. In 1838 he endured the loss of his father. In May 1840 Carnot Posey married Mary Collins. The couple soon had two sons, but the marriage ended tragically when Mary Collins Posey passed away in 1844. In 1848 Posey also suffered the death of his mother.[3]

Meanwhile, the 1846 arrival of war with Mexico led Carnot Posey to enlist in the 1st Mississippi Rifles. Posey rose to the rank of 1st lieutenant during the course of the conflict. Serving under the command of future Confederate President Jefferson Davis, 1st Lieutenant Posey took part in the Buena Vista charge that is often regarded as one of the most brilliant of the war. The February 1847 attack saved the day for the Americans, but the victory was not without cost. During the charge, Posey, who "took a manly part," was seriously wounded.[4]

The end of the Mexican-American War enabled Carnot Posey to return to his Mississippi law firm. President James Buchanan later appointed Posey to the position of District Attorney for Mississippi's Southern District, a post that carried a great deal of political power. Posey remained in that position until the onset of the American Civil War.[5]

Aside from his post-Mexican War business expansion, Carnot Posey ended his five-year status as a widower in February 1849 when he married Jane White. Carnot Posey and Jane produced six children in their years of matrimony.[6]

The arrival of the War Between the States created Carnot Posey's desire to recruit a militia company, the Wilkinson Rifles. The company soon joined others to form the 16th Mississippi Infantry Regiment. The veteran of the Mexican War and successful lawyer was quickly elected as the colonel of the regiment, and he remained in that capacity when the unit saw its initial combat in a skirmish near Corinth, Mississippi.[7]

Colonel Posey and his regiment were transferred to the Eastern Theater in August, 1861. They arrived in time to take part in the action at First Manassas. In October 1861 Colonel Carnot Posey also participated in the battle of Leesburg or Ball's Bluff.[8]

Additional combat experience for Colonel Posey took place at Richmond, Virginia in 1862. In June of that year he was slightly wounded during the battle of Cross Keys. Among the other sites where he saw action were Second Manassas, Harper's Ferry, and Sharpsburg. It was stated that Posey was among the Confederates troops who "bowled over Pope at Manassas" and was present with the Confederate wing that "kept McClellan in check and repulsed him" at the deadly confrontation at Sharpsburg. Colonel Posey temporarily led Brigadier General Winfield Featherston's brigade during the Northern Virginia and Maryland Campaigns.[9]

In the spring of 1863 Posey received a promotion to brigadier general, effective to November 1, 1862. The elevation in rank had come from his "meritorious and gallant conduct" during the aforementioned conflicts. As a newly-commissioned brigadier general, Carnot Posey was in charge of four Mississippi regiments that were in Anderson's division of A. P. Hill's corps. The regiments in Brigadier General Posey's command were the 12th, 16th, 19th, and 48th Mississippi Infantry Regiments.[10]

Brigadier General Carnot Posey "conducted himself with the gallantry for which he had always been distinguished" during the May 1863 battle of Chancellorsville, Virginia. He initially held a reserve position near Salem Church, but Brigadier General Posey received a comment from his division commander. In his official report of the battle, General Anderson said, "Posey's brigade gallantly maintained its position against great odds, and checked the farther advance of the enemy."[11]

In his report of the action at Chancellorsville, Brigadier General Carnot Posey wrote, "We concluded to leave five companies of my brigade and one regiment of General Mahone's brigade to watch and defend the United States Ford...we moved...to Chancellorsville...I formed a line of battle in Aldrich's field, between the Plank road and old Pike..."[12]

Regarding the ensuing action, Brigadier General Posey continued, "The advanced line of skirmishers soon encountered the enemy...I advanced another line...drove the enemy's skirmishers back in gallant style until we encountered the enemy in heavy force, drawn up in line ...on the Furnace road. This line was soon broken by the vigorous onset of my skirmishers."[13]

The later activities of his regiment were noted in the following sentences, "My command moved down the Furnace road, and formed a line of battle with three regiments being left behind as skirmishers... On the morning of the 3rd...I advanced my command by the furnace, capturing many prisoners and arms...and after a short time was ordered to advance by flank to the right and attack the enemy, who were in strong on a hill in front."[14]

Posey's concluding remarks were, "The next day, my command was moved...in the afternoon formed a line of battle near Hazel Run... my command moved across to the Plank road...under heavy fire...I remained near Banks' Ford during the balance of the night, and the next evening, in a severe storm of wind and rain, advanced to within 2 miles of Chancellorsville, and bivouacked for the night...My command was on foot from April 29 to May 7, inclusive, and bore the privations, fatigue, labor, and fighting without a murmur."[15]

Similar results as those at Chancellorsville awaited Posey at Gettysburg, in July 1863. Posey's brigade was assigned to Major General Richard Anderson's Division of General A. P. Hill's Third Corps. On July 2, 1863, Posey joined Anderson in the attack on Cemetery Ridge that was described as "feeble, disjointed attack that was repulsed."[16]

In relation to the lackluster attack Posey's brigade conducted at Gettysburg, a clear description is found on the Confederate brigade marker on Gettysburg's West Confederate Avenue, north of the Spangler Woods. The monument proclaims, "Through some misunderstanding of orders, instead of the brigade advancing in compact ranks...the regiments were ordered forward at different times...they pushed back the Union outposts and drove some artillerists...but did not join in the attack upon... Cemetery Ridge."[17]

Brigadier General Carnot Posey remarked on his brigade's activities at Gettysburg in his July 29, 1863 official report. Posey wrote, "My position was to the right of the cemetery, about which the enemy's lines of battle were formed...I received an order...to advance but two of my regiments... and at once sent out the Forty-eighth and Nineteenth Regiments...These regiments advanced some 200 or 300 yards beyond the barn and house, which were burned...When I reached the barn, I found my three regiments well up in advance...I sent the major-general a message, informing him of my position. He then ordered me to fall back to my original position, in the rear of Pegram's battery."[18]

Tragedy befell Brigadier General Carnot Posey and his family at the battle of Bristoe Station on October 14, 1863. During that military engagement that has been called "the Third Corps debacle," a shell fragment struck Posey in his left thigh, creating a wound that was initially determined to be minor. The general was taken to Culpepper for medical treatment and was then moved to room 33 West Lawn at the University of Virginia. Infection set in, and on November 13, 1863 the forty-five year-old Posey succumbed to his wound. Sadly, "he was one of thousands who died of infected wounds" during the war, a seemingly senseless tragedy in the larger travesty of the American Civil War.[19]

Brigadier General Carnot Posey was moved from the facility where Dr.

John Davis had cared for him. His remains were then buried in the Davis family plot at the University Cemetery in Charlottesville, Virginia. An attempt to preserve the memory of the brigadier general occurred with the 1875 founding of the Carnot Posey Lodge #378 of the Free and Accepted Masons in Ethel, Mississippi. His home, located in Woodville, Mississippi, is a modern-day bed and breakfast and special events center.[20]

WILLIAM PRICE SANDERS, U. S. A.
1833-1863

William Price Sanders was born in Kentucky. He eventually considered Mississippi his home state. Interestingly, he is buried in Tennessee where, unlike the vast majority of his fellow Mississippians, he was killed while fighting for, and not against, the United States of America.

August 12, 1833 is usually regarded as the birthday of William Price Sanders. Various sources claim the event took place either at Lexington, or near Frankfort, Kentucky. Slightly more certain are the names of the infant's parents, Lewis Sanders, Jr. and Margaret Sanders. Indications are that Lewis was approximately thirty-six and Margaret near thirty-one when William Price Sanders entered the world. The couple also had a daughter named Eliza.[1]

In 1839 the Sanders family moved to Natchez, Mississippi where William spent the majority of his young years. Records indicate William's childhood nickname was Doc, although he was not known to have ever studied or practiced medicine. However, one of the boy's uncles was a doctor, and that individual was presumably the source of the pseudonym.[2]

William Price Sanders entered the United States Military Academy at West Point in 1852. Among his classmates were other future Civil War officers such as Orlando Poe, William Hicks Jackson, and Fitzhugh Lee. An 1854 letter from Robert Edward Lee, West Point Superintendent at the time, recommended that Sanders be dismissed. The reason for Lee's determined effort is difficult to determine. However, the intervention of Mississippian Jefferson Davis, a Sanders family friend, enabled William Sanders to remain at the academy. Sanders overcame the dispute and graduated in 1856, ranked forty-first from forty-nine cadets.[3]

On July 1, 1856, William Price Sanders received his commission as a Brevet Second Lieutenant with the 1st United States Dragoons. Less than a year later, on May 27, 1856, Second Lieutenant Sanders was transferred to the 2nd United States Dragoons.[4] Sanders remained with that unit and held that rank until the beginning of the American Civil War.

Abandoning his fellow Mississippians' tendency to serve the Confederate States of America, Sanders remained loyal to the United States. On May 10, 1861 he received a promotion to first lieutenant; within a week he became a captain. He held that rank while the 2nd United States Dragoons gained the new designation of the 6th United States Cavalry in August 1861.[5]

Captain William Price Sanders served in the Peninsula Campaign and saw action at Antietam before transferring to Cincinnati. As a member of the Department of the Ohio, Sanders was promoted to the rank of colonel in the 5th Kentucky Cavalry in March 1863. Colonel William Sanders also sought to capture Morgan's Raiders. Locations of additional military activities for Sanders included Blue Lick Springs and Lenoir's Station. In September 1863 Colonel Sanders made his way to Knoxville, Tennessee where his life forever changed.[6]

In October 1863 Sanders was promoted to brigadier general. The officer also reportedly found love while in Knoxville where he was said to have experienced a mutual affection with Sue Boyd. Boyd was nineteen years old, eleven years younger than Brigadier General Sanders. The general was described as "dashing." In addition, Sue was known to possess a beautiful singing voice. Sue Boyd's father was Samuel Beckett Boyd, the owner of the Blount Mansion. Captain Orlando Poe, a West Point cadet with Sanders and an officer who was with Sanders at Knoxville, wrote home and noted that the beautiful Sue Boyd was "smitten with Sanders."[7]

A Knoxville adversary of Brigadier General Sanders was Colonel A. P.

Alexander, a man who Sanders also knew outside of military respects. One of Alexander's sharpshooters was positioned in a tower that was part of the Bleak House, a Knoxville residence that was serving as the headquarters for Confederate general James Longstreet. On November 18, 1863, the sharpshooter fired at Brigadier General Sanders and struck the young general in his side.[8]

Having effectively used a limited command of only seven hundred troops, Brigadier General Sanders had managed to hold his position along the Kingston Road for some twenty-four hours. That time frame had allowed additional Federal fortifications to be established in preparation for an inevitable Confederate assault.[9]

Captain Orlando Poe witnessed a conversation in which Sanders was ordered to hold his position. Poe recalled Sanders "dutifully acknowledged" the order and that "every spadeful of earth turned while Sanders was fighting aided in making" the Federal position stronger.[10]

Unfortunately Sanders suffered a mortal wound. He was taken to the Lamar House where he succumbed to his wound the following day, November 19, 1863. From the Federal earthworks, soon to be named Fort Sanders, a twenty-pound Parrot gun fired toward the Bleak House. Allegedly, at least one sharpshooter in the tower was killed in the cannon fire that was projected in retaliation for the mortal wounding of Sanders.[11]

Federal troops used the safety of darkness to bury Sanders in the Second Presbyterian Church Cemetery. However, his corpse was later reinterred in the Chattanooga National Cemetery. There, the lifelong bachelor rests in grave 1601 of Section C. In addition to the posthumously named Fort Sanders, other locations were named for the young brigadier general. Fort Sanders Presbyterian Church and an East Tennessee chapter of the Sons of Union Veterans have attempted to preserve his memory.[12]

CLAUDIUS WISTAR SEARS, C.S.A.
1817-1891

Claudius Wistar Sears was born on November 8, 1817. His birthplace was Peru, Massachusetts, a community located in Berkshire, County, an area of the Berkshire Hills region of Western Massachusetts. Little is recorded about his early life, but he gained an appointment to the United States Military Academy in 1837. Interestingly, the state which supplied his admission to West Point was New York, and not his home state of Massachusetts.[1]

Cadet Sears entered West Point on July 1, 1837 and remained there until his July 1, 1847 graduation. Other members of his West Point class included future Civil War officers Don Carlos Buell, Abraham Buford, John Reynolds, and Richard Garnett. Cadets who graduated with Sears were Julius Garesche, Nathaniel Lyon, and Samuel Anderson. In 1841 Sears completed his West Point studies, ranked thirty-first of fifty-two cadets.[2]

Claudius Sears received a promotion to the rank of second lieutenant. His July 1, 1841 commission sent Second Lieutenant Sears to the garrison at Ft. Columbus, New York. Sears remained at Ft. Columbus until orders required him to report to Florida. From late 1841 through October 10,

1842, Sears participated in the Florida Wars, also known as the Seminole Wars. The end of his tenure in Florida came with his abrupt resignation from the Army.[3]

Having resigned from the United States military, Sears adjusted to civilian life by entering the field of education. For two years, beginning in 1844, Sears taught mathematics at St. Thomas Hall in Holly Springs, Mississippi. In 1845 he secured a new job, and served as a professor of mathematics, physics, and civil engineering at the University of Louisiana. He held that position until 1860, when he returned to Holly Springs and was the president of St. Thomas Hall. Sears led the faculty and staff at St. Thomas Hall through the spring of 1861.[4]

In the meantime Claudius Sears had married Texas native Alice Gray in 1853. Claudius and Alice Gray Sears had one son, Peter Gray Sears. Alice and Claudius maintained a long relationship; she also survived her husband by two years. Peter lived until the early 1940s.[5]

Foregoing his Northern birth, and siding with his adopted home state of Mississippi, Sears enlisted in the 17th Mississippi Infantry Regiment in May 1861. He was elected captain of Company G of the 17th Mississippi Infantry Regiment at that time. His time in the 17th Missisippi enabled Captain Sears to gain combat experience at the July battle of First Manassas.[6]

During the fall of 1861, Captain Sears and the 17th Mississippi Infantry Regiment participated in the battle of Ball's Bluff, in addition to the well-documented Peninsula Campaign engagements. Afterwards, Sears earned additional experience through his activities during the Seven Days Battles. In September 1862 Captain Sears joined his comrades of the 17th Mississippi Infantry Regiment as they fought at Antietam, Maryland.[7]

In December 1862 Sears was promoted to the rank of colonel. As such, Colonel Claudius Sears was transferred to the 46th Mississippi Infantry Regiment and left the Eastern Theater for the Western. The majority of his time in the following months was filled with a number of battles associated with the Vicksburg Campaign and included Chickasaw Bayou and Port Gibson.[8]

Most notable was the commendation Colonel Sears received for his action during the siege of Vicksburg. Although he was captured with the large number of Confederates who surrendered on July 4, 1863, Sears was positively mentioned in the official report of his brigade commander, Brigadier General William Baldwin. Baldwin wrote, "Colonel Sears, Forty-sixth Mississippi, merits favorable notice for his conduct during this trying time."[9]

Colonel Claudius Sears remained a prisoner of war until his exchange in October 1863. He fought a series of illnesses in the coming months. Having recovered from diseases contracted during his incarceration, Colonel Sears returned to his regiment in the spring of 1864.[10]

In March 1864 Sears was promoted to the rank of brigadier general and was assigned to the Army of Tennessee. Having briefly led a brigade prior to his increase in rank, Brigadier General Sears was moved from Selma, Alabama to Tuscaloosa and then to Rome, Georgia. Given command of several regiments and a battalion of Mississippi troops, Sears advanced to Resaca in May. On May 19 Sears was wounded during the battle of Adairsville, Georgia.[11]

Although he soon returned and saw a large amount of military action from May through September of 1864, Brigadier General Claudius Sears spent most of July in medical care. His intermittent service did garner praise in a superior's report, as Sears was commended for his "valuable services."[12]

In November 1864 Brigadier General Sears led his soldiers into the vicious struggle at Franklin, Tennessee. Sears received accolades for the significant number of men and officers who successfully reached the primary line of Federal defenses.[13] From Franklin, Brigadier General Sears encountered his next significant military action at Nashville, a battle that would forever change his life.

At Nashville, Brigadier General Claudius Sears continued to command a brigade of five regiments and one battalion; all of the units were from Mississippi. Those brigade elements were the 7th Mississippi Battalion, as well as the 4th, 35th, 36th, 39th, and 46th Mississippi Infantry Regiments. In addition, Sears's Brigade combined with those of Brigadier Generals Francis Cockrell and Matthew Ector to form Major General Samuel French's Division. Major Generals William Loring and Edward Walthall commanded two other divisions that comprised Lieutenant General Alexander Stewart's Corps at Nashville.[14]

R. N. Rea recalled the tragic incidents that befell Brigadier General

Sears during the battle of Nashville. Rea's 1903 *Confederate Veteran* article was titled "Gen. C. W. Sears, a pathetic incident." Rea wrote, "While there have been recorded...countless deeds of heroism and fortitude of the Confederate soldier, in my humble opinion none has surpassed that of Gen. Claudius W. Sears at the battle of Nashville, during Gen. Hood's Tennessee Campaign."[15]

Rea, an eyewitness to the events, noted, "I write...of that gallant old Confederate soldier and his faithful horse Billy. I was present...Federal forces had succeeded in turning the right and left wings of the Confederate Army. Sears's Brigade occupied a central position, and when his command yielded to the inevitable, it passed under fire from front, right, and left."[16]

Rea added, "After extricating his command from this position, Gen. Sears rode to a small eminence in order to get a better view of the enemy. He removed his field glass from its case, and began his inspection." For Sears, the personal tragedy of the battle was proclaimed in Rea's statement, "While seated upon his horse and with the glass to his eyes, the enemy fired a shell at him. It carried away one of his legs below the knee, and it also killed his horse."[17]

Rea remarked that, "...the ground was frozen hard and was covered with deep snow, and it seemed the coldest as well as the saddest day I had ever experienced. No surgeon was near to administer to his pressing need, everything was in confusion, and in the midst of all the sad surrounding scenes of a fierce battle, the grand old hero stood upon one foot..."[18]

The admiration Brigadier General Sears held for his steed was explained in the words, "...with tears running down his cheeks, like a child, exclaimed, 'Poor Billy! Poor Billy!' He did not seem to notice his own sad condition, but his whole attention and sympathy were directed toward the faithful steed which he had ridden during the entire war."[19]

Rea's concluded, "An ambulance was secured to carry him...after making him as comfortable as possible, we bade him adieu, never expecting to see him again. Many of us never did. They say, 'Fortune favors the brave.' In this case it certainly did, for he recovered..."[20]

Brigadier General Claudius Wistar Sears was taken prisoner in Pulaski, Tennessee while recuperating from the amputation of his leg. His December 21, 1864 capture, for all purposes, marked the end of military service for Sears. He was paroled on June 23, 1865.[21]

The years following the American Civil War enabled Sears to return to the educational sector. From 1865 until the late 1880s, he was a professor of mathematics at the University of Mississippi. Making Oxford, Mississippi his home, Sears also taught civil engineering at the University of Mississippi from 1872 to 1874. In 1889 he retired.[22]

On February 15, 1891, the seventy-three year-old Sears passed away in Oxford. He was buried in the Oxford Memorial, Saint Peter's, Cemetery in Lafayette County, Mississippi.[23]

JACOB HUNTER SHARP, C.S.A.
1833-1907

Jacob Hunter Sharp was the third and final child born to the Pickensville, Alabama couple of Elisha Hunter and Sallie Carter Hunt Sharp. Jacob's older siblings included Thomas Sharp, a future Confederate officer, and Caroline Sarah Sharp Walker. Sallie Carter Hunt Sharp, the matriarch of the family, was a daughter of Isaac Carter, a major in the American Revolution.[1]

The Sharp family made an exodus from Alabama moved to Lowndes County, Mississippi when Jacob was a child. As a result, Jacob spent his formative years in Lowndes County, but he returned to Alabama in 1850 in order to attend college. After he graduated from the University of Alabama, Sharp returned to Columbus and established a law practice.[2]

From a personal perspective, Jacob Hunter Sharp became a husband when he married Sarah Hunt Harris, the daughter of a judge. The couple produced two children, Willie Sharp Askew and Thomas Hunter Sharp. Willie passed away prior to the family patriarch's death; Thomas lived into the 1950s. Sarah survived her husband by a decade.[3]

Soon after the American Civil War started, Jacob Sharp enlisted in what eventually became Company A of the 44th Mississippi Infantry

Regiment. The 44th Mississippi Infantry Regiment was also known as Blythe's Regiment, and held that designation from Lieutenant-Colonel A. K. Blythe. Originally associated with the 1st Mississippi Battalion, the company was raised in Lowndes County and was known as the Tombigbee Rangers. Within a short time after the company was formed, Jacob Sharp was elected as its captain.[4]

Captain Jacob Sharp initially experienced combat at Belmont, Missouri in November 1861. It was stated that the 44th Mississippi "displayed the greatest coolness and determined courage, and although under fire for the first time, bore themselves like veterans, sustaining the reputation of Tennesseans and Mississippians..."[5]

Captain Jacob Sharp received mention in Colonel Preston Smith's report of the battle of Shiloh. During the action of April 6, 1862, the regiment's namesake, Colonel Blythe, was, "shot dead from his horse while gallantly leading his regiment..." With Sharp gaining some leadership responsibilities in the aftermath of Blythe's death, Colonel Smith noted that Captain Sharp was among the company officers whose conduct was favorable during the two days of fighting.[6]

In the weeks following Shiloh, the 44th Mississippi Infantry Regiment was in Trapier's Brigade for a short time before being transferred to Chalmers's Brigade. Captain Sharp and his comrades in Chalmers's Brigade took part in the attack against the Federal fort at Munfordville. Of the two hundred eighty-one men who reported for duty at Munfordville, four were killed and thirty-eight wounded. At Murfreesboro, the regiment endured four killed, thirty-one wounded, and seventeen missing. The regiment was noted as having, "rallied, reformed, and fought gallantly" during the Murfreesboro campaign.[7]

Jacob Sharp was promoted to the rank of colonel in August 1863 and gained leadership experience at Davis's Crossroads on September 11, 1863. Colonel Sharp actually led the brigade during a skirmish at the crossroads, but was noted for a similar role in the battle of Chickamauga. With the wounding of General Thomas Hindman, "Colonel Sharp took command of the Mississippi Brigade."[8]

Colonel Jacob Sharp's report of the battle at Chickamauga stated, "We went into action with 272 officers and enlisted men and lost 81 killed and wounded." Sharp also commented that his soldiers charged "up and hill on which the Federal line was wavering, carrying everything, taking no note of guns taken or the prisoners who passed through the line in great numbers, advanced two miles, captured two stands of colors. Next attacked a blue line strongly posted on a hill...repulsed three times...each time reformed and went in again."[9]

Regarding the May 8, 1864 action at Rocky Face Ridge, General Walthall praised both Brigadier General W. F. Tucker and Colonel Sharp. Walthall stated, "To both these efficient officers I am indebted for valuable suggestions and repeated offers of assistance, for which their command was kept in a constant state of readiness."[10]

Evidently as a result of his valor at Rocky Face Ridge and the previous engagements for which he gained praise, Sharp was promoted in July 1864.[11] From that point forward, Brigadier General Jacob Hunter Sharp would be the title by which the pre-war lawyer would be known.

General John C. Brown noted the conduct of Brigadier General Sharp following the battle of Ezra Church. Brown wrote, "To...Sharp...I am especially indebted for...prompt obedience to every order and cheerful cooperation in everything tending to promote the efficiency of... commands and the good of the service."[12]

The August 1864 action at Jonesboro, Georgia earned Brigadier General Sharp more accolades. Regarding that action, it was reported, "Sharp's gallant Mississippians could be seen pushing their way in small parties up to the very slope of the enemy's breastworks. Officers could be plainly observed encouraging the men to this work. One on horseback, whom I took to be General Sharp, was particularly conspicuous."[13]

Sharp's Brigade also fought at Franklin, Tennessee in late November 1864. A commentary on the unit's relevance in that engagement stated, "Sharp's Brigade was distinguished in the desperate struggle, taking three battle-flags and leaving their dead and wounded in the trenches and along the works."[14]

After the December 1864 battle of Nashville, Tennessee, Sharp's Brigade was furloughed until the following February. By April 3, 1865 the brigade contained only four hundred twenty men and officers. It was also consolidated with several other regiments and battalions prior to its surrender with General Joseph Johnston at Durham Station on April 26, 1865.[15]

The majority of Sharp's post-war career was largely dedicated to the resumption and restoration of his law practice. He also took time to publish and edit the Columbus, Mississippi *Independent*. Residing in the state capital of Jackson for a brief period of time Sharp also served four years in the Mississippi House of Representatives.[16]

Jacob Hunter Sharp passed away on September 15, 1907, and was buried in Friendship Cemetery in Columbus, Mississippi. Ten years later Sarah was interred next to him.[17]

PETER BURWELL STARKE, C. S. A.
1815-1888

Brunswick County, Virginia was the location of Peter Burwell Starke's 1815 birth. Unfortunately, a more specific date has been lost to time. Peter's siblings included an older brother, William Edwin Starke, who was also destined to become a Confederate brigadier general. Peter and William spent their early years assisting with the family's means of livelihood, a stagecoach business that ran from Petersburg to Lawrenceville, Virginia.[1]

In 1840 Peter Starke moved to Bolivar, Mississippi. At the time Bolivar, a small town on the banks of the Mississippi River, was the county seat of Bolivar County, Mississippi. In the near future Peter became involved in Mississippi politics. He unsuccessfully sought a seat as a congressman in 1846, but four years later he won an election for the House of Representatives. In 1856 Peter Starke ran for and entered the Mississippi State Senate.[2] The beginning of the American Civil War postponed Starke's continuation of his political public service.

Having joined the Confederate Army, Peter Burwell Starke was given the rank of colonel in the 28th Mississippi Cavalry Regiment in February 1862. The cavalry regiment was initially assigned to the command of General Morgan Lewis Smith. By September Colonel Starke was serving in Arkansas and alerted other Confederates of Federal movements from the state. As a result, Starke and his cavalrymen took part in skirmishes in the area.[3]

Tragedy struck the Starke family in the fall of 1862. Peter's brother, Brigadier General William Starke, had been a cotton merchant in New Orleans and Mobile before the war. William had climbed the ranks quickly, and was serving as the division commander at Antietam in September 1862. The older Starke was shot three times in the early morning of September 17 while leading Confederate troops against Federals. Succumbing to his multiple wounds within an hour, William was carried to Richmond, Virginia for burial. His body was interred in Hollywood Cemetery, next to his son who had been killed at the battle of Seven Pines two months earlier.[4]

A decision in Vicksburg, in the spring of 1863, created a reassignment of Colonel Peter Starke's regiment to the brigade of General William Hicks Jackson. Starke's troopers joined those of a battalion and three other regiments to complete Jackson's brigade. Starke was soon following the command of Earl Van Dorn during the battle of Thompson's Station, Tennessee.[5]

General William Hicks Jackson was given command of a cavalry division, and Colonel Peter Starke assumed the leadership role of the brigade. Three brigades, as well as a company and an artillery battery were at Starke's disposal. However, at that time, in February 1864, Starke was serving as a general, but continued to hold the rank of colonel.[6]

Colonel Peter Starke later led the brigade in the Meridian expedition as well as at Sharon, where the Confederates "inflicted considerable loss on the enemy." Generals Jackson and S. D. Lee praised Starke's conduct in the events, with Lee writing, "Colonel Starke, commanding brigade, showed skill and gallantry on every occasion, and won my confidence."[7]

The acknowledgement from Jackson and Lee, combined with Starke's efficient command of a regiment in the Atlanta Campaign, led to a promotion for the acting general. In November 1864 Starke's cavalrymen took part in Hood's Tennessee Campaign. In the spring 1865 Starke reported to General Nathan Bedford Forrest and was given command of all or part of seven units. Those included the 4th, 6th, 8th, and 28th Mississippi Cavalry as well as the 8th Mississippi Cavalry, the 18th Battalion, and a portion of the Fifth Regiment.[8]

Brigadier General Starke served in Alabama with Chalmers's Division for the remainder of the war. His command surrendered with Lieutenant General Richard Taylor at Citronelle, Alabama on May 4, 1865.[9] With his service completed, Starke returned to Mississippi.

During his post-war life, Peter Starke managed to gain a number of public appointments. He served on the Board of Mississippi Levee Commissioners as well as the sheriff of Bolivar County for one term. Sadly, his children passed away in the years after the war, and Starke married a second time. In the early 1870s Starke left Mississippi and returned to the family farm that was located near Lawrenceville, Virginia.[10]

On July 13, 1888 Peter Burwell Starke died at his farm; the cause of his death was reported as "debility." His corpse was taken to Brunswick County, Virginia in the Lawrenceville vicinity. At that location Starke was buried in the Percival Family Cemetery, situated on the farm of his second wife, Elizabeth J. Percival Starke.[11]

WILLIAM FEIMSTER TUCKER, C. S. A.

1827-1881

William Feimster Tucker was born in Iredell County, North Carolina May 9, 1827. Little is recorded in relation to his childhood, but there is evidence regarding his teen years and the education he received. Tucker eventually entered Emory and Henry College in Emory, Virginia. He graduated in 1843, but financial difficulties initially comprised his unforeseen reward.[1]

In an effort to gain some semblance of financial stability, Tucker moved to the Chickasaw County, Mississippi settlement of Houston. Houston was a North Mississippi frontier town. Tucker began a teaching career, and used his spare time to study law. He also managed to found the Okolona Male Academy in 1852. In 1855, he became a county probate judge, although he lacked any training to do so. Tucker eventually completed the required education to become a lawyer, secured his admission to the Mississippi bar, and entered a practice of law.[2] Tucker continued seeking his livelihood in that profession until he entered the American Civil War.

In 1861 William Tucker became a captain in a company known as the Chickasaw Guards. The Guards were soon made a part of the Mississippi State Militia, but the relationship was short-lived. The Chickasaw Guards were then attached to the 11th Mississippi Infantry Regiment, and Tucker was given command of Company K. As such, Tucker and his compatriots of the 11th Mississippi were assigned to General Bernard Bee's brigade in service of the Confederate States of America.[3]

Tucker's combat indoctrination took place at Manassas, Virginia in July 1861. The 11th Mississippi played a significant part in the Confederate victory. Captain Tucker received recognition for his leadership of Company K, while the Confederate Army endured total casualties of less than two thousand. The Federals suffered almost 2,900 casualties.[4]

Captain Tucker made a May 1862 recruiting trip to Pontotoc, Mississippi, where he embarked upon a successful effort to raise a regiment. The unit Tucker established eventually became the 41st Mississippi, a group destined to see their share of heated conflicts. Having raised the 41st Mississippi Infantry Regiment, Tucker was elected to the rank of colonel.[5]

The fall of 1862 found Colonel Tucker and the 41st Mississippi in a brigade composed largely of Florida members. The other regimental members were the men of the 1st and 3rd Florida Infantry Regiments, as well as Battery A of the 14th Battalion, Georgia Light Artillery.[6] With that assignment, Tucker and the 41st Mississippi Infantry Regiment moved into Kentucky.

During the battle of Perryville, Kentucky, thirty-five year-old Brigadier General John Calvin Brown commanded the brigade containing the 41st Mississippi. Brigadier General Brown was wounded in his thigh, and brigade leadership fell to Colonel William F. Tucker. Unfortunately for Colonel Tucker, he also received an arm wound, and command went to Colonel William Miller of the 1st Florida Infantry Regiment.[7]

Additional insight into the activities of Colonel Tucker and the men of the 41st Mississippi at Perryville can be gained in reading an excerpt from a veteran's reminiscences. W. C. Hearn, a post-war preacher, was a lieutenant colonel with the 41st Mississippi. Lieutenant Colonel Hearn praised Tucker and recalled the officer's wounding.[8]

Lieutenant Colonel Hearn wrote, "I have seen little concerning the service of the regiment…and yet a more gallant command did not enter the field in defense of the South. It was raised and organized by the lamented Gen. W. F. Tucker…I…mention one engagement only, in which there was shown courage worthy of a place in history."[9]

Hearn continued, "It was at Perryville…October 8, 1862. As we crossed the creek...we found ourselves on a piece of table land of a few acres, where we were held under a most disastrous fire from the enemy, from behind a fence on the hill, for perhaps thirty minutes."[10]

Detailing the brigade's leadership, Hearn noted, "Gen. John C. Brown...fell from his horse with a shot through the thigh, and was soon followed by Col. W. F. Tucker, with a shot through the right arm, from which he fainted, and was carried by his adjutant off the field."[11]

Many other members of the 41st Mississippi became Perryville casualty statistics with Colonel Tucker. The regimental losses for the battle were reported as eighteen killed and seventeen wounded. The completeness of those figures has been noted as incomplete.[12]

Colonel Tucker's severe wound eventually healed, and he was able to rejoin his command in time to participate in the battle of Murfreesboro. During the action at Murfreesboro, the 41st Mississippi was temporarily assigned to the brigade of Brigadier General James Chalmers. A part of the action Tucker and the 41st Mississippi encountered at Murfreesboro was duly recorded. The recollection stated, "The storm of lead and iron that met the Mississippians...shattered the line." By the end of the battle Tucker's regiment had suffered twenty-five killed, one hundred twenty-three wounded, and eight missing.[13]

George W. Leavell was a private in Company B of the Forty-first Mississippi at Murfreesboro. In his recollections, Leavell wrote, "Perhaps there was no part of the Confederate army that might not claim some special distinction. It was the distinction of the Forty First Mississippi Regiment that, in all its long list of battles fought, it was never led to the charge without moving the enemy. In one instance alone, at the battle of Murfreesboro, a part of this regiment was repulsed, and, when ordered to retreat, retired under fire...it would be hard to express that experience. This regiment was organized and disciplined into the service by Col. W. F. Tucker. No man of truer heart or braver spirit ever drew sword in battle."[14]

At Chickamauga and Chattanooga, Tucker led an entire brigade. The troops of the 7th, 9th, 10th, 41st, and 44th Mississippi Infantry Regiments, as well as the 9th Mississippi Battalion Sharpshooters, were at his disposal in these campaigns, as were the members of Garrity's Alabama Battery. In turn, the regiments compiled Brigadier General Patton Anderson's Brigade, a unit in Major General Thomas Hindman's Division of Major

General William Walker's Corps. The casualties for the 41ˢᵗ Mississippi at Chattanooga were twenty-four killed, one hundred sixty-four wounded, and nine missing from the five hundred two officers and enlisted men.[15]

In May 1864, William Tucker was promoted to the rank of brigadier general, effective from March 1, 1864. With that designation, he gained command of the units he had led in the previous battles. During the subsequent Atlanta Campaign, Brigadier General William Feimster Tucker led his troops against General William Sherman's Federals at Resaca, Georgia. During the action a shell exploded near Tucker and "shattered his left arm."[16]

General John Bell Hood reported Tucker's wounding in writing, "Walthall's Brigade, occupying the left of Hindman's division suffered severely from an enfilade fire of the enemy's artillery...displaying conspicuous valor...Brigadier General Tucker, commanding brigade in reserve, was severely wounded."[17]

General Walthall also recalled the incident, "The fine brigade which was posted in my rear for support...sustained considerable loss, mainly from the enemy's artillery. Its commander, Brig. Gen. W. F. Tucker, was severely wounded, while observing the enemy's movements...and was succeeded in command by Col. Jacob H. Sharp...their command was kept in a constant state of readiness."[18]

The critical wound, received three days after his promotion to brigadier general, forced Tucker to prematurely end his field service. Brigadier General Tucker's left arm was rendered useless for the remainder of the general's life.[19]

Evidently not willing to let his wound negate his service to the Confederate States of America, Tucker held an administrative post for the duration of the war. His position was primarily relegated to the District of Southern Mississippi and East Louisiana.[20]

A major responsibility of Brigadier General Tucker was to negotiate with Federal Major General Napoleon Dana. With the "end of hostilities," Tucker was paroled in Jackson, Mississippi in May 1865, Tucker returned to his law practice.[21]

During the following decade, William Tucker entered a two-year term in the Mississippi State House of Representatives. One of his major legislative acts was to serve on the committee that recalled Mississippi's

Reconstruction Governor. Despite this prominent task, Tucker's 1880 bid for the United States Senate proved unsuccessful. Again, he returned to his law practice.[22]

On September 14, 1881, Tucker was lying in his Okolona, Mississippi bed, reading a letter from his son. With a knock on the bedroom window, Tucker asked, "Who's there?" He was mortally shot in the chest. Rumors abounded that the incident was in response to Tucker's disclosure of an individual's misuse of trust fund money. There was a man who was the subject of a pending case, and he may have hired assassins to eliminate Tucker. Various people were tried for the crime, all were found innocent, and the murder remained unsolved.[23]

Tucker was buried in the Odd Fellows Cemetery in Okolona, Mississippi. Martha Josephine Shackelford Tucker and the couple's children survived him.[24]

EARL VAN DORN, C.S.A.
1820-1863

Earl Van Dorn was born in Port Gibson, Mississippi on September 20, 1820, he was the son of Mississippi State Representative Peter Aaron Van Dorn and his wife, Sophie Donelson Caffery Van Dorn. Peter and Sophie Van Dorn eventually had nine children, two daughters and seven sons. Interestingly, Mrs. Van Dorn was a niece of Andrew Jackson's wife Rachel.[1]

Legend holds that Van Dorn, who was sixteen and attending school in Baltimore, made an appeal to Andrew Jackson, seeking his influence in helping the teen gain admission to West Point. An article said, "...soon the name of Earl Van Dorn was enrolled for the four years' training which prepared him for his chosen...work in the United States Army."[2]

General James Longstreet recalled that he, as well as fifteen other future generals was among Van Dorn's classmates who graduated from West Point in 1842. Some of the other members of that illustrious class were John Newton, William Rosecrans, George Sykes, and Abner Doubleday. Destined to serve as Confederate generals were Lafayette McLaws, D. H. Hill, Gustavus Smith, Mansfield Lovell, A. P. Stewart, and R. H. Anderson.[3]

Earl Van Dorn was largely regarded as a poor student during his time at West Point, and he was regularly cited for misconduct. Despite his shortcomings, the native Mississippian was noted as possessing potential with skills in drawing, field soldiering, and horsemanship.[4]

Regarding Van Dorn's 1842 graduation from the United States Military Academy, one historian wrote, "At the age of twenty-one he left the institution with the rank of lieutenant, and was assigned to duty with the 7th United States Infantry Regiment." Van Dorn spent time stationed at Mount Vernon Arsenal and at Pensacola, in Alabama and Florida respectfully.[5]

In a more personal aspect, twenty-three year-old Earl Van Dorn married sixteen year-old Caroline Godbold soon after his graduation. Caroline was the daughter of a wealthy Alabama plantation owner, James Godbold and his wife Olivia. Caroline, also known as Carey or Cary, was unable to spend much time with Van Dorn; his presence at their home was limited due to his frequent and prolonged absences resulting from military deployments. However, the couple did manage to have a son, Earl, Jr., and Olivia, their daughter, named for Van Dorn's mother.[6]

The 7th U. S. Infantry Regiment, in which Lieutenant Earl Van Dorn served, was reported as being among the first to venture to the Texas border in preparation for military action against Mexico. An early Twentieth Century historian wrote about Van Dorn's activities in the 7th U. S. Infantry, "The first daring act of this young officer occurred at Fort Brown, which was under siege. The United States flag had been shot down. The pole being some distance outside the fort, the commanding officer called for volunteers to rehoist the flag. Lieutenant Van Dorn promptly answered the call. With the aid of a soldier, he went out, and while shot and shell tore the ground under his feet he raised the flag, threw it to the breeze, and amid the huzzahs of his comrades returned as by a miracle safely within the fort."[7]

Earl Van Dorn wrote to his wife, "I dodged several bomb-shells which threatened to fall on my head. I skipped out of the way of a rolling howitzer ball...musket balls flew around me at one time like a thousand hummingbirds...I had the sound of all kinds of music."[8]

Van Dorn received additional commendations for his actions at the battles of Fort Texas, Chapultepec, Cerro Gordo, Vera Cruz, and Mexico City. Additional praise for his efforts at Contreras and Churubusco earned

Van Dorn a promotion to major in 1847. He had also survived a foot wound at Mexico City and another injury when storming the Belen Gate.[9]

Upon the completion of the Mexican War, Van Dorn joined other Mexican War veterans in protecting the Texas frontier from Comanche Indians. It was said that among those who joined Van Dorn in Texas were "Albert S. Johnston, Robert E. Lee, Joseph E. Johnston, George H. Thomas...John B. Hood, and others no less renowned." These men were considered to be some of the best the U. S. Army had to offer, and were assigned to the 2nd U. S. Cavalry, a unit formed in 1855. Among the tasks Van Dorn, who served as a company commander, undertook was the assignment to "pursue and put to rout the savage enemies of the plains. Many of these expeditions resulted in fearful and bloody encounters. Twice Major Van Dorn was severely wounded with arrows, which he pulled from his body, 'the blood flowing like wine from a drunkard's tankard'."[10]

On October 1, 1858 Van Dorn joined in an attack on a combined Comanche and Kiowa group near Wichita Village. In the ensuing action, he was shot through the stomach and lung, as well as hit in an arm, when a duo of arrows slammed into his body. Van Dorn's initiative exhibited in attacking a force that was approximately two times that of his own earned him praise from his superiors. Unfortunately, his recovery period for the wounds he received took a period of some five weeks of the winter.[11]

Accolades for the young officer were frequent in the press of the day. It was written, "He had received brevets for gallantry on the battlefields of Mexico and in honor of his successful Indian campaigns. His native state and county recognized with pride his fame as a Mississippian, and presented him with jeweled swords, which in accepting he pledged to the service of the State should they ever be needed."[12]

The services of Van Dorn, who was a reported "ardent advocate of the right of secession," were needed and offered when Mississippi became the second Southern state to secede from the United States. The veteran of the Mexican War then resigned from the United States Army and offered his military experience to the state of Mississippi. Van Dorn served as a brigadier general and major general in command of Mississippi State troops, his rank changed when his tenure with the Confederate States of America began. In March 1861 Earl Van Dorn was given the rank of colonel and started his service to the Confederacy. One historian issued the statement related to Van Dorn, "His record for bravery and daring in the Mexican War and in fighting the Seminoles and Comanches led to high expectations."[13]

Mixed opinions were given in regard to Earl Van Dorn's persona. Confederate officer Dabney Maury wrote, "He craved glory beyond everything." A biographer described Van Dorn as a "rash young commander with a one-dimensional mind." Another stated that Van Dorn's "dashing manners and courage led most people to overlook his faults, which were egregious. Bold beyond prudence, he had no patience with reconnaissance, staff work, logistics, or anything else that might keep him from closing quickly with the enemy."[14]

An 1861 description of Earl Van Dorn came from a Virginia reporter. The correspondent noted, "The General is rather undersized, of a spare frame, erect and graceful in his movements; his mustache is long but light; otherwise he is closely shaven, which is one cause of his youthful appearance.[15]

Colonel Earl Van Dorn received instructions regarding his Confederate duties on April 11, 1861. The officer was ordered to "intercept and prevent the movement of the United States troops from the State of Texas." His official assignment in the Department of Texas lasted from April 21 to September 4, 1861. In turn, an early success for Van Dorn took place, as he led the capture of some eight hundred fifteen men and officers. Some of the private soldiers, by some accounts, remained prisoners for two years. The property and supplies Colonel Van Dorn managed to capture were reportedly valued at $1,209,500 and included "mules, wagons, horses, harness, tools, corn, clothing, commissary and ordnance stores."[16]

The success of Colonel Earl Van Dorn's Texas escapades contributed to a promotion in rank. In June 1861 Earl Van Dorn received the designation of brigadier general in service of the Confederate States of America. With that rank, Brigadier General Van Dorn commanded Forts St. Philip and Jackson in the New Orleans vicinity.[17] Another promotion was soon to come for the man who had made a name for himself in the Mexican War, fighting against the Seminoles, and exhibiting potential in the early months of the American Civil War.

Earl Van Dorn's appearance in battle was described in the words of Major General Dabney Maury. Major General Maury recalled, "He used to ride a beautiful by Andalusian horse, and as he came galloping along the lines, with his yellow hair waving in the wind and his bright face lighted with kindliness and courage...his figure was lithe and graceful, his stature did not exceed five feet eight inches, but his clear blue eyes, his firm set mouth, with white strong teeth, his well-cut nose...gave assurance of a man whom men could trust and follow."[18]

By the early days of 1862, Van Dorn held the rank of major general in the Confederate Army, having attained that rank in September 1861. Major General Earl Van Dorn was sent to Virginia and briefly commanded the First Division of the Confederate Army of the Potomac, serving there from October 4 through January 1862. On January 10, 1862 Confederate President Jefferson Davis appointed Major General Van Dorn to lead the Trans-Mississippi Military District. Interestingly, Confederate generals Braxton Bragg and Henry Heth had both declined earlier offers to hold the same responsibility. Having accepted the post, Van Dorn made his headquarters in Pocahontas, Arkansas. From that location Major General Earl Van Dorn made it clear that he intended to conduct a raid into Missouri. The plan was made more evident with Van Dorn's declaration to his wife, "I must have St. Louis!"[19]

In moving toward the Boston Mountains Major General Van Dorn literally fell into the Little Red River; the result was a fever that hampered him during the Pea Ridge Campaign. On March 2, 1862 Van Dorn arrived with his command that he had renamed the Army of the West. In addition, Van Dorn called for Albert Pike's Indian troops to avoid the treaties that specifically stated they would not serve outside the borders of the Indian Territory.[20] With a force of some sixteen thousand troops and sixty-five cannon, Van Dorn prepared to attack the Federal troops at Pea Ridge, Arkansas, a battle that would also be known as Elkhorn Tavern.

Colonel Thomas Snead held different ranks and unit assignments during the American Civil War. In serving as the Adjutant-General of the Missouri State Guard, Chief-of-Staff of the Army of the West, and also a member of the Confederate Congress, he was able to have intermittent contact with Major General Van Dorn. In that set of positions, Snead remarked that Van Dorn "unwisely divided his army, and leaving McCulloch with his own command and Pike's to attack Curtis in front, himself made with Price and the Missourians a long circuit to the rear of

Curtis, and out of communication with McCulloch...morning revealed the enemy in a new and strong position, their forces united and offering battle...Van Dorn ordered a retreat."[21]

Evaluating Van Dorn's performance and leadership at Pea Ridge, one historian wrote, "Van Dorn was a poor choice...impulsive, reckless, and lacked administrative skills." Little argument can be made against this statement as the major generals venture into the waters and mountains of Arkansas had resulted in the illness of almost one-fourth of his sixteen thousand troops. Additionally, Pea Ridge had cost him another two thousand troops killed, wounded, and missing. General McCulloch was among the dead, and General Sterling Price was "wounded and narrowly escaped death."[22]

A more positive evaluation of Van Dorn came from Major General Franz Sigel, a Federal commander at Pea Ridge. Sigel stated, "It was... fortunate for the Confederates that...Van Dorn was appointed...to the command of the Trans-Mississippi Department, and that he took charge of the combined forces about to confront Curtis."[23]

Sigel also commented that, while Pea Ridge was not a battle in the caliber of Gettysburg or Chattanooga in respect to the territory or foothold the Federals gained, "it virtually cleared the Southwest of [Confederates]... and made it possible...[for the Federal army]to reinforce "the armies under Buell, Rosecrans, Grant, and Sherman...Van Dorn was...surprised when he found his plan to take St. Louis...was anticipated...was greatly surprised to find himself...attacked in front and rear and compelled to retreat."[24]

Pea Ridge resulted in a great deal of dislike, even disdain, for Van Dorn, particularly on the part of the soldiers in his command. One historian noted that in the aftermath of Pea Ridge, "Van Dorn's stock plummeted...men muttered threats of mutiny and ridiculed Van Dorn openly. In an apparent means of reassuring himself, Van Dorn wrote to Albert Sidney Johnston from his camp along the Arkansas River and stated that at Pea Ridge, "I was not defeated, but only failed in my intentions." However, as would also happen after loss at Corinth, Major General Earl Van Dorn was accused of failing to plan his campaign satisfactorily, and he was said to have neglected his duties and his troops, as well as showing no regard for their welfare.[25]

Unfortunately, for Major General Earl Van Dorn and the Confederate soldiers in his command, the loss at Pea Ridge was a predecessor to another Southern defeat at Corinth, Mississippi. In a post-battle account of the engagement he waged at the Southern rail center, Van Dorn explained his rationale for moving against Corinth. With his field returns estimating his strength at twenty-two thousand men, and the Federals of General William Rosecrans reportedly at fifteen thousand troops, and an additional eight thousand twelve to fifteen miles from Corinth, Van Dorn determined an attack upon Corinth was logical.[26]

Major General Van Dorn also noted, "...the taking of Corinth was a condition precedent to the accomplishment of anything of importance in west Tennessee. To take Memphis would be to destroy an immense amount of property without any adequate military advantage...The line of fortifications around Bolivar is intersected by the Hatchie River, rendering it impossible to take the place by quick assault...if a successful attack could be made upon Corinth from the west and north-west...Bolivar and Jackson would easily fall...west Tennessee would soon be in our possession...I determined to attempt Corinth..."[27]

The Army of West Tennessee, under Major General Earl Van Dorn's command at Corinth, contained Major General Sterling Price's Corps. Brigadier Generals Louis Hebert and Martin Green led the First Division of Price's Corps, while Brigadier General Dabney Maury's three-brigade division added additional manpower. Major General Mansfield Lovell's First Division contained another three infantry brigades, as well as a cavalry brigade, and Brigadier General Frank Armstrong's Cavalry and Hoxton's Tennessee Battery rounded out the men at Van Dorn's disposal.[28]

Regarding the positive situation provided at various times during the first days' fighting at Corinth on October 3, 1862, Van Dorn remarked, "I had been in hopes that one days' operations would end the contest and decide who should be the victors on this bloody field; but a ten miles' march over a parched country on dusty roads without water, getting into line of battle in forests with undergrowth, and the more than equal activity and determined courage displayed by the enemy, commanded by one of the ablest generals of the United States army, who threw all possible obstacles in our way that an active mind could suggest, prolonged the battle until I saw with great regret the sun sink behind the horizon...One more hour of daylight and victory would have soothed our grief for the loss of the gallant dead who sleep on that lost but not dishonored field..."[29]

After the subsequent failure of the Confederates to push the Federals from their strong position on the second day of battle at Corinth, Major General Van Dorn wrote, "A hand-to-hand contest was being enacted in the very yard of General Rosecrans' headquarters and in the streets of the town...A heavy fire from fresh troops...poured into our thinned ranks. Exhausted from loss of sleep, wearied from hard marching and fighting, companies and regiments without officers, our troops, let no one censure them, gave way. The day was lost..."[30]

Major General Earl Van Dorn's Confederates reported their losses from the action at Corinth as five hundred five killed, two thousand one hundred fifty wounded, and approximately two thousand two hundred missing. Historian Peter Cozzens theorized that since Van Dorn had counted on a Corinth victory to "erase the stigma of Pea Ridge," the resulting loss had left him "near collapse." Additionally, Cozzens remarked, Corinth had wrecked Van Dorn's military career.[31]

Rumors abound that Major General Earl Van Dorn had been drunk at Corinth. The conversations that took place after the battle and contained his name seldom revealed positive comments in relation to Van Dorn. A Mobile, Alabama newspaper contained the statement that the general had been lured into a trap and "made to fight against heavy odds without the hope of any advantage for this waste of blood and life."[32]

Sadly, Mississippi Senator James Phelan lambasted Major General Van Dorn by telling Confederate President Jefferson Davis, "The army is in a most deplorable state...called 'Van Dorn's Army', and the universal opprobrium which covers that officer and the 'lower than the lowest depth' to which he has fallen in the estimation of the community of all classes, you cannot be aware of."[33]

Earl Van Dorn informed his wife Emily that "All that valor attempted was won but the enemy was too strong for us...I have lost nothing...Do not be mortified at what they say..." In contrast, another individual penned, "Van Dorn's incompetence...turned the battles of Elkhorn Tavern...and Corinth...into important Union victories."[34]

In the meanwhile, Major General John Pemberton received the recommendation of President Davis, as well as the Confederate Senate's confirmation, to assume command of the Department of Mississippi and East Louisiana. As such, Pemberton was placed in charge of Major General Earl Van Dorn, a situation that contributed with the recent resounding defeats and sent the Mississippian into a state of depression.[35]

From November 7 to November 28, 1862, a court of inquiry investigated Major General Earl Van Dorn's conduct in the Corinth fiasco. A host of witnesses for and against his conduct during the campaign offered emotional testimony regarding the general. The final defense witness was Van Dorn himself. Van Dorn stated, "I am a Mississippian...My blood has always been ready for her, yet in the midst of my struggles for her, my name has been blighted by her people. My trust is that the investigation of this court will vindicate it from dishonor."[36]

The court, with Lloyd Tilghman, Dabney Maury, and Sterling Price in judgment, found Major General Earl Van Dorn innocent of any allegations against his leadership flaws. In an act of celebration, Van Dorn paid for the printing and circulation of one thousand pamphlets that contained the proceedings of the recent trial.[37]

A comment on the long-term effects of Major General Earl Van Dorn's loss at Corinth, Mississippi was provided in an article from Colonel Thomas Snead. The officer remarked, "The disastrous defeat of Van Dorn at Corinth in October 1862 opened the way for Ulysses Grant to move overland against Vicksburg."[38] In an effort to make amends for the disaster at Corinth, Van Dorn, with incentive with others, planned to strike the Federal supply base at Holly Springs, a location that was being used as a stockpile area for Grant.

In the aftermath of the Corinth defeat, Lieutenant Colonel John Griffith of the 6th Texas formed a petition, with the support of other Confederate officers, and sent it to General John Pemberton. The purpose of the petition, according to a veteran of Van Dorn's brigade, was to seek Pemberton's permission for Major General Van Dorn "to organize a cavalry raid for the purpose of operating in General Grant's rear, and to place General Van Dorn in command of it."[39] The event that lay ahead would arguably become the pinnacle of Van Dorn's Civil War career.

S. B. Barron was with Major General Earl Van Dorn in the early stages of the preparation for the raid on Holly Springs. Barron recalled, "...in light marching order, without artillery, we left the vicinity of Grenada soon after dark on the night of December 18, and, moving rapidly all night... passed Pontotoc next day, when the good ladies stood on the streets with dishes, baskets, and waiters filled with all manner of good things to eat." Barron noted that the hungry Confederates grasped the foodstuffs from the ladies without slowing down.[40]

The subsequent moves of Major General Van Dorn's command were remembered, "In going north from Pontotoc...instead of taking the Holly Springs road, passed all Holly Springs roads, going east of that place... headed the column toward Bolivar, Tenn., so the Federals concluded that we were aiming to attack Bolivar. Stopping long enough to feed at night, we remounted our horses, and by a quiet movement and countermarching during the night were placed on the roads leading to Holly Springs."[41]

Having divided the force into two parts, Major General Earl Van Dorn used what was described as a rough and seldom used road. A Confederate who served with Van Dorn at Holly Springs remembered the events of the raid in writing, "At day dawn, being perhaps three miles from town, we struck a gallop, which was soon increased to full speed...pouring into the infantry camps near the railroad depot...infantry soon came running out of their tents in their night clothes, held up their hands, and surrendered without firing a gun."[42]

The Confederate veteran continued remarking on the Holly Springs raid that served as the bright spot on the mixed successes of Earl Van Dorn's Civil War record by noting, "And so on this bright frosty morning, December 20, 1862, the town, with its immense stores of army supplies, was ours...a long train of box cars loaded with rations and clothing for the army at the front...waiting to get up steam enough to pull out. This was burned where it stood and the engine crippled."[43]

The citizens of Holly Springs, Mississippi realized it was Major General Van Dorn's Confederates who were arriving, and the town's residents were "wild with joy." Reportedly the ladies regularly "in their night robes came running out of their houses...long hair streaming...shouting and clasping their hands." One account declared that the female residents of Holly Springs forgot everything other than Confederates had come to town and began shouting, "Hurrah for Jeff Davis! Hurrah for Van Dorn! Hurray for the Confederacy!"[44]

The reward Major General Earl Van Dorn and his Confederates

received at Holly Springs was described in a report of the raid. The writer said, "A mere glance at the stores, heaps upon heaps of clothing, blankets, provisions, arms, ammunition, medicine, and hospital supplies for the winter, for the use and comfort of a vast army was overwhelming to us… every available space that could be used, was packed full to overflowing… For about ten hours we labored… destroying, burning this property, and in order to do this effectually we had to burn a good many houses…wagons and ambulances were cut down and burned."[45]

A participant's comments on the success of the raid noted that some one thousand five hundred Federals were captured and paroled. Van Dorn estimated approximately one and a half million dollars of property was destroyed at Holly Springs, while General Ulysses Grant valued the losses at less than one-third that amount. Perhaps that discrepancy could be clarified with an evaluation from a Confederate who proposed, "Doubtless one was too high and the other too low."[46]

W. H. Loving was with Van Dorn in the Holly Springs raid, and Loving offered praise for the success of the event, and he gave credit for the victory to the Mississippi general. Loving reminisced, "Gen. Earl Van Dorn…planned and executed that grand victory…that has no parallel in the history of the world. General Van Dorn, with less than two thousand poorly mounted and poorly equipped soldiers, defeated an army flushed with many victories…The raid was a success in every detail."[47]

Additional comments on the accomplishments of Van Dorn's successful raid on the supply base at Holly Springs came from a participant in the endeavor. The individual stated, "We destroyed the army stores of every kind…captured the infantry…had a hand to hand fight with the cavalry in the old fair ground, defeating them. They retreated in great disorder…"[48]

A critic of Van Dorn reluctantly made a positive, but seemingly sarcastic, comment on the general in noting, "For the only time during the war Van Dorn was properly matched to an assignment." From January 13, 1863 until his death, Major General Earl Van Dorn served in various cavalry units in the Army of the Department of Mississippi and East Louisiana as well as the Army of Tennessee.[49]

The last major contribution Major General Earl Van Dorn made to the Confederate effort took place at Thompson's Station, Tennessee in early March of 1863. Utilizing Brigadier Generals W. H. Jackson and Nathan

Bedford Forrest, Van Dorn managed to obtain the surrender of Federal Colonel John Coburn's wagon train and several thousand troops.[50]

Aside from the aforementioned skills as an artist and his performance when riding a horse, Earl Van Dorn was also described as a poet. However, an oft-discussed and scrutinized characteristic that had been attached to Earl Van Dorn since his days at West Point was his fondness, if not an obsession, of women. A period reporter had even labeled the Confederate general as "the terror of ugly husbands."[51]

Strong evidence exists that Earl Van Dorn may have had a second family, sired during his years spent in Texas. Martha Goodbread and Van Dorn allegedly had three children, two sons and one daughter. The sons were presumably born in 1857 and 1860, while the daughter was said to have arrived in 1858.[52] The rumors of affairs and a second family eventually cost Major General Earl Van Dorn more than he likely imagined.

Van Dorn had established his headquarters in Spring Hill, Tennessee. There, as at other locations in his past, it was reported that the general was spending his spare time in the company of women. During his lengthy time in Spring Hill Major General Van Dorn had been rumored to be exhibiting a strong interest in twenty-five year-old Jessie McKissack Peters, the wife of a doctor. Gossip was wide-spread that Mrs. Peters and Van Dorn had been seen riding in her carriage, and that the two had spent several nights together while Doctor Peters was out of town.[53]

On May 7, 1863, Major General Earl Van Dorn met his death at the hand of the jealous doctor. Van Dorn was reportedly alone in his office in the Matt Cheairs's home, and Dr. Peters entered the room and fired a fatal shot into Van Dorn's head. There are conflicting accounts that the two men had exchanged heated words or that there may have been threats from Van Dorn to the doctor. In addition, Dr. Peters exclaimed that Van Dorn had "violated the sanctity" of the Peters home.[54]

Additional insight into the circumstances surrounding Van Dorn's murder appeared in a 1911 *Confederate Veteran* article. The author of that piece wrote, "General Van Dorn…was planning to retake Nashville and cross the Ohio into Cincinnati. For two weeks a cavalry force encamped at Spring Hill, Tenn., where preparations for this campaign were daily being made… the movement was about ready."[55]

Turning to the aspect of Dr. Peters, the author of the *Confederate*

Veteran article noted, "A physician living near, accustomed to riding through the country on passports from the commanding officers, was known to be a Union man. He had lost his property on the Arkansas side of the Mississippi River, and he remarked that he would soon recover it. To remove, the daring and alert commander...that was to carry out the obvious plan...for the movement upon Nashville, he saw his opportunity and acted accordingly."[56]

Dr. Peters's assassination of General Van Dorn was summarized, "Feigning darker and baseless reasons, under the pretest of obtaining a passport to the country, he entered the room of General Van Dorn and asked for a passport. Moving back of the table on which the general was writing, he shot the unsuspecting officer in the back of the head and fled."[57]

A comment on the effect of Major General Earl Van Dorn's death came from M. W. Searcy, a one-time member of the general's Confederate command. Searcy said, "The death of General Van Dorn was a serious blow to the Confederate cause, as he was one of the most brilliant cavalry commanders on either side and a perfect soldier in every detail."[58]

S. B. Barron was another Confederate, and he had joined Van Dorn in the career highlight at Holly Springs. Remaining with the general until the latter's death at Spring Hill. Barron wrote, "In his memory, and speaking from the experience and observation of four years' service under various commanders, I will say that a more gallant soldier than Earl Van Dorn was never found in any army, and as a cavalry commander, I do not believe he had a superior."[59]

Other comments regarding Major General Earl Van Dorn's death were not as complimentary. One account stated, "The country has sustained no loss in the death...He was unfit to live..." Another commented, "He was never at his post when he ought to be. He was either tied to a woman's apron strings or heated with wine." Lastly, a soldier wrote to his wife, "General Van Dorn was killed...for tampering with a fellow's wife. If that be the case he was served right."[60]

A set of words of praise for Van Dorn came from General W. H. Jackson's General Order No. 3. Jackson pronounced, "Upon the battlefield, he was indeed the very personification of courage and chivalry...none was ever more generous and humane to the sufferers...As a commanding officer he was warmly beloved and highly respected...his social qualities were of the rarest order and for goodness of heart he had no superior. His deeds have rendered his name worthy to be enrolled beside the proudest in the Confederate Capitol and will ever be fondly cherished in the hearts of his command."[61]

The fact that Port Gibson, Mississippi was Federally-occupied at the time of Van Dorn's death resulted in his original burial place being in the family plot of his in-laws. The Godbold Cemetery in Mount Vernon, Alabama was the location where the general's daughter served as the major mourner, as his "wife being too prostrated with grief to leave her room."[62]

In November 1899 Earl Van Dorn's sister, Emily Miller, and her son oversaw the disinterment of the general's body. The corpse was transferred aboard a train to Port Gibson, Mississippi. Upon arrival the casket was opened and a discussion related to the high level of preservation took place. Major General Earl Van Dorn was then reburied at the Wintergreen Cemetery in Port Gibson, Mississippi. His grave is beside that of his father.[63]

EDWARD CAREY WALTHALL, C.S.A.

1831-1898

Edward Carey Walthall was born in Richmond, Virginia on April 4, 1831. Eight years after his birth Walthall's family, reportedly "seeking to repair reverses of fortune," moved Holly Springs, Mississippi. In Holly Springs the Walthall's had a lifestyle recalled as, "Idyllic, wealth, leisure, inspiration, the grand old mansions where upper class Southern life was lived..."[1]

Walthall's primary education took place in Holly Springs, and one biographer noted that he had a "limited education, but with rare natural gifts and high practice." Another writer contradicted that point and stated that Edward Carey Walthall attended a Holly Springs military school known as St. Thomas Hall. At St. Thomas, Walthall reportedly had future Confederate generals Kit Mott and James Chalmers as two of his classmates.[2]

Walthall later studied law in a manner sufficient enough to secure admission to the bar in 1852. That same year his successful studies and dedication paid off, and he secured a license and began to practice law in Coffeeville, Mississippi. Walthall's law career was lucrative from the onset; and, in 1856, he was elected District Attorney of the Mississippi Tenth

Judicial District. In 1859 he was reelected to the post and held it until the onset of the American Civil War.[3]

A soldier who later served under Edward Carey Walthall's command recalled the sacrifices Walthall made in order to join the Confederate military. E. A. Smith joined the 29th Mississippi Infantry Regiment, a unit that would eventually be in the brigade Walthall commanded in the early phase of the war. Smith wrote that Walthall, "...was a young lawyer in Coffeeville...rising rapidly in...his profession...had he not laid aside his pen for the sword, would much sooner have reached the eminent distinction to which he afterwards attained."[4]

A late 1800's biography of Walthall recorded the ensuing events, "He resigned that office in the spring of 1861, and entered the Confederate service as a lieutenant in the Fifteenth Mississippi Regiment...[he] was soon afterward elected lieutenant colonel..." With that rank, Lieutenant Colonel Walthall was in command of the 15th Mississippi Infantry Regiment.[5]

The early stages of Walthall's service in the Confederate Army were recorded in a 1904 *Confederate Veteran* article. E. A. Smith wrote, "He was a natural born soldier, and entered that splendid regiment, the Fifteenth Mississippi, first with the rank of lieutenant, whence he rose to that of captain, then to that of lieutenant colonel."[6]

The 15th Mississippi Infantry Regiment, with Lieutenant Colonel Walthall leading, was initiated into the bloodshed at Fishing Creek, Kentucky, "where the fall, through treachery, of the lamented Zollicoffer threw the Confederate forces into confusion." A post-war article stated that the Confederates at Mill Springs, a name by which the Fishing Creek engagement was also known, "were only saved from disaster by the gallant stand of the Fifteenth under the rally and superior military ability of" Lieutenant Colonel Edward Carey Walthall.[7]

An article of the period recalled Walthall's conduct in the battle, "His first baptism was at Fishing Creek, Ky...In the midst of disaster and confusion, Lieut. Col. Walthall, in the absence of his colonel, took conspicuous part in the battle, and brought off his regiment in almost perfect order. The promise of military genius there displayed was afterward more than fulfilled."[8]

During a Confederate charge at Mill Springs, the flag of the Yalobusha Rifles, a company in the 15th Mississippi, was captured. The silk flag bore the inscription of the company's name, and had been a gift from the ladies of Coffeeville. Colonel James R. Binford of the 15th Mississippi reminisced, "We were receiving the fire from troops we thought were Confederates, and Col. Walthall placed the flag on a cabin to…show them who we were. We soon discovered our mistake…Col. Walthall ordered a charge, and in the hurry and excitement, it being our first engagement, we left the flag on the cabin."[9]

The company flag's story did not end then, as Binford added, "…advancing…and driving the enemy in our front, the Tenth Indiana Regiment moved around in our rear, and…was in line very near the spot where we had left our flag." In the early 1900s the flag was offered to the survivors of the company when Daniel Neal, the captor of the flag, passed away.[10]

The loss of the flag was not the most tragic event of Mill Springs. In addition to the loss of General Zollicoffer, the Confederates endured a great deal of casualties. Walthall's regiment, the 15th Mississippi, suffered casualties of two hundred twenty-seven soldiers of the four hundred fifty who entered the battle. It was noted that that rate of killed, wounded, and missing was forty-five percent, a significantly high number for any unit during the entire war.[11]

Following his performance in the Battle of Fishing Creek, Lieutenant Colonel Walthall reportedly, "…received a commission from the War Department to organize a regiment." In turn, Walthall resigned from the 15th Mississippi, "hurried home and soon organized the Twenty Ninth [Infantry Regiment Regiment]."[12]

During the spring of 1862, Walthall was elected colonel of the 29th Mississippi Infantry Regiment, and he continued serving in Kentucky. Colonel Walthall took part in the "desperate and much criticized assault upon Munfordville, where so many valiant Mississippians found bloody graves…"[13]

In December 1862, Walthall received a promtion to the rank of brigadier general. The 24th, 27th, 29th, 30th, and 34th Mississippi Infantry Regiments compiled the brigade that Brigadier General Walthall commanded at that stage of the War Between the States. A record of the brigade stated that the unit was "known to the end of the war as Walthall's Brigade." The same recollection noted that Walthall's brigade's fighting record was "unsurpassed by any other command of the Western army."[14]

Perhaps the success of Walthall's brigade can best be attributed to the respect his men held for him. A member of the unit remarked that Brigadier General Walthall, "Asked no advice and took none. A rigid disciplinarian and intolerant of any deficiencies of conduct, he was beloved by his men. Though he fought them with dash and spirit, it was always with care and skill. His men gave to him their confidence from start to finish, accepted his orders, and fought without reproach or the slightest question of the danger incurred."[15]

In November 1863, Brigadier General Walthall arrived at Missionary Ridge. The regiments in his command on the afternoon of November 25 were under the leadership of two colonels and one each of a major, a captain, and a lieutenant. Walthall led his troops to Missionary Ridge where they aligned on the right of Cheatham's Division, a major segment of Hardee's Corps. Union troops managed to gain a foothold and pushed back two Confederate brigades from Cheatham's Division as they attempted to slow the onslaught from the men in blue. Walthall's brigade realigned itself at a right angle to where it had originally set up, and stood strong against the Federal advance. The intense fire lasted past dark, at which time Walthall withdrew his troops to Chickamauga Station.[16]

Brigadier General Walthall used the men of his brigade and another to hold Lookout Mountain "against...heavy corps during the whole day and far into the night, inflicting serious loss, as, rock by rock, he yielded a position untenable before such superior numbers...on Missionary Ridge, he did not withdraw until after support had been driven from right and left, and, although painfully wounded, being disabled for many weeks afterward, kept his saddle until after nightfall, when the army withdrew in an orderly manner."[17]

Brigadier General Walthall reported on Lookout Mountain, where his brigade "bore a conspicuous part in that misunderstood battle." Walthall stated, "The battle above the clouds, the explanation of this poetic name... is found that during most of the day...a dense fog enveloped the sides of the mountain and hung in the valley...obscuring the view from below..."[18]

General Walthall readily gave credit to his comrades in noting, "Gen. Pettus came to my support with three regiments...to save the position, which my depleted command, whose ammunition was exhausted, would very soon have been forced to yield."[18]

At Chickamauga, Walthall and his command were primarily part of a reserve division, but they were also involved in the early stages of the battle at Alexander's Bridge. It was said of Walthall's command, "This brigade...capture[d] a battery early in the engagement...no individual command contributed more in securing the victory than the Mississippians."[20]

In June 1864, Walthall was promoted to the rank of major general. In that capacity, Major General Walthall led a division in General John Bell Hood's Army into Tennessee.[21] The effects of that campaign were devastating to Hood's Army and arguably cast the outcome of the war for the beleaguered Confederates.

As a major general, Walthall was "assigned to a division composed of D. H. Reynolds' Arkansas Brigade, Canty's Alabama Brigade, and Quarles's Tennessee Brigade...a stranger to every officer and soldier in the division when he came to it, his splendid presence and military bearing at once secured the admiration of his new command..."[22]

In 1903, a writer offered insight into Major General Walthall's leadership, "Walthall was a knightly leader among unpaid and starving soldiers whose banners only went down in the smoke of battle...He was regarded by his friends and political enemies alike as the embodiment of every sentiment which out to make the ideal statesman and soldier."[23]

Major General Walthall's conduct in battle was recalled in an article written after his death. It stated, "Whenever he waved his sword, galloped to the front, and called on his men to charge, they caught the inspiration of his sublime fearlessness, and with the wild Rebel yell followed him into the very jaws of death."[24]

With the Confederate forces engaged in a retreat created with the heavy losses at Franklin, where Major General Walthall had two horses shot from under him, and Nashville, Walthall, "was assigned to the command of a meager force of eight skeleton brigades, numbering three thousand men, charged with the duty of covering the retreat." Many of the participants feared that serving in the capacity of rear guard in such a dire condition meant certain capture for Major General Walthall and the men of his division.[25]

It was said that Major General Walthall, who met a member of Hood's staff at the Nimrod Porter home, "...made the prompt and characteristic reply, 'Make your order Gen. Hood. I never sought a hard place for glory nor a soft place for comfort.' With the assistance of Forrest...the shattered army, with all of its trains, and also the protecting rear guard...reached the south bank of the Tennessee [River] in safety."[26]

At the time, Edward Carey Walthall was the youngest major general in Hood's army, and he had reportedly been concerned that his senior officers "may complain that the place was not offered to them." Only the reassurance of General Nathan Bedford Forrest's desire to serve with Walthall led Walthall to endeavor to perform the task which he so successfully completed.[27]

Accolades for Major General Walthall's performance also came from an adversary. General Thomas stated, "He had formed a powerful rear guard...With the exception of his rear guard...army had become disheartened and a disorganized rabble of half armed and barefooted men who sought opportunity to...desert...The rear guard, however, was undaunted and firm, and did its work bravely..."[28]

Another statement of praise for Walthall's stand during the retreat from Nashville, said, "Walthall with his incomparable infantry, together with the magnificent cavalry and artillery under Forrest, saved Hood's army from annihilation and enabled...escape..."[29]

E. W. Tarrant was an artilleryman at Nashville. He recalled an incident in the December 15, 1864 action prior to the retreat. Tarrant wrote that he was "in command of two...guns stationed on an eminence... with no infantry support...we discovered that our forces on the left were falling back in great disorder...our ammunition was almost exhausted...a courier..." ordered Tarrant and his fellow artillerymen to limber his guns and make for safety.[30]

Aware that the wheel horses for one of his guns had been killed, Tarrant made the decision to spike one gun and move another to the rear. He described his encounter with Walthall, "It had not gone more than a hundred yards when one of the wheel horses was shot down...and the gun brought to a dead halt...I spiked it and pushed on to get together with my scattered men...Seeing Gen. Walthall...I rode alongside and, saluting him, said, 'General, I held my position until I was ordered to retire, but it was too late to save my guns.' Instead of getting a withering rebuke...he in the kindest manner possible consoled me for my loss, and said...that

I had done everything that a man could do, and that he had no fault to find with me."[31]

Major General Walthall's last engagement of the war took place at Cole's Farm, near Bentonville, North Carolina. One of his corps commanders described the battle, "The enemy, in overwhelming numbers, was upon us...Walthall's Division, at the edge of an open field...[went] forward to the encounter. It was an inspiring sight...to see their intrepid commander, in whom all had unbounded confidence, towering above them on his own horse, advancing under a shower of bullets into the storm of battle. The enemy gave way before their invincible attacks."[32]

J. M. Dunn of Company F, 29th Mississippi, paid a tribute to Major General Walthall, "We followed him as a colonel, as brigadier general, and as major general...A braver man, a truer man...never wore the honors... As an illustration...after the war...when he would meet with any of his old regiment, he would say, 'You boys served me faithfully during the war, in return, if any of you need the services of an attorney, I am yours to command without charge.'"[33]

After the war, Walthall returned to Coffeeville and resumed his law practice. Walthall later moved to Grenada, Mississippi and served as the general attorney for the Mississippi Central Railroad Company. A biographer noted that Walthall was able to see the rail line become part of a larger system and, "he took rank with the great corporation lawyers of the day."[34]

Walthall had attended every National Democratic Convention from 1868 through 1885, but he had never sought nor attempted to hold any political office. That set of circumstances changed when Walthall's longtime friend, Senator Lucius Quintus Cincinnatus Lamar, was appointed Secretary of the Interior in President Cleveland's cabinet. Lamar's assignment created a Senate vacancy. Mississippi Governor Lowry determined Walthall should hold the Senate seat. On March 12, 1885, Senator Walthall began his service in the U. S. Senate.[35]

Senator Walthall's service to his fellow Mississippians appeared in an 1898 *Confederate Veteran* article. The author said, "This seat he held by successive elections, without opposition, to the day of his death, with the exception of fourteen months of one term, when he resigned, because of ill health, but returned to his place the following year."[36]

In the years of his service in Congress, Walthall served on a number of committees. Those included the Revolutionary Claims, of which he was chairman in 1897, and Military Affairs, which he chaired in 1893. He was also on the Civil Service and Retrenchment, Education and Labor, Public Lands, and Indian Depredations Committees. Others included Improvement of the Mississippi and its Tributaries and the Organization, Conduct and Expenditures of the Executive Department. The 1890 Federal Elections Bill, also known as the Force Bill, sought to protect the suffrage of Freedmen through threat of federal supervision.[37]

The last official Senatorial act of Walthall's career was his delivery of a eulogy for J. Z. George, a colleague of Walthall's in the 1890 Federal Elections Bill. Little did the who witnesses of that day know Walthall would share the same fate as George in less than two weeks.[38]

Senator Edward Carey Walthall passed away in Washington, D. C. on April 21, 1898. A memorial service took place at the same location where he had given George's eulogy. The President, members of the Senate, House of Representatives, and the Supreme Court attended the ceremony before the transfer of Walthall's remains. His body was returned to Holly Springs, where a massive funeral took place at Christ Episcopal Church. An article said, "The funeral train brought, besides the family, the Congressional delegation of eight Senators, six Congressmen, several judges, and a host of others honored in Mississippi and in the nation. Another train brought three hundred and fifty citizens of Yalobusha County. A vast procession... followed the hearse. Among them were many of his old brigade..."[39]

Bishop Thompson conducted the funeral service and said, "The great white light that beats upon the throne and blackens every blot had found not one blot upon Gen. Walthall's character. He was open, manly, frank, absolutely sincere, and was ever beyond the reach of fear or flattery."[40]

Evidence of the admiration Walthall held among his constituents is shown in the words of an obituary, "His standing and influence and the personal esteem in which he was held...evidenced by the fact that he was the first of the Senators from the South after the war to be honored with the appointment of chairman of the Senate Committee on Military Affairs. Superb in his mental, moral, and physical endowments, he had no occasion for ambitions."[41]

The obituary continued, "With a cool head and a warm heart, fully equipped, when duties were laid upon him he discharged them with courage and promptness. When honors were bestowed, he wore them with dignity and grace." Lamenting Walthall's passing, a writer penned, "He rests where his childhood and youth were spent, under the dews that make green the graves of his kindred...With him there was no blot to darken, no reflection that did not give back warmth and radiance. He was true to all the ties that make home sacred, to all the bonds that guard friendship as a treasure, to all the duties that in their fulfillment ennoble life."[42]

Senator and Presidential Cabinet member L. Q. C. Lamar praised Walthall in saying, "Of all the great men Mississippi has produced, Gen. Walthall stands out in boldest relief, in moral purity, strength of mind, heroism of soul, and commanding influences among men." Massachusetts Senator George Hoar added, "If I were to select the man of all others with I have served in the Senate, who seemed to me to be the most perfect example of the quality and character of the American Senator, I think it would be Edward C. Walthall, of Mississippi." Hoar concluded, "He was a very modest man...When he did speak the Senate listened to a man of great ability, eloquence, and dignity."[43]

Edward Carey Walthall was buried in Hill Crest Cemetery in Holly Springs, Mississippi. Mary Leckie Walthall, his beloved wife, died on December 10, less than eight months after her husband. She is buried beside him.[44]

In 1902 Mrs. John B. Ross, Walthall's daughter, presented a flag to the survivors of Walthall's brigade. The lone survivor of the general stated, "A younger generation has grown up since you soldiers wore the gray, and fought beneath the folds of the Southern Cross, but we know that your hearts are as warm as ever, and that the impulses of early manhood and loyal friendships will throb in your bosoms as long as life itself."[45]

A 1904 *Confederate Veteran* article announced that General E. T. Sykes, a member of Walthall's wartime staff, had completed the text for book about Walthall. The article noted, "This work was given him by Gen. Walthall...to be written and published after his death, and Gen. Sykes regarded the request as a sacred trust." The intended dedication of the book was the friends and survivors of Walthall's Brigade.[46] The manuscript was published in 1916.

In 1910, Walthall County, Mississippi was created from portions of Marion and Pike Counties. Named for the Confederate general, the county contains four hundred four square miles; the town of Tylertown serves as the county seat.[47] In keeping with Walthall's contributions to the Confederate States of America, a Sons of Confederate Veterans Camp in Grenada, Mississippi bears the name of Edward Carey Walthall.

THOSE WITH NOTEWORTHY MISSISSIPPI CONNECTIONS

DANIEL WEISIGER ADAMS (1821-1872)

Known as Dan among his friends and family, Daniel Weisiger Adams was born to George and Anna Weisiger Adams on May 1, 1821. Accounts differ as to the precise location of his birth, with both Frankfort, Kentucky and Lynchburg, Virginia being listed on various accounts of the event. His brother was William Wirt Adams. The boys' family moved to Mississippi while Daniel was a youngster, and he later used the setting as a location to read law. He also gained an education at the University of Virginia and, having passed the bar, began practicing law in Louisiana.[1]

Dan Adams joined a group of his fellow Louisiana citizens in objecting to the 1860 election of Abraham Lincoln as President. Initially serving on the military board for the state of Louisiana, Adams left the position in order to serve in the First Louisiana Infantry Regiment. Adams eventually rose to the rank of lieutenant in the Confederate Army and, in 1862, brigadier general. While he saw action at locations such as Mobile, Alabama and Perryville, Kentucky, Dan Adams earned a new level of respect after suffering the loss of his right eye at Shiloh and at Chickamauga, where he was captured after receiving another wound.[2]

A superior officer wrote of the Chickamauga wounding of Adams, "General Adams, who is as remarkable for his judgment on the field as for his courage, was severely wounded and fell into the hands of the enemy." Other sites of military engagements in which Brigadier General Daniel Weisiger Adams served included Murfreesboro, where he was again wounded. Regarding Adams, General Daniel Hill stated, "It was difficult for me to decide which the most to admire, his extraordinary judgment as an officer, his courage on the field, or his unparalleled cheerfulness under suffering." Additional battlefields that supplied experience for Adams included Selma, Alabama and Columbus, Georgia. Commanding the Department of the Gulf in the war's final months, Dan Adams led the resistance against the final Federal attacks in the region.[3]

Following the Confederate surrender and his parole, Adams visited England before returning to his New Orleans law practice. In 1872 Adams died in New Orleans and was buried in an unmarked grave in the Greenwood Cemetery at Greenwood, Mississippi.[4]

JAMES PATTON ANDERSON (1822-1872)

Born in Winchester, Tennessee, on February 16, 1822, Patton Anderson was one of seven children of William and Margaret Anderson. The death of William, when Patton was only nine years old, devastated the family in many respects, none of which was less evident than from a financial perspective. Margaret Anderson eventually remarried, and Joseph Bybee, the doctor she wed, saw it as appropriate for Patton to attend school in Pennsylvania. Financial problems later resulted in the Bybee family moving to DeSoto County, Mississippi, but Patton Anderson chose to migrate to Kentucky where he attended law school.[5]

In 1843, Anderson, having returned to Mississippi, passed the bar and established a practice in Hernando. He left the law profession to serve in the Mexican War, doing so as a member of the Mississippi Rifles. The end of the war enabled him to resume his law practice and, in 1849, he was elected to the Mississippi House of Representatives.[6]

In 1853, Patton Anderson moved to the Washington Territory and became the territorial marshal. He married Henrietta Buford Adair that same year, and was active in the area's politics through 1857. President James Buchanan made an offer for Anderson to serve as the governor of the Washington Territory, but Anderson refused. At that point, Anderson moved to Florida and settled in Jefferson County. Anderson quickly rose the ranks of political prominence in the Sunshine State where he served as a delegate to the secession convention.[7]

Anderson was elected colonel of the First Florida Regiment at the point of the unit's formation, and by mid-February 1862 he had attained the rank of brigadier general. Anderson saw action at Perryville, Knoxville, Chattanooga, and Murfreesboro. In February 1864, newly-promoted Major General James Patton Anderson briefly served in the Army of Tennessee before being transferred to the Florida District.[8]

During the Atlanta Campaign, Anderson was seriously wounded at the battle of Jonesboro. A *Confederate Veteran* article noted, "At Jonesboro, under a hail of bullets, Gen. Anderson was shot…He lived several years, but never recovered from the painful wound." Although sources vary as to the location of the wound, alternating between his jaw and upper chest, it was stated that Anderson was, "unable to work actively because of his war wound."[9]

Anderson returned in time to lead his troops in North Carolina, where they surrendered at Greensboro. He returned to Memphis, where he was in the insurance business, collected delinquent taxes, and served as the editor of an agricultural publication. Unfortunately, Anderson was financially devastated, and he often battled the issue that had plagued his family most of his life.[10]

James Patton Anderson passed away in Memphis on September 20, 1872 and was buried in Elmwood Cemetery. An article in the *Memphis Appeal* praised Anderson in saying, "Gen. Anderson was the soul of honor...His generosity was only limited by his means...A purer man in thought and action never lived..."[11]

NATHAN BEDFORD FORREST (1821-1877)

One of the most written-about and controversial figures of the American Civil War, Nathan Bedford Forrest was born near Chapel Hill, Tennessee on July 13, 1821. The poor family moved to Tippah County, Mississippi in 1834, and the Forrest patriarch passed away three years later. As the eldest son who was given the responsibility of bearing the responsibility of providing for the family, Nathan Bedford Forrest received limited education. However, his physical presence and outgoing personality allowed him to achieve success despite the shortcomings of his youth.[12]

In 1841, Forrest joined a group of Mississippians headed for Texas. The unit intended to assist in the Lone Star Republic securing its independence. Although he returned to Mississippi as soon as he discovered the services of his group were not needed, Forrest made an impression upon another future Confederate general, James Chalmers. Chalmers recalled, "I remember well a small company of volunteers which marched out of the town of Holly Springs, Mississippi...In that little band stood Bedford Forrest, a tall, black-haired, and gray-eyed youth...who then gave the first evidence of the military ardor he possessed."[13]

In 1845, Forrest married Mary Ann Montgomery, five years his junior. He worked in the mercantile business in Hernando, Mississippi until 1851. In the meantime, Mary Ann and he produced two children. His son, William, later served with him in the American Civil War. Sadly, Fannie, the couple's daughter, passed away at a young age.[14]

A move to Memphis was deemed necessary, as Forrest became actively involved in the slave trade. He liquidated his Hernando, Mississippi holdings and was elected to the Memphis Board of Aldermen in 1858. Dabbling in real estate, Forrest purchased land in Coahoma County, Mississippi and found the slave trade was fast becoming a secondary source of income. By 1861, Forrest's Mississippi farms were producing an annual income of thirty thousand dollars and were yielding almost one thousand bales of cotton.[15]

Forrest set aside his lucrative business interests in June 1861 and joined the Confederate military, enlisting as a private in Josiah White's Mounted Rifles, a unit also designated as Company D of the 6th Tennessee Battalion. Forrest soon used his political influence to secure permission to raise a regiment for the Confederate government. Asking for the volunteers to meet at the Gayoso Hotel in Memphis, Forrest's ad in the *Memphis Daily Appeal* called for, "five hundred able-bodied men, mounted and equipped with such arms as they can procure, shot-guns and pistols preferable, suitable to the service." By October 1861, Forrest had organized eight companies, and he was promoted to lieutenant colonel.[16]

In his first battle at Sacramento, Kentucky on December 28, 1861, Forrest's tenacity in battle became legendary. He engaged in a struggle with four Federal cavalrymen, killing three of them and capturing the fourth. His subsequent decision to escape, rather than surrender, at Fort Donelson, in February 1862, made his name more familiar, as he led over one thousand Confederates to safety.[17]

At the 1862 battle of Shiloh, Forrest witnessed the arrival of Federal reinforcements on the night of April 6, but he was hastily ordered to return to his regiment. The next day he was seriously wounded while serving as a member of the Confederate rear guard, but he managed to pick up a Federal soldier and use the unwilling warrior as a human shield. The act enabled Forrest to reach the safety of the Confederate lines. He recovered from the wound, but precious time was lost in the process.[18]

An outstanding performance at Murfreesboro enabled the newly promoted Brigadier General Forrest to capture over one thousand prisoners. In December 1862, Forrest began his infamous West Tennessee campaign, in which he achieved victories at locations such as Trenton, Humboldt, and Lexington. On December 31, 1862, he found himself surrounded while processing prisoners at Parker's Crossroads, Tennessee. When asked what his troops should do, Forrest reportedly responded with, "Charge 'em both ways." The order was obeyed, and Forrest achieved military notoriety and praise across the region.[19]

A series of victories in 1863 solidified Forrest's reputation and legendary status. A second battle near Fort Donelson, as well as engagements at Thompson's Station and Brentwood, aided in the escalation of his status. Unfortunately, a dark spot emerged when it became known that Forrest had stabbed Lieutenant A. Wills Gould, a would-be assassin. Later victories at Shelbyville, Tullahoma, and Sand Mountain tended to repair the damage the Gould incident had created.[20]

In the February 1864 battle of Okolona, Mississippi, General Forrest killed three Federal soldiers in hand-to-hand combat in retaliation for the death of his younger brother Jeffrey. Two months later, as Fort Pillow, Tennessee, Forrest's troopers killed a large number of Federal soldiers who had reportedly surrendered prior to the majority of casualties being inflicted. With many of the dead being members of the Colored Regiments defending the fort, calls of racism and other atrocities arose and prevail to this day.[21]

In June 1864, Federal soldiers wearing badges that said, "Remember Fort Pillow" approached the town of Baldwyn, Mississippi. During a resulting battle also known as Brice's Crossroads, the Federals met Forrest's cavalrymen in what became one of the most lopsided victories of the war. Forrest's men had total casualties of less than five hundred, while Federal losses were over two thousand two hundred.[22]

In the remaining months of the war, Forrest's major engagements took place at Tupelo, Mississippi, as well as Columbia, Spring Hill, and Franklin, Tennessee, and a raid into Memphis. Mixed results were outcomes, but all were minor in comparison to the amount of Federal property Forrest's men neutralized at Johnsonville, Tennessee in November 1864. Over seven million dollars in supplies and weapons were captured or destroyed, the Federal depot was burned, and Federal morale was dealt a serious blow. General William Tecumseh Sherman proclaimed "the devil Forrest" had to be stopped before ruining the Federal supply network.[23]

Forrest was promoted to lieutenant general in February 1865. That escalation in rank made Nathan Bedford Forrest the only man, North or South, to rise from private to lieutenant general in the course of the war. Two months later, Lieutenant General Forrest fought his last battle of the American Civil War; the struggle took place in Selma, Alabama.[24]

After his surrender at Gainesville, Alabama in May 1865, Forrest, known as the "Wizard of the Saddle," informed his troopers, "It is your duty and mine to lay down our arms…and to aid in restoring peace and establishing law and order throughout the land."[25]

In his post war life, Nathan Bedford Forrest received a Presidential pardon, but the effects of the war had taken a serious toll on his body. He returned to farming out of financial necessity, leasing President's Island near Memphis, and using convict labor to work it and another plantation in the north portion of Shelby County, Tennessee. Alleged Forrest connections to the Ku Klux Klan have hampered modern perceptions of Forrest, with differing opinions holding to his level of involvement or lack thereof.[26]

Diabetes and dysentery began to ravage Forrest's body, and he passed away October 29, 1877. Having earlier made a profession of faith, Forrest was given a Christian funeral before his burial in Memphis. Over twenty thousand people lined the three-mile procession route that led to Elmwood Cemetery. In 1905, Forrest and his wife were reinterred in Forrest Park, with a large equestrian statue marking their graves.[27]

JOHN WESLEY FRAZER (1827-1906)

John Wesley Frazer was born in Hardin County, Tennessee on January 6, 1827. The family surname was alternately spelled Fraser or Frazier, and John Wesley shared that with his brother Charles, also a future Confederate general. The Frazer family eventually moved to Marshall County, Mississippi where they bought twelve acres in Holly Springs. The death of the family's patriarch resulted in the Frazers relocating to DeSoto County, Mississippi.[28]

Earning an eventual appointment to West Point from Mississippi, John Wesley Frazer graduated in 1849, ranked thirty-fourth in his class. Cadet Frazer managed to successfully complete his years at the United States Military Academy despite the receipt of over ninety demerits. Absenteeism and the introduction of "spirituous liquors in the barracks" served as the bulk of these charges. Following his matriculation, Second Lieutenant Frazer served two years at Ft. Columbus, New York, as assignment that preceded tenures in California and Washington. Following a leave of absence in 1860-1861, Frazer resigned his commission as captain in March 1861, and he offered his services to the Confederate States of America.[29]

Initially assigned to the rank of captain, Frazer was sent to Louisiana and given the task of recruiting in the areas of New Orleans and Baton Rouge. In June 1861, he was promoted to lieutenant colonel and assigned to the 8th Alabama Infantry Regiment. He soon resigned, but returned to the Confederate military in November 1861 and was given the rank of colonel.[30]

Colonel Frazer served at Shiloh, Corinth, and Munfordville, Kentucky, but resigned again in late 1862. In March 1863, Frazer returned and attained the rank of brigadier general. With that rank he was given command of the Fifth Brigade in the Army of East Tennessee. Controversy surrounds the events of that September as Brigadier General John Frazer surrendered his command to General Ambrose Burnside. While supporters of Frazer hold to the view that Frazer surrendered only after determining the situation he faced was hopeless, detractors claim the capitulation was not necessary. The Confederate Congress revoked Frazer's rank of brigadier general in February 1864.[31]

During his time as a prisoner of war at Fort Warren, Massachusetts, Frazer began corresponding with a Confederate sympathizer. After the war and his parole Frazer met the individual, a Utica, New York resident named Kate Tiffany. The couple married in 1870, but their years of marriage were marred due to Kate's poor health.[32]

Frazer's primary post-war vocations were the varied jobs of a merchant and farmer in Memphis, operating a plantation in Arkansas, and owning a business in New York City. The latter location was reached due to a difficult situation. John Frazer had suffered from the effects of tongue cancer for a lengthy period of time. Urged to seek radium treatment in New York City, Frazer agreed that doing so would offer the only possibility of a cure. In February 1906, a fire engine struck Frazer as he crossed 23rd Street; the result was a fractured hip. Other complications developed from the incident, and Frazer died on March 31, 1906. The former Confederate general was buried next to his wife in Clifton Springs, New York.[33]

SAMUEL GIBBS FRENCH (1881-1910)

Samuel Gibbs French is uncommon among those who had strong Mississippi ties in that he was born in New Jersey. The location of his birth was Gloucester, New Jersey, and the event took place on November 22, 1818. His parents were Samuel and Rebecca Clark French; they would eventually have five other children. Most of French's education took place in Burlington, and his major educational catalyst occurred with his admission to the United States Military Academy. He graduated from West Point in 1843 with Ulysses S. Grant as a classmate.[34]

Upon his matriculation, French was brevetted a second lieutenant in the 3rd Artillery. He was given the responsibility of preparing Fort Macon, North Carolina and remained at that post from July 1, 1843 to November 1844. At that point, Second Lieutenant French went to Fort McHenry and remained there until he participated in the occupation of Texas. French gained a great deal of combat experience during the Mexican War, serving from 1846 to 1847.[35]

French took part in the September 1846 battle of Monterrey and was promoted to First Lieutenant soon afterward. The two events are related in that his promotion was noted to have occurred "for gallant and meritorious service in the several conflicts at Monterrey."[36]

On February 23, 1847, French was wounded at Buena Vista. His contributions in the engagement also led to a subsequent promotion to captain. French discussed his wound in his 1901 autobiography in writing,

"Unfortunately some of Lane's troops gave way and fled, and this enabled the enemy to gain our left flank and rear. At this time I was struck with an ounce musket ball in the upper part of the right thigh while my left foot was in the stirrup in the act of mounting my horse. The shot was not painful at all, and the sensation was that of being struck with a club. I was put on my horse, as I could not walk. Soon after, to prevent being entirely surrounded, we were ordered to fall back toward the road, and came into line facing toward the mountain, and opened fire, now taking the enemy in flank and rear as they were crossing the plain. I refused to be taken from my horse and put in a wagon, knowing I would be 'lanced' by the Mexicans in case of disaster, so I sat on my horse all the rest of the day walking him sometimes to the battery when it remained in one place any length of time."[37]

French explained the eventual onset of pain, "Weary, tired, and weakened by loss of blood, with my leg stiff and useless, I rode into the court of the hacienda, and was taken from my horse and carried into a very large room and laid on the floor. The whole floor was covered with wounded. I was placed between two soldiers. One had both legs broken below the knee. The scene almost beggars description. The screams of agony from pain, the moans of the dying, the messages sent home by the despairing, the parting farewells of friends, the incoherent speech, the peculiar movements of the hands and fingers, silence...On the field I was twice taken from my horse by the surgeons and had the wound probed, but no probe could reach the ball. No surgeon was at the hacienda, so there I remained until after dark...I was taken to our camp at Saltillo, put on the ground in my tent with but little covering, and left alone. Where my servant was I know not. The camp was silent, every one being away on or near the field of battle. It was to me a night of bodily suffering. About daylight I heard footsteps and called aloud, and was answered by a passing soldier coming to my relief. That morning I was moved to a hospital and received medical attention, and soon after I was sent to a private house occupied by the wife of one of our soldiers, where I received every care and was made comfortable."[38]

Following his service and related promotions during the Mexican War, Captain French was assigned the task of quartermaster, initially for Washington, D. C. and then for New Orleans. In March 1847, he received another promotion and became known as 1st Lieutenant Samuel Gibbs French. He continued to serve with than rank until his May 1856 resignation from the military at which time he became engaged in planting near Vicksburg, Mississippi.[39]

At the onset of the American Civil War, French left the plantation he acquired through his 1853 marriage to Matilda Roberts. French's appreciation for Southern culture led him to volunteer his services to the Confederate States of America, and he was given the responsibility of serving as chief of ordnance for the State of Mississippi. In October 1861, Samuel Gibbs French was promoted to brigadier general.[40]

Brigadier General French was sent to the Eastern Theater, where he participated in engagements taking place in the Peninsular Campaign and in North Carolina. His performance in these battles must have been tremendous, as French was promoted to major general in August 1862. With that rank, French led a division in the Army of Tennessee as they fought in Jackson, Mississippi, Atlanta, and in and around Nashville. Health issues with his eyes resulted in Major General French returning to his Mississippi home in December 1864, but he recovered in time to serve in Mobile, Alabama during the war's final months.[41]

Having lost his first wife, French married Mary Fontaine Abercrombie in January 1865. The couple made their post-war home in Florida, where he became a planter. In 1901, the former Confederate general wrote his autobiography entitled *Two Wars*. He passed away on April 20, 1910 and is buried in Pensacola, Florida.[42]

DANIEL CHEVILETTE GOVAN (1829-1911)

Born on July 4, 1827, Daniel Govan would become one of the last surviving generals from the American Civil War. His life was filled with adventure, accomplishments, success, and personal tragedy at a level not many of his peers experienced. The child of a one-time South Carolina politician, he joined his parents as they moved to Marshall County, Mississippi when he was five years old.[43]

Following private tutoring received at home, Daniel Govan left Marshall County and became a student at South Carolina College. However, for some unknown reason, he left prior to fulfilling the requirements for graduation. He ventured to California to participate in the gold rush of the late 1840s, making the trip with his cousins Ben and Henry McCulloch, both of whom also later served as Confederate generals. Govan abandoned the dream of quick wealth in order to serve as the deputy sheriff of Sacramento, California. Another change in vocations took place in 1852 as Govan returned to Marshall County and became a planter. Never one to remain in one place too long, he moved to Arkansas the following year in order to run a plantation.[44]

While in Helena, Arkansas, Daniel Govan met Mary Fogg Otey, the daughter of an Episcopal bishop. The couple married after a short courtship and had fourteen children in the course of their marriage. Govan outlived eleven of his offspring.[45]

The onset of the American Civil War caused Govan to raise a company of soldiers from Helena, and he was made captain of the group. By the end of 1861, he held the rank of lieutenant colonel in the 2nd Arkansas Infantry. Within a month, Govan was promoted to colonel and led troops at Shiloh, Perryville, Murfreesboro, and Chickamauga. In late December 1863, Daniel Govan received another promotion, that time to brigadier general. Brigadier General Govan commanded four Arkansas regiments in a brigade that came to be known as Govan's Brigade.[46]

While experiencing and enduring the bloodshed of the Atlanta Campaign, Govan was captured at Jonesboro in September 1864. Some six hundred of his troops had been captured with Govan, but his duration as a prisoner of war was far less than many of them. Only one month after his capture, Brigadier General Govan was exchanged for a Federal general.[47]

Brigadier General Govan spent the remainder of the Civil War in the Army of Tennessee. The major engagement in which Govan participated was the November 30, 1864 battle of Franklin, Tennessee. Ordered to advance a mile toward strong Federal earthworks centered on the Carter House, Govan paused for a short conversation with fellow Arkansan and division commander Patrick Cleburne. Cleburne informed Govan he held doubts about following the directive from General John Bell Hood. Govan stated, "Well, General, few of us will ever return to Arkansas to tell the story of this battle." According to Govan, the Irish immigrant, one of the most respected officers in the Confederate army, replied, "Well, Govan, if we are to die, let us die like men." In the assault that followed, Cleburne was killed near the Federal center.[48]

Although he suffered a throat wound at Nashville two weeks after the battle of Franklin, Brigadier General Govan continued to lead his troops. With General Joseph Johnston in April 1865, Govan joined in the surrender of his troops as the war came to an end. In December 1865 Govan received a pardon from the United States and returned to his Arkansas farm.[49]

In 1894, President Grover Cleveland appointed Govan as the Indian agent in Everett, Washington. Having served effectively in that post, Govan retired in 1898 and spent the remainder of his life traveling across the nation and visiting his surviving children. Another position Govan held with high regard and fulfilled with extreme professionalism was as a member of the United Confederate Veterans, an organization for which he was a speaker at a reunion of Federal and Confederate veterans.[50]

While visiting his daughter at her Memphis, Tennessee home, Govan passed away on March 12, 1911. His body was returned to his childhood home of Holly Springs, Mississippi where he was buried in the family plot in Hillcrest Cemetery.[51]

HIRAM BRONSON GRANBURY (1831-1864)

Hiram Granbury was born in Copiah County, Mississippi on March 1, 1831. The son of a Baptist minister, Hiram Granbury graduated from Oakland College, a prominent institution located near Rodney, Mississippi. In the 1850s, Granbury moved to Waco, Texas and became, after his admission to and fulfillment of the requirements of the bar, the chief justice of McLennan County, Texas.[52]

The twenty-seven year old Granbury married twenty year-old Alabama-born Waco resident Fannie Sims in 1858. Health issues hampered Fannie, and the couple had no children. Their marriage was forever changed with the arrival of the American Civil War and Granbury's raising of the Waco Guards to enter the Confederate service.[53]

In mid-February 1862, Major Hiram Granbury was captured at Fort Donelson and sent to Johnson Island, Ohio. Granbury was soon transferred to Fort Warren in Boston Harbor, and remained there until his parole later that year. Sadly, in the meantime Fannie was diagnosed with ovarian cancer. She was soon sent to her family's home in Tuscaloosa, Alabama where she died at the age of twenty-five in March 1863. Due to the financial situation of the time, Fannie Granbury was buried in an unmarked grave.[54]

Making intermittent visits to his ill wife, Granbury was promoted to the rank of colonel after his release from prison. Subsequent action involved the battles of Raymond, Mississippi and Chickamauga. Granbury was wounded in the latter engagement, but recovered in time to participate in the battle of Ringgold, Georgia. Granbury's performance at Ringgold earned him a promotion to brigadier general.[55]

Brigadier General Hiram Granbury was killed at the battle of Franklin, Tennessee on November 30, 1864. Having charged the Federal center with Patrick Cleburne, Granbury fell on the edge of the Federal earthworks and became one of six Confederate generals sacrificed at Franklin. After his initial burial in Franklin, Granbury's remains were moved to Ashwood Cemetery, property of St. John's Episcopal Church in Columbia, Tennessee. On the thirtieth anniversary of his death at Franklin, Granbury was reinterred in Granbury, Texas, a town named in his honor. Ironically, Granbury is the county seat of Hood County, named for Granbury's commanding officer at the time of his death.[56]

ELKANAH GREER (1825-1877)

Born in Paris, Tennessee on October 11, 1825, Elkanah Greer moved to Marshall County, Mississippi as a young man. He chose the community of Potts Camp as his home, and left the area in to serve in the Mexican War. Greer gained military experience at Buena Vista and Monterrey as a private in the Marshall Guards, also known as Company I of the 1st Mississippi Infantry, under the command of Jefferson Davis. The end of the war witnessed Greer leaving Mississippi and moving to Marshall, Texas where he owned a business and engaged in farming. On a personal note, he visited Tennessee and married Francis Wilkinson Pickens in 1851, and the couple eventually produced five children. In 1859, he was elected grand commander of the Knights of the Golden Circle. He also entered a legal partnership, serving as an attorney with Pope, Stedman, and Greer.[57]

In the months before the onset of war, Greer called for Texas to secede as he opposed the election of Abraham Lincoln. The American Civil War beckoned Greer, and he offered his services to the Confederate States of America. Entering the military as a colonel in the 3rd Texas Cavalry, a unit he helped raise, Greer saw action at Wilson's Creek and Pea Ridge. During the latter engagement, he received a minor arm wound from which he fully recovered.[58]

Having resigned his commission in 1862, Greer was recalled in 1863 and received a promotion to brigadier general in October 1863. Brigadier General Greer served as the chief of the Conscripting Bureau for the

Department of the Trans-Mississippi where he attempted to streamline draft laws in the area. He also served as the commander of the Texas Reserve Corps and was given the responsibility of keeping Texas troops prepared to defend against a possible coastal invasion. Doing so caused Greer to organize slave laborers to erect fortifications and build roads capable of handling troops and supplies.[59]

When the war concluded, Brigadier General Greer returned to Marshall, Texas and remained a farmer and merchant there for the majority of his life. In 1877, he was visiting his sister in DeVall's Bluff, Arkansas, and a sudden illness resulted in his death. His remains were buried next to his parents in Elmwood Cemetery in Memphis.[60]

JAMES EDWARD HARRISON (1815-1875)

James Edward Harrison was born to Isham and Harriet Kelly Harrison on April 24, 1815. The family soon left the Greenville District in South Carolina and moved to Jefferson County, Alabama. When James was fourteen years old, the Harrison family, which then included brother Thomas, another future Confederate general, relocated to Monroe County, Mississippi.[61]

While in Monroe County, Mississippi, Harrison met and married Mary Evans in 1841. The Harrison couple eventually had five children, three sons and two daughters. Harrison also served two terms in the

Mississippi Senate before moving his family to Waco, Texas in 1859. Harrison and his wife purchased a six thousand acre plantation located on the east side of the Brazos River, some ten miles south of Waco. His apparent high level of knowledge concerning the languages and lifestyles of the Choctaw and Creek soon led to Harrison's appointment as Texas Commissioner for Indian Affairs.[62]

Harrison was a member of the state secession convention and more actively exercised his stance when joined the 1st Texas Infantry Battalion as the Civil War began. The unit was reorganized as the 15th Texas Infantry in 1862, and James Harrison was appointed as the lieutenant colonel. That same year Mary Ann Harrison passed away, as did the couple's son Thomas. After the burials of his family members Harrison returned to his post and received a promotion to colonel of the regiment in the ensuing months and participated in the Louisiana campaigns of 1863 and 1864.[63]

Leading his troops at Fordoche Bridge, Harrison participated in capturing five hundred prisoners and a large amount of weapons. General Thomas Green wrote, "To Lieut.-Col. J. E. Harrison, commanding Spaight's Brigade...all honor is due, and to the officers...who displayed great coolness in the action. Many of them had never been under fire before, but moved like veterans up the enemy under a heavy fire and succeeded in driving them from house to house...The heavy loss...shows the desperate nature of the conflict."[64]

On December 22, 1864, Harrison was promoted to brigadier general and was placed in command of his old regiment as well as the 17th, 22nd, and 31st Texas Dismounted Cavalry. Among his duties was the negotiation of Texas troops surrendered in the final days of the war. The end of the Civil War enabled Harrison to return to Waco where he was active in the Baptist church and local politics. In 1874, Harrison was appointed as a trustee to Baylor University, but he died the following year. Harrison is buried in Waco's First Street Cemetery. His name was memorialized through the naming of Harrison, Texas, in McLennan County.[65]

THOMAS HARRISON (1823-1891)

Thomas Harrison, the younger brother of fellow Confederate general James Edward Harrison, was born in Jefferson County, Alabama May 1, 1823. The family soon moved to Mississippi, and Thomas moved to Texas at the age of twenty. He married Sarah Elizabeth MacDonald, with whom he had two sons. Although he had established a successful career as an attorney, Thomas left Texas in order to serve with the 1st Mississippi Rifles, under the leadership of Jefferson Davis, in the Mexican War.[66]

Harrison later entered politics, serving a term as a Harris County representative in the Texas legislature. Calling Waco his home, Harrison also became a captain in a local militia.[67]

Harrison's militia company became part of the 8th Texas Cavalry Regiment, also known as Terry's Texas Rangers. During the Civil War, the unit fought at Shiloh, Corinth, and Perryville, with Harrison rising in rank from captain, to major, and then colonel. During the battle of Murfreesboro, Tennessee, Colonel Harrison was wounded one of the three times in the war, but he recovered in time to participate in the Tullahoma Campaign.[68]

The majority of the remainder of the war for Colonel Harrison was spent leading brigades who primarily served as scouts. Locations of Harrison's service included Chickamauga, Knoxville, Atlanta, and the Carolinas. On February 18, 1865, Harrison was promoted to brigadier general. Serving in Hampton's Cavalry Corps, Brigadier General Thomas

Harrison was wounded at Monroe's Crossroads, North Carolina in March 1865. Two months later he was paroled, and his pardon was issued the following month.[69]

After the war Harrison returned to Waco, Texas where he held the post of a district judge until he was removed under the decision of the Reconstruction government. Ready to serve his local townspeople, Harrison was a trustee for Waco University and was active in church. He also was an 1872 elector to the Democratic Convention and was known as an opponent of Reconstruction. On July 14, 1891 Harrison died in Waco as was buried in Oakwood Cemetery in that Texas town.[70]

STEPHEN DILL LEE (1833-1908)

Although he was born in Charleston, South Carolina September 22, 1863, Stephen Dill Lee's post-war settlement, death, and burial in Mississippi earn him the designation as holding significant Mississippi ties. A relative of such noted Americans as Light Horse Harry Lee and Robert E. Lee, Stephen Dill Lee entered the United States Military Academy at the age of seventeen. He graduated four years later, in 1854, ranked seventeenth of forty-six cadets. Future Confederate general J. E. B. Stuart was one of his West Point classmates.[71]

Upon his graduation, Lieutenant Stephen Dill Lee entered the U. S. Army as an officer in the 4th U. S. Artillery. His subsequent assignments sent him to various military installations in Texas, the Dakota Territory, Florida, and Kansas. When South Carolina seceded from the United States, Lee felt an obligation to join his fellow statesmen and, resigning his commission, offered his services to the Confederate States of America.[72]

Stephen Dill Lee's first assignment as a Confederate officer was at Charleston, where he served as an aide-de-camp for General P. G. T. Beauregard. Lee joined Colonel James Chesnut as the duo rowed to Fort Sumter and delivered a demand for surrender. Federal officer Robert Anderson's refusal to do so resulted in the ensuing Confederate barrage of the fort. Rumors abound that Stephen Dill Lee may have been the individual who fired the first shot that literally signaled the beginning of the cataclysmic war that lasted four years.[73]

Lee's biography from the Stephen D. Lee Institute acknowledges, "As the war really got under way, Lee's assignments and promotions came quickly." As proof of this declaration, Lee was given command of a battery in Hampton's Legion where he was under the leadership of General Joseph Johnston. In a short period of time, Lee had become Chief of Artillery in General Lafayette McLaw's command in the Army of Northern Virginia.[74]

The Peninsula Campaign and Second Bull Run served as locations of Lee's early combat experiences, with the recently promoted Colonel Lee receiving praise from the Confederate President Jefferson Davis. President Davis wrote of Lee at Manassas, or Bull Run, "I have reason to believe at that great conflict on the field of Manassas that Colonel Lee served to turn the tide of battle and consummate the victory."[75]

At Antietam, September 17, 1862, Lee participated in the action at several locations during the bloodiest day of the war. The West Woods, the Cornfield, and Dunkard Church served as sites of Lee's activities on that day. In the Antietam aftermath, President Jefferson Davis requested that Robert E. Lee select his "most accomplished and efficient artillery officer" to be sent to serve in Mississippi. General Lee selected Colonel Stephen Dill Lee for the task.[76]

Serving with General John Pemberton in the defense of Vicksburg, Colonel Stephen Dill Lee was promoted to brigadier general on November 6, 1862. Brigadier General Lee gained command of Pemberton's artillery during the early action at Vicksburg, but that series of events suffered with Lee's shoulder wound received during the battle of Champion Hill. Having partially recovered, Lee was captured when Vicksburg fell in July 1863; he was exchanged on October 3, 1863.[77]

After his release, Lee was promoted to major general and given the leadership role of cavalry in Mississippi, Alabama, Eastern Louisiana, and West Tennessee. When John Bell Hood took command of the Army of Tennessee in June 1863, Lee's promotion to lieutenant general took place. With that promotion in rank, thirty year-old Lieutenant General S. D. Lee became the youngest man to hold such a rank in the Confederate service and provided Lee with a resume of complete experience in infantry, cavalry, and artillery.[78]

The Atlanta Campaign served as S. D. Lee's next test of leadership, and he was given the task of attacking Sherman's supply lines. As the fighting continued in the Atlanta area, Lieutenant General Lee was ordered to lead the corps which General John Bell Hood once commanded in the Army of Tennessee. The fall of Atlanta resulted in Lee moving northward where additional engagements waited.[79]

Wounded during the Tennessee Campaign, Lieutenant General Lee managed to participate in action at Spring Hill, Franklin, and Nashville, with Lee having supervised the initial time frame of the Army of Tennessee's rear guard as it exited Middle Tennessee. A wound at Nashville rendered Lee incapable of service for some time, but he later served with General Joseph Johnston in the Carolina Campaign, surrendering his command in April 1865.[80]

Although Lee received praise and accolades from the majority of his peers and is held in high regard among modern historians, there were, and continue to be, critics. One pundit, speaking of Lee's loss at Tupelo, Mississippi in July 1864, proclaimed that the Confederates, "...with Lee personally commanding, an ill-conceived and ill-executed assault on a superior and well-entrenched Union force...suffered a bloody repulse." The detractor added, in discussing the Atlanta Campaign, "...in what became known as the battle of Ezra Church...a severe defeat...in the assault at his behest, suffered 3,000 casualties, compared with the enemy losses of 632."[81]

Paroled in May 1865, Lee moved to Columbus, Mississippi. He had married Regina Harrison, a Columbus resident, three months earlier. S. D. Lee became a Mississippi planter and that served as a major source of income for several years after the war. In 1878, he became a Mississippi senator, and served from 1880 to 1899 as the first president of Mississippi Agricultural and Mechanical College, known today as Mississippi State University.[82]

Following his resignation as college president, Lee's additional post-war activities included the heralded establishment of Vicksburg National Military Park. He also authored articles related to the American Civil War, with *Battles and Leaders of the Civil War* containing a Lee-authored article in the publication's first volume. Lee published *Sherman's Meridian Expedition and Sooy Smith's Raid to West Point* in 1880. In addition, Lee, the highest ranking Confederate general alive at the time, was the founder and commander in chief of the United Confederate Veterans. A significant number of Sons of Confederate Veterans camps bear Lee's name, marking lasting tributes to the organization's long-time leader.[83]

In 1906, Lee issued a charge to the Sons of Confederate Veterans, "To you, Sons of Confederate Veterans, we will commit the vindication of the Cause for which we fought. To your strength will be given the defense of the Confederate soldier's good name, the guardianship of his history, the emulation of his virtues, the perpetuation of those principles he loved and which you love also, and those ideals which made him glorious and which you also cherish…it is your duty to see that the true history of the South is presented to future generations."[84]

Lee held the post of Confederate Veteran commander in chief until his death on May 28, 1908. Having survived his wife by five years, he left a son, Blewett Harrison Lee. Stephen Dill Lee was buried in Friendship Cemetery in Columbus. Additionally, the Lee home in Columbus, Mississippi is on the National Register of Historic Places with the related historical marker located on 7th Street North.[85]

PHILIP DALE RODDEY (1826-1897)

The Lawrence County, Alabama town of Moulton was the location of Philip Dale Roddey's 1826 birth. It was noted, "His parents were in humble circumstances and able to give him but scanty educational advantages." He spent his early years working in a tailor shop in Moulton, but in his adult life he won the first of three years as sheriff of Lawrence County. He also spent time working on a steamboat based in Chickasaw, Alabama.[86]

Roddey helped raise a company, the Tishomingo Rangers, to serve the Confederate cause, and his efficient tactics as a scout earned praise from his commanding general. Philip Dale Roddey was given the rank of captain and quickly earned the intense trust of his superiors. His performance at Shiloh also earned comments for Roddey's gallantry.[87]

General Braxton Bragg wrote to General Sterling Price, "Captain Roddey is detached with a squadron of cavalry on special service in northwest Alabama, where he has shown himself to be an officer of rare energy, enterprise and skill in harassing the enemy and procuring information of his movements....has the entire confidence of the commanding general, who wishes to commend him to you as one eminently worthy of trust."[88]

During the latter months of 1862, Roddey saw action at Corinth and Iuka before being promoted to colonel in December. Colonel Roddey participated in battles at Tuscumbia and Columbia, Tennessee in early 1863; he and was promoted to brigadier general on August 3, 1863. In October 1863, Brigadier General Roddey joined General Joseph

Wheeler in raids into Tennessee where Confederates sought to destroy Federal communications. Roddey was also present at Chickamauga and Chattanooga, where he continued to serve under Wheeler.[89]

During 1864, Brigadier General Roddey fought at Athens, Alabama and Lebanon. After those battles, Wheeler ordered Roddey to Dalton, Georgia where Roddey was given the responsibility of leading a cavalry division. Having spent the spring months of 1864 in north Alabama, Roddey was sent to North Mississippi to support General Nathan Bedford Forrest.[90]

On June 10, 1864, Brigadier General Roddey performed what is often regarded as his most valuable service to the Confederate States of America when he joined Forrest at Brices Crossroads, Mississippi. A short biography on Roddey proclaimed, "…he distinguished himself in the Battle of Brice's Cross Roads."[91] The victory was Forrest's largest, and one of the most one-sided of the entire war.

Brigadier General Roddey continued his alignment with Forrest when the duo led troops at Tupelo or Harrisburg, Mississippi. A biographer stated of the fall 1864 engagement, "Part of his troops were with Forrest in the September-October raid in Alabama and Tennessee."[92]

The North Alabama District was placed under Roddey's command in September 1864, and the general also managed to play a role in the Atlanta Campaign. It was noted of Roddey, "During the Atlanta campaign he fought a heavy Federal raiding party at Moulton." He also aided in keeping General John Bell Hood's communications open in the latter part of 1864.[93]

The last months of the war provided a period of additional service for Brigadier General Roddey. A writer said, "In 1865 he offered a stout, though vain, resistance to Wilson's column, and was engaged under Forrest in the gallant attempt to defend Selma against the overwhelming numbers of the enemy." Roddey surrendered his command in May 1865.[94]

With the end of the Civil War, Roddey moved to New York City, where he lived the majority of his remaining years. In 1881, he lost his wife Margaret, and apparently never remarried. Roddey engaged in the business of a commission merchant, during which he invested in a new design of a pump. Seeking investors, Roddey made a trip to Europe in 1897. During his time in Europe, Roddey passed away in London. Accounts vary as to the date of his death, with both July and August, 1897 being provided. However, July 19 is the date on his headstone marking his grave at Greenwood Cemetery in Tuscaloosa, Alabama.[95]

ALFRED JEFFERSON VAUGHAN, JR. (1830-1899)

Born in Virginia in May 1830, Alfred Jefferson Vaughan entered Virginia Military Institute in 1848. Vaughan managed to graduate fifteenth of twenty-nine cadets three years later, having spent his final cadet year commanding a company and holding the position of cadet captain. Upon his graduation, Vaughan became a civil engineer and moved to Missouri before relocating to California. During that period of his life, Vaughan was a surveyor for the Hannibal and St. Louis Railroad and subsequently became a Northern Pacific Railroad executive.[96]

Vaughan's association with Mississippi began when he moved to Marshall County and became a farmer. There he met and married Martha Jane Hardaway. The couple had eight children together and farmed at the time the American Civil War began.[7]

Alfred Jefferson Vaughan abandoned his strong pro-United States sentiments and joined the Confederate cause. While the Mississippi-based company he helped raise lacked the ability to obtain weapons and proper equipment, Vaughan advanced northward to Moscow, Tennessee. Having originally been elected captain of the 13th Tennessee Infantry Regiment,

Vaughan was promoted to lieutenant colonel following the regiment's reorganization in the summer of 1861.[98]

As he climbed through the ranks, Vaughan and his varied commands saw action at Belmont, Missouri, Shiloh, and in Kentucky. Wounded at Shiloh, Vaughan managed to heal enough to participate in additional 1862 battles at Richmond, Kentucky as well as Perryville and Murfreesboro. After the battle of Chickamauga, Vaughan was promoted to brigadier general. President Jefferson Davis provided the field promotion in noting Vaughan's "service to the Confederacy at Chickamauga."[99]

During the Atlanta Campaign, Brigadier General Vaughan saw action at a host of locations. H was seriously wounded in a skirmish at Vining's Station in July 1864. An artillery shell exploded near him and tore off one of his legs. Vaughan saw no additional combat. In May 1865 he was paroled and returned to Mississippi.[100]

Vaughan's post-war activities included farming ventures in Mississippi and being a merchant in Memphis. Political activism centered on the Grange Movement, with Vaughan serving as the group's liaison for Mississippi, Tennessee, and Arkansas. Vaughan also held a post as Shelby County, Tennessee's criminal court clerk and was the United Confederate Veterans president for the state of Tennessee. A major accomplishment of Vaughan was to publish his memoirs in 1897. Vaughan passed away in Indianapolis two years later and was buried in Elmwood Cemetery in Memphis.[101]

WILLIAM HENRY CHASE WHITING (1824-1865)

Whiting was born to Captain Levi and Mary A. Whiting in Biloxi, Mississippi, March 22, 1824. His father was a Massachusetts native who served forty years in the service of the United States and was an artillery officer at the time W. H. C., a name by which William Henry Chase was known, was born.[102]

Young Whiting was considered a genius, and entered Boston English High School at the age of twelve. Two years later he graduated at the top of his class and subsequently entered Georgetown College. At sixteen, Whiting completed Georgetown, ranked second in his class.[103]

W. H. C. Whiting's academic prowess continued, as he was admitted to the United States Military Academy in 1841. In 1845, he completed his tenure at West Point and graduated first in his class. An indication of his designation as a genius is shown in the fact that Whiting maintained the highest academic average in all subjects for his entire term at the academy. Also, his grades were the highest of any student to have attended West Point to that time.[104]

Commissioned as second lieutenant, Whiting was sent to Pensacola, Florida where he was to serve as an assistant engineer. In 1848, he was transferred to Texas where he provided valuable work in scouting a transportation route from El Paso to San Antonio. The effort, accomplished while battling the Comanche, was deemed the Whiting and Smith Expedition and managed to identify a military and commercial road between the two cities. In January 1850, Whiting provided an invaluable service when he surveyed forts on the Texas frontier. Whiting lost his father in 1853, with the elderly Whiting having served forty years in the military by that point, and had achieved the rank of lieutenant colonel.[105]

His engineering expertise took Whiting throughout areas of Texas and eventually resulted in him making periods of service in Maryland, California, Georgia, Florida, and the Carolinas. Whiting took a major step in his personal life when he married Kate Walker in 1857. Kate accompanied him as he served in Georgia and Florida prior to Whiting's resignation, having attained the rank of captain, from the United States Army in February 1861.[106]

During his early months of Confederate service, Whiting inspected the Charleston works, fortified Morris Island, served as inspector-general of the North Carolina defenses, and led the destruction of the Harper's Ferry arsenal. By July 1861, having received a field promotion from President Davis, Whiting was given the rank of brigadier general and was in charge of two brigades. Whiting's promotion had come after Davis was highly impressed with Whiting's performance at Manassas, and the rise in rank enabled Whiting to pass three other officer grades. Whiting battled Federal troops and chronic fatigue in the early engagements around Richmond, namely First Manassas and Seven Pines, but he was allowed to take a medical furlough due to the latter condition. An alleged dislike and sense of jealousy regarding "Stonewall" Jackson had also led to Whiting's superiors granting the leave.[107]

In February 1863, Whiting was promoted to major general. Within a year of achieving the rank of major general, Whiting was recommended for lieutenant general status, but the request failed. General Joseph E. Johnston remarked, "The reason for putting aside the recommendation was an odd one to me. It was that you were too valuable in your present place." A biographer noted that Whiting's personality was considered abrasive, and he had become somewhat of a political outcast due to his strong critical remarks regarding government officials. Another point of contention regarding Whiting lay in the prevalent rumors regarding his tendency to abuse alcohol.[108]

Known as "Little Billy" among his troops, Whiting was a relatively short man. He not only lacked the ability to work well with his fellow officers, but the general was also regarded to possess a pessimistic nature.[109]

Assignments to Wilmington and Richmond occupied several months of Whiting's career, but the continued accusations of alcohol abuse led to short tenures in each location. In addition, remarks about Whiting's fondness of narcotics lessened his effectiveness. The combination reportedly contributed to the general's failure to properly defend Richmond from the eastward approaching Federals. In turn, Whiting asked for a transfer to Wilmington.[110]

Having seen action around Petersburg, Whiting's military career was dealt a major setback when he suffered a leg wound at Fort Fisher. Major General Whiting had joined in a hand-to-hand struggle within the fort, and attempted to take down the Federal flag when he received two wounds. He was taken to Fort Columbus, on Governors Island, New York for imprisonment.[111]

The effects of his wound, coupled with dysentery and diarrhea, proved devastating, and he became too weak to sign a letter. Brigadier General W. H. C. Whiting passed away on March 10, 1865, twelve days before his forty-first birthday. Originally buried in Brooklyn's Greenwood Cemetery, Whiting's body was exhumed in 1900, under the request of his widow, and reinterred in Oakdale Cemetery in Wilmington, North Carolina.[112]

INDEX

CPSIA information can be obtained
at www.ICGtesting.com
Printed in the USA
LVOW11s0239110817
544612LV00001B/41/P